Material Discourse— Materialist Analysis

Material Discourse—Materialist Analysis

Approaches in Discourse Studies

Johannes Beetz and Veit Schwab

LEXINGTON BOOKS
Lanham • Boulder • New York • London

Published by Lexington Books
An imprint of The Rowman & Littlefield Publishing Group, Inc.
4501 Forbes Boulevard, Suite 200, Lanham, Maryland 20706
www.rowman.com

Unit A, Whitacre Mews, 26-34 Stannary Street, London SE11 4AB

British Library Cataloguing in Publication Information Available

Library of Congress Cataloging-in-Publication Data Available

ISBN 978-1-4985-5815-0 (cloth : alk. paper)
ISBN 978-1-4985-5816-7 (electronic)

∞™ The paper used in this publication meets the minimum requirements of American
National Standard for Information Sciences—Permanence of Paper for Printed Library
Materials, ANSI/NISO Z39.48-1992.

Printed in the United States of America

Contents

Acknowledgments

Born out of a desire to explore and revitalize materialist approaches in the field of Discourse Studies, this volume took shape in a series of collective discussions during a workshop on *Materialist_Discourse_Analysis: Methodological entanglements* (University of Warwick, UK, July 2016), a winter school on *Discourse, Ideology, and Political Economy* (University of Valencia, Spain, January 2017), and in a series of conversations in the DiscourseNet research group on *Discourse, Ideology, Political Economy (DIPE)*.

This book would not exist without everyone who helped to make these encounters such a pleasant and stimulating experience and contributed to our collective discussion of the issues at stake—thank you!

We would also like to thank Johannes Angermuller, Malcolm MacDonald and Vicki Squire for their ongoing support; as well as Iwona Janicka, Nawel Aït Ali and Alexandra Zierold for their uncomplicated help with translations and last-minute corrections.

We are immensely grateful to the anonymous reviewer who provided us with detailed and encouraging feedback.

Rachel Weydert and Jana Hodges-Kluck at Lexington have supported this publication project throughout with great enthusiasm, and always had an open ear for us. Thank you!

Last but not least, we thank our friends and comrades—the Birmingham crowd, everyone at Coventry Peace House, Marie, Julia, Andrea, Broder, Georg, Palscal, and all those who had to deal with us. This book is dedicated to you.

Introduction

Material-Discursive Entanglements

Locating Materialist Discourse Studies

Johannes Beetz and Veit Schwab

The discursive and the material are entangled. This entanglement lies at the foundation of every materialist approach to discourse. A cognate concern for linguistic phenomena, symbolic practices, discourse as well as materialism can look back on a long tradition in the Social Sciences and Humanities. It was, however, only recently that their relation was made a more explicit stake again through the consolidation of two new fields—Discourse Studies and New Materialism(s). While discursivity and materiality have been placed at the centers of these fields of research, they are often regarded as conceptually disentangled and separated aspects of the Social.

This book adopts a different perspective. It contributes to the ongoing debates revolving around materiality, materialism, discourse, and language, by making the relation between them an explicit focus. Located at the intersections of materialism and Discourse Studies, it highlights the materiality of discourse and the entwinement of matter and meaning.

The Social is a messy place. Grasping it in its material reality and investigating the processes and practices which constitute and reproduce it is approached in a multitude of ways. Over the past few decades, an assemblage of perspectives working on the intersections of language and society has emerged. What they share is a theoretical and empirical concern for the production of meaning and the constitutive role of discourse(s) in the social world. The highly diverse and transdisciplinary field of Discourse Studies looks at how (material) realities are made meaningful, and explores (material) consequences of discursive practices and processes. To this end, it brings together various strands and permutations of discourse analyses and theories.

In the broadest sense, discourse analysis scrutinizes semiotic material that is appropriated and processed through practices embedded in specific material contexts. Simultaneously, discourse analysis always proceeds against the background of a discourse-theoretical framework, which provides an ontological and epistemological foundation that needs to be made explicit. Taking its departure in the 1960s, research decidedly concerned with discourse(s) and the production of meaning has now become an integral part of the academic landscape (Angermuller, Maingueneau, and Wodak 2014).

Today, Discourse Studies brings together approaches from linguistics, sociology, political sciences, gender studies, cultural studies, and many others. They reach from micro-analytical camps that analyze discourse as a set of situated practices and processes, to socio-historical and macro-sociological strands, which are more interested in the (re)production of large scale social phenomena. While this diversity is reflected in the contributions to this volume, they are united in two important ways: They share an interest in discourse and discursive practices, and they all adopt a decidedly materialist perspective.

In many ways, discourse and language are fundamentally material (Beetz 2016, 82ff). Furthermore, meaning making practices take place in material conditions (e.g., conditions and relations of production/reproduction), and are infused with power relations and inequality, which they also shape. The materiality of discourse and its embeddedness in material conditions are but two aspects of a materialist discourse analysis, which posits the primacy of the material over the ideational or "immaterial" when empirically or theoretically investigating meaning making practices in contexts.

The present volume investigates the methodological and conceptual implications materialism has for Discourse Studies. Simultaneously, the contributions show how discourse-analytical and theoretical concepts and methods contribute to a genuinely materialist understanding of the social world. Thus, what follows can be located on the intersection of Discourse Studies and materialism. With Discourse Studies constituting an ever-growing area of research and with questions of materiality and materialism experiencing a remarkable revival, *Material Discourse—Materialist Analysis* is an intervention in, as well as an expression of these ongoing discussions.

MAPPING THE BORDERS OF MATERIALIST DISCOURSE STUDIES

Some of the earliest forms of Discourse Studies started out as materialist and political endeavors. This is especially true for the beginnings of discourse analysis in France: Associated with figures such as Michel Pêcheux (Pêcheux 1982, 1995; Conein et al. 1981) and heavily influenced by Louis Althusser's reading of Marx (Althusser 1971, 2005; Althusser et al. 2015), they were decidedly Marxist and materialist (also see Courtine 1981; Maldidier 1990; Williams 1999).

Conversely, a concern for discursivity and discursive materialities figures prominently in the Marxist critique of ideology (Eagleton 1991), materialist semiotics (Rossi-Landi 1983), Russian formalism (Bennett 2003, Jameson 1974, pp 43ff), Critical Theory (Benjamin 1996–2003), and psychoanalysis (Freud 2010; Lacan 1981). Michel Foucault, who is readily identified with the label "discourse analysis" today, was heavily influenced by materialist scholarship on the intersection of historical materialism, psychoanalysis, and linguistics. While it might not always be evident on the textual surface of Foucault's writing, a materialist gaze is present throughout his work, for example in his conception of discursive formations in the *Archaeology of Knowledge* (2002).

However, many aspects of the complex and contentious history of materialist discourse analysis seem to have gotten lost in contemporary approaches to discourse, or only live on as a spectral undercurrent. According to Marie-Anne Paveau (2007), discourse analysis is marked by a particular form of forgetting. She notes that current discourse analysis is either relying on "a linguistic analysis of language that has forgotten history (reduction to language without context), or extended to a sociology of speaking that has forgotten the materiality of language (extension to interaction in general)." That way, it has basically "'dematerialized' by demarxisising itself" (ibid., 8–9; our translation). This, we believe, is not only true for the French context, but characteristic of a broader development that we seek to challenge with this volume.

Materialism and materiality remain an important, if often implicit, concern in Discourse Studies. Critical Discourse Analysis (Chouliaraki and Fairclough 1999; Fairclough and Graham 2002; Fairclough 2013; Flowerdew and Richardson 2017), the Essex School (Laclau and Mouffe 2001; Torfing 1999; Wodak and Meyer 2001; Critchley and Marchart 2004), enunciative pragmatics (Angermuller 2014), feminist and queer theory (Butler 1990, 1993, 1997; Hennessy 1993), and other strands and debates within Discourse Studies (Butler, Laclau, and Žižek 2000; Jones 2004) avail themselves to materialist theories and could be dubbed materialist in the sense introduced above.

Furthermore, there is a whole set of literatures dealing with discourse, language and communication that qualify as materialist and acknowledge the materiality of the semiotic material they engage with. This is true for Stuart Hall's seminal work on racism and cultural identities (Hall 1980, 1985, 1997; Hall and Du Gay 1996), as well as discursive strands of psychoanalysis (Parker and Pavón-Cuéllar 2014; Stavrakakis 1997, 1999). Equally, a concern for discursive materiality is present in research on the production of knowledge in the field of Cultural Political Economy (Jessop 2004; Sum and Jessop 2014). Moreover, Conversation Analysis (Sacks 1992) as well as research drawing on speech act theory (Austin 2009) cannot easily be dismissed as ignoring discourse, nor is their conception of discourse necessarily idealist.

It lies outside the scope of this volume (let alone this introduction) to map the above fields by presenting an anthology of materialist approaches in Discourse Studies. Such handbooks are unquestionably essential for the presentation and formation of fields such as (Critical) Discourse Studies. This is reflected in the exhaustive nature of Angermuller, Maingueneau and Wodak's *Discourse Studies Reader* (2014) as well as Flowerdew and Richardson's *Handbook of Critical Discourse Studies* (2017), to name just two prominent examples. The present volume is different in scope and aim: It neither claims to be a comprehensive overview, nor does it suggest an authoritative theory and methodology of a materialist discourse analysis. Rather, the different contributions in this book offer various *specific* takes on a common problematic, namely the relation between materialism, materiality, and discourse.

This problematic can look back on a long tradition. However, some strands within Discourse Studies tend to partially efface their materialist heritage by relegating materialism to the realm of a mere "prehistory." On the one side, citing Marx, Althusser, or Pêcheux feeds into practices of demarcation that insist on the prefix "post-" (-materialism, -marxism). On the other, "Marxism" and "materialism" are conceived of as separate bodies of literature that can be articulated with a concern for "discourse."

Ernsto Laclau and Chantal Mouffe's *Hegemony and Socialist Strategy* (2001), one of the foundational text for the Essex School of discourse theory, provides an excellent case in point: Laclau and Mouffe present their version of discourse analysis as a "post-marxist" actualization of "Althusserianism," "radicalizing *some* of its themes in a way that will explode its basic concepts" (Laclau and Mouffe 2001, 97). To this end, they resort to the discourse-analytical concepts of articulation, discursive formation and suture (stitching). What is strangely absent from their argument, however, is that precisely this combination (and the concomitant interlacing of linguistics, psychoanalysis, and historical materialism) had indeed been discussed previously, is present within these basic concepts, and played a crucial role in the very emergence of discourse analysis.

Against this background, we do not claim to describe an entanglement thus far invisible or altogether disregarded. Neither does the present volume attempt to reverse engineer an apparatus for a materialist discourse analysis which has been forgotten over the last decades. In many ways, materialist perspectives in the Social Sciences and Humanities as well as discursive approaches to the Social are thriving, and there are fruitful encounters across disciplinary boundaries and theoretical as well as ontological commitments.

Still, we believe that the relationship between discourse analysis and materialism has not been explored enough with regard to the *methodological and conceptual consequences* a materialist view on discourse entails. In many cases, materialism (often used synonymously with Marxist historical materialism) is treated as a dusty and outdated body of literature that needs to be rearticulated or jazzed up with other theories and methods. This results not only in an anecdotal and thus incomplete appraisal of the materialist legacy in Discourse Studies. Much worse, it leads to a severe misjudgment regarding its ongoing influence and development. Materialism is indeed alive and kicking, in and beyond Discourse Studies.

[NEW] MATERIALISM(S) AND DISCOURSE

When considering the nexus of materialism and discourse from the other side, it seems like contemporary materialism and research on materialities is generally not overly concerned with discourse and language, and on occasion even posits the latter as *the other* of the concrete and material. Especially with the emergence of New Materialisms (Coole and Frost 2010b; Dolphijn and van der Tuin 2012; Bennett 2010), material semiotics (Law 2009; Haraway 2004), or material cultural studies (Miller 2005; Woodward 2007; Hicks and Beaudry 2010), and a renewed interest in the materiality of discursive, social, and political realities (Bruno 2016; Pink, Ardévol, and Lanzeni 2016; Bleich 2013), what exactly "materialism" and "materiality" denote has become the subject of intense debate in the Social Sciences and Humanities again.

While these debates contribute a fresh and intriguing perspective on materialism and challenge some of its theoretical and methodological orthodoxies, it often replicates the aforementioned effacement by relying on a differentialist understanding of materiality and discourse. Such an understanding frequently results in a generally dismissive attitude toward discourse theory and analysis (see Lundborg and Vaughan-Williams 2015 for a compelling critique).

The charge sometimes raised against New Materialisms—namely, that the approaches assembled under this umbrella term disregard the symbolic and discursive dimensions of material reality and thus posit "matter" against (dialectical, historical) materialism (see e.g., Noys 2015)—finds its complement in the accusation that Discourse Studies disregards those material instances not immediately identified with the discursively constituted Social.

The latter can be found in Coole and Frost's *New Materialisms: Ontology, Agency, and Politics* (2010a). While they acknowledge that a "radical constructivism" has contributed considerable insight in the workings of power, they diagnose "an allergy to 'the real' that is characteristic of its more linguistic or discursive forms" leading to "overtures to material reality [being] dismissed as an insidious foundationalism" dissuading "critical inquirers from the more empirical kinds of investigation that material processes and structures require" (ibid., 6).

We can take a brief look at the discussion around the all too often embraced binary of "the discursive" and "the material" to illustrate the dangers of such an effacement, which obscures that the two have often constituted a cognate concern evading any dichotomization. In a nutshell, both (new) materialisms and (linguistic) Discourse Studies regularly accuse each other of playing materiality off against discourse or vice versa—thus reproducing the assumed incommensurability of the two and implicitly or explicitly favoring one of them. One such accusation is frequently aimed at the discourse theory of Laclau and Mouffe (2001) and takes the following form: If, for them, everything is discursive, then it seems like the (non-discursive) material is either excluded from inquiry or delegated to the realm of yet another dichotomy, that of *being* and *existence*, which still favors the discursive over material instances. No wonder some (new) materialists take issue with such a theory—caught up as they are in a practice of demarcation that strains to keep discourse and materiality separate.

And the reverse can be seen as well. Where the primary concern is *Vibrant Matter* (Bennett 2010) and the "vital materiality" (ibid., vii) of all *things* included in the flat ontologies of newer approaches, there seems to be no place for discourse and meaning, some Discourse Studies scholars argue. So the allergy diagnosed by Frost and Coole appears to be a mutual one, if we insist on keeping materiality and discursivity quarantined in their own pre-defined fields.

In our view, this goes hand-in-hand with an unfortunate overstatement of what is allegedly "new" in the materialist debate, much to the detriment of a careful appraisal of "old" and "new" materialist theories of language and discourse. "Older" materialist philosophy before Marx did certainly not emphasize and elaborate on the material character of language and was not very much concerned with developing a materialist theory of language. While the same is true for Marx and early Marxism, it should be pointed out—or recalled, where it has been forgotten—that the *practice* and sensual human activity of Marx's 1st thesis on Feuerbach (Marx 2010, 3) does not exclude linguistic activity and that there are important interventions throughout the history of Marxist materialism which developed materialist notions of language, symbolic practice, and discourse (see, e.g., Vološinov 1973, Pêcheux 1982, Bakhtin 1981, Marx 2002, Jessop 2002).

Vice versa, "new" materialist perspectives by no means all exclude discourse, meaning, or concerns shared with "older" materialisms either. Karen Barad's work constitutes an example for such a take. While contributing to the field of New Materialism, her work on "agential realism" is explicitly concerned with "the relationship between discursive practices and the material world" (Barad 2007, 24) and includes—albeit in a limited manner—questions of class and relations of production in her investigation (35). Her book *Meeting the Universe Halfway* (2007) takes an important step toward (re)articulating the centrality of discursive practices and the production of meaning to those approaches concerned with materiality and a "renewal" of materialism. Conversely, her insistence on the fundamental materiality of (discursive) practices (ibid. 45) and the role of materializations in the production of knowledge and meaning are an important intervention in the field of Discourse Studies.

We believe that the partial effacement of the deep entanglement between "materialism" and "discourse" constitutes a problem which goes beyond Discourse Studies or (new) materialism as fields of knowledge production.

It thwarts a more careful investigation of how the encounter continues to provide different strands of discourse theory and analysis with complex, in many ways even contradictory conceptions of materiality and materialism. Thus, notions of materiality in Discourse Studies range from essentialist/substantialist understandings which conceptualize materiality as matter or matter in motion over to representationalist and post-foundationalist conceptions with a less reductionist view on materiality. Equally, materialism may appear in its historical, dialectical, or interventionist forms or draw on the post-Deleuzian materialism of some of the new materialisms.

This unaddressed conceptual diversity risks resulting in a confusion that seriously impedes the reception and collaboration within and beyond Discourse Studies. This is exacerbated by the construction of alleged incompatibilities (between "materialism" and "post-structuralism," or "discourse analysis" and "materialist analysis"), and a range of essentialist dichotomies (materiality/discourse, discourse/reality, language/materiality, etc.), which constitute a prominent topic in theoretical debates.

In our view, disquieting these prevalent dichotomies should be one of the focal projects of a materialist discourse analysis that is worth its salt. While this can happen *neither* by positing that everything is simply matter or material *nor* that everything is discursive, we can trouble or conceptually halt the privileging of one over the other by highlighting the materiality of discourse and the entanglement of matter and meaning.

THE BOOK AND ITS CHAPTERS

Against widespread practices of demarcation and compartmentalization in subfields—which might be beneficial from the point of view of academic marketing, but certainly do not contribute to an inspiring and intriguing intellectual climate—this volume seeks to open up the debate on materialist discourse analysis. This is reflected in the composition of the volume, which brings together contributions from a whole range of disciplines, fields and academic contexts in a truly transdisciplinary and global manner. The contributions are united by a materialist understanding of discourse, as well as a rejection of static dichotomies such as discursive/material, language/materiality or reality/symbolic representation. Rather than presenting materialism and Discourse Studies as distinct from one another, they are shown to be intimately entwined and mutually beneficial, both in terms of their historical development and analytical gaze.

Several chapters put a decidedly materialist discourse analysis in practice by analyzing empirical material including journalistic texts (Oliveira), political video montages (Araújo, Ruiz and Leiser Baronas), or forum discussions and blog entries (Zimmermann). The contributions demonstrate the conceptual and analytical handling of discursive materialities (Herzog; de Araújo, Ruiz and Leiser Baronas; Pantzerhielm; Zimmermann) and articulations (Glasson; Pantzerhielm). They tackle questions of materiality from a discourse analytical standpoint, and investigate how the materiality of discourse can be conceptualized. Overall, the volume delineates the close relation between discourse analysis and materialism. This relation is explored with regard to Marxist materialist dialectics (Herzog), historical materialism (Courtine; Beetz and Schwab; Borrelli; Iretzberger), as well as new materialisms (Zimmermann). Furthermore, the relation between discourse analysis and materialist critique is discussed from different perspectives (Herzog; Courtine; Beetz and Schwab; Oliveira; Iretzberger).

The volume is opened by Benno Herzog's chapter on *Materialist Discourse Analysis as Social Critique.* Herzog combines Discourse Studies with Critical Theory in the tradition of the Frankfurt School in order to develop an immanent critique of processes of social reproduction. He shows how a dialectic mode of critique can help overcome the "empirical deficit" of critical theory and furnish discourse analysis with a more coherent understanding of critique. Herzog's contribution outlines eight steps for a materialist discourse analysis working toward social change, which are illustrated with the issue of meritocracy.

The following chapter features Jean-Jacques Courtine's *The Second Disappearance of Michel Pêcheux,* which is here first published in English. Courtine is a pioneer of discourse analysis in France. In his contribution, he reflects on the disappearance of materialist discourse analysis through the lens of the theoretical and political forgetting of Pêcheux and his work in the French context. Courtine questions the disciplinary politics behind the label of "French Discourse Analysis," which very much relegated its materialist beginnings to the status of a distant past. Against the dehistoricized versions of discourse analysis that dominate the field today, his contribution inspires to rediscover and embrace the original problematic of materialist discourse analysis that grappled with the encounter between a "real of language" and a "real of history," and challenges the now common distinction between discourse analysis and materialism.

In *Materialist Discourse Analysis: Three moments and some criteria*, Johannes Beetz and Veit Schwab explore moments of such an encounter across the work of Marx, Bakhtin, Vološinov, Althusser, and Pêcheux. They show that the border between "materialism" and "discourse," and the way it is policed in theory, methods, and academic debates are effects of discourse. Working against the oblivion of materialist discourse analysis helps uncovering some limits of contemporary knowledge production at the intersections of the linguistic, the social, and the political, and questioning the institutional structures within which it operates. In their chapter, they draft a preliminary set of criteria that aims at making the combination between discourse, ideology, and political economy matter (again).

Helio Oliveira shifts the focus to discursive materialities in his materialist-enunciative analysis of *The Black Consciousness Movement in Brazil*. Combining enunciative pragmatics with materialism in the tradition of Althusser and Pêcheux, Oliveira demonstrates how the formula "Black consciousness" is constituted in Brazilian debates on racism, a context that is marked by a historical "myth of racial democracy," which persistently covers up the brutal realities of everyday racism in the country. Against the background of an analysis of journalistic and activist texts, he shows that the media are biased toward a view that attributes racism to socioeconomic problems of the Black population and limits its treatment to celebrations of diversity, instead of listening to those who are affected by racism in the first place, thereby masking its historical and material conditions.

Ligia Mara Boin Menossi de Araújo, Marco Antonio Almeida Ruiz and Roberto Leiser Baronas continue the engagement with discursive materialities in their analysis of multimodal discourse on YouTube. In *Heterogeneous Materialities on YouTube,* the authors combine French theories on enunciative heterogeneity with more recent methodological developments in Brazil to analyze the political discourse in the context of the presidential elections of 2010. They show how "French" discourse analysis in the tradition of Pêcheux and Authier-Revuz can be used to scrutinize new discursive materialities that emerged in the twenty-first century. They particularly focus on how ridicule manifests itself as a special type of material-discursive heterogeneity that is not strictly bound to text or spoken language.

In *Unspeakable Articulations: Steps towards a Materialist Discourse Theory,* Benjamin Glasson addresses the problem of the "extra-discursive" and material in materialist theories of discourse. Focusing on Laclau and Mouffe's discourse theory, he highlights the paradoxes of the notion of "discursive totality" and of the being/existence binary to overcome some shortcomings of discourse theory concerning the status of matter and the "extra-discursive." Glasson draws on Badiou's dialectical materialism to enrich discourse theory with a genuinely materialist outlook, which locates that which is not discursive but material in the space obscured by the empty signifier and the subject.

Laura Pantzerhielm's contribution continues the engagement with discourse theory in the tradition of the Essex School and argues for a post-foundationalist/anti-essentialist approach to discourse which acknowledges the productive—yet contingent—role of materiality in structuring the Social. Challenging the prevalent assertion of a dichotomy of materialism and radical constructivist epistemology, *Contingent Materialities as Sedimented Articulations* proposes a combination of Foucauldian mapping of outer epistemic borders with a concern for instances of political sedimentation and articulation which draws on Laclau and Mouffe's conceptual instruments, while using the field of International Relations (IR) as an example to show how such a perspective can be put to work.

The next chapter proposes a "Critical Materialist Discourse Analysis" (CMDA) which draws on Marxist materialism and is informed by the metatheory of Critical Realism. Manuel Iretzberger critiques contemporary (constructivist) approaches to discourse by exemplarily presenting drawbacks in Laclau and Mouffe's discourse theory and Fairclough's Critical Discourse Analysis. The problematization of the status given to the non-discursive and material in discourse theory as well as the dichotomy of the discursive field and the non-discursive field in Critical Discourse Analysis echoes Glasson's critique, albeit with a different focus. Arguing for a stratified ontology that conceptualizes the material and extra-discursive as instances that discourse is embedded in, *Marxism and Discourse: On the Meta-Theoretical Foundation of a Critical Materialist Discourse Analysis* offers a re-evaluation of the role of discourse within Marxism and outlines an alternative to current (critical) approaches within Discourse Studies.

Semiosis and Discursivity of the Commodity-Form explores the question of how a materialist semiotic and discursive method can be conceptualized. Giorgio Borrelli critically engages with the theory of the Italian scholar Ferruccio Rossi-Landi to delineate a semiotics which proposes a fundamental similarity between the production of material artifacts (commodities) and the production of signs and messages (discourse). By outlining Rossi-Landi's *homological method* and presenting the Marxian category of the commodity as a sign-vehicle, Borrelli contributes to a materialist theory of discourse, which draws on the Marxian critique of political economy as well as Italian semiotics.

The volume closes with Julia Maria Zimmermann's chapter on *Desire, Queer Politics, and the Materiality of Experience*. Against the background of New Materialism(s) in empirical queer theory, she explores the status given to matter in constructivist and queer research. This is done by looking at the materiality of absence through the lens of bottom-up discourses on asexuality in online communities. Zimmermann argues for a non-reductionist understanding of materiality in and beyond queer theory and Discourse Studies, which pushes the latter to account for unintelligible forms of materiality without essentializing these across different subjects and contexts.

Altogether, the contributions in this volume offer a reappraisal of the intricate relation between materiality, materialism, and discourse by challenging some widespread theoretical and analytical positions and demarcations. Evidently, the scope of this book is limited. Rather than constituting an exhaustive presentation of materialist Discourse Studies and accounting for the myriad pertinent approaches that theorize and empirically analyze discourse as a material phenomenon, our aim is to facilitate debates and interventions around one focal point:

What matters in discourse?

BIBLIOGRAPHY

Althusser, Louis. 1971. "Ideology and Ideological State Apparatuses (Notes Towards an Investigation)." In *Lenin and Philosophy and Other Essays*, edited by Ben Brewster, 127–86. New York, London: Monthly Review Press.

———. 2005. *For Marx.* London, New York: Verso.

Althusser, Louis, Étienne Balibar, Roger Establet, Pierre Macherey, and Jacques Rancière. 2015. *Reading Capital: The Complete Edition.* London, New York: Verso.

Angermuller, Johannes. 2014. *Poststructuralist Discourse Analysis: Subjectivity in Enunciative Pragmatics.* Houndmills: Palgrave Macmillan.

Angermuller, Johannes, Dominique Maingueneau, and Ruth Wodak. 2014. "The Discourse Studies Reader: An Introduction." In *The Discourse Studies Reader: Main Currents in Theory and Analysis*, edited by Johannes Angermuller, Dominique Maingueneau, and Ruth Wodak, 1–14. Amsterdam: John Benjamins.

Austin, John L. 2009. *How to Do Things with Words.* Cambridge, MA: Harvard University Press.

Bakhtin, Mikhail M., and Michael Holquist, eds. 1981. *The Dialogic Imagination: Four Essays.* Austin: University of Texas Press.

Barad, Karen M. 2007. *Meeting the Universe Halfway: Quantum Physics and the Entanglement of Matter and Meaning.* Durham, NC: Duke University Press.

Beetz, Johannes. 2016. *Materiality and Subject in Marxism, (Post-)Structuralism, and Material Semiotics.* London: Palgrave Macmillan.

Benjamin, Walter. 1996–2003. *Selected Writings.* Edited by Howard Eiland, Michael W. Jennings, and Gary Smith. Cambridge, MA, London: Belknap Press of Harvard University Press.

Bennett, Jane. 2010. *Vibrant Matter: A Political Ecology of Things.* Durham: Duke University Press.

Bleich, David. 2013. *The Materiality of Language: Gender, Politics, and the University.* Bloomington: Indiana University Press.

Bruno, Giuliana. 2016. *Surface: Matters of Aesthetics, Materiality, and Media.* Chicago: University of Chicago Press.

Butler, Judith. 1990. *Gender Trouble: Feminism and the Subversion of Identity.* Thinking gender. New York: Routledge.

———. 1993. *Bodies That Matter: On the Discursive Limits of "Sex."* New York: Routledge.

———. 1997. *The Psychic Life of Power: Theories in Subjection.* Stanford: Stanford University Press.

Butler, Judith, Ernesto Laclau, and Slavoj Žižek, eds. 2000. *Contingency, Hegemony, Universality: Contemporary Dialogues on the Left.* London: Verso.

Chouliaraki, Lilie, and Norman Fairclough. 1999. *Discourse in Late Modernity: Rethinking Critical Discourse Analysis.* Edinburgh: Edinburgh University Press.

Conein, Bernard, Jean-Jacques Courtine, Françoise Gadet, Jean-Marie Marandin, and Michel Pêcheux, eds. 1981. *Materialités Discursives: Colloque des 24, 25, 26 avril 1980, Université Paris X - Nanterre.* Lille: Presses Universitaires de Lille.

Coole, Diana H., and Samantha Frost. 2010a. "Introducing the New Materialisms." In *New Materialisms: Ontology, Agency, and Politics,* 1–43. Durham: Duke University Press.

———, eds. 2010b. *New Materialisms: Ontology, Agency, and Politics.* Durham: Duke University Press.

Courtine, Jean-Jacques. 1981. "Quelques problèmes théoriques et méthodologiques en analyse du discours, à propos du discours communiste adressé aux chrétiens." *Langages* 15 (62): 9–128.

Critchley, Simon, and Oliver Marchart, eds. 2004. *Laclau: A Critical Reader.* London, New York: Routledge.

Dolphijn, Rick, and Iris van der Tuin, eds. 2012. *New Materialism: Interviews and Cartographies.* New Metaphysics. Ann Arbor: Open Humanities Press.

Eagleton, Terry. 1991. *Ideology: An Introduction.* London, New York: Verso.

Fairclough, Norman. 2013. *Critical Discourse Analysis: The Critical Study of Language.* London, New York: Routledge.

Fairclough, Norman, and Phil Graham. 2002. "Marx as a Critical Discourse Analyst: The Genesis of a Critical Method and its Relevance to the Critique of Global Capital." *Estudios de Sociolingüística* 3 (1): 185–229.

Foucault, Michel. 2002. *Archaeology of Knowledge.* London, New York: Routledge.

Freud, Sigmund. 2010. *The Interpretation of Dreams.* Edited by James Strachey. New York: Basic Books.

Hall, Stuart. 1980. "Race, Articulation and Societies Structured in Dominance." In *Sociological Theories: Race and Colonialism*, edited by UNESCO, 305–45. Paris: UNESCO.

———. 1985. "Signification, Representation, Ideology: Althusser and the Post-Structuralist Debates." *Critical Studies in Mass Communication* 2 (2): 91–114.

———. ed. 1997. *Representation: Cultural Representations and Signifying Practices.* Culture, Media and Identities. London: Sage.

Hall, Stuart, and Paul Du Gay, eds. 1996. *Questions of Cultural Identity.* London: Sage.

Haraway, Donna J. 2004. *The Haraway Reader.* New York: Routledge.

Hennessy, Rosemary. 1993. *Materialist Feminism and the Politics of Discourse.* New York, London: Routledge.

Hicks, Dan, and Mary C. Beaudry, eds. 2010. *The Oxford Handbook of Material Culture Studies.* Oxford Handbooks. Oxford, New York: Oxford University Press.

Jameson, Fredric. 1974. *The Prison-House of Language: A Critical Account of Structuralism and Russian Formalism.* Princeton, NJ: Princeton University Press.

Jessop, Bob. 2004. "Critical Semiotic Analysis and Cultural Political Economy." *Critical Discourse Studies* 1 (2): 159–74. doi:10.1080/17405900410001674506.

Jones, Peter. 2004. "Discourse and the Materialist Conception of History: Critical Comments on Critical Discourse Analysis." *Historical Materialism* 12 (1): 97–125.

Lacan, Jacques. 1981. *The Four Fundamental Concepts of Psychoanalysis.* The Seminar of Jacques Lacan 11. New York: W.W. Norton.

Laclau, Ernesto, and Chantal Mouffe. 2001. *Hegemony and Socialist Strategy: Towards a Radical Democratic Politics.* 2nd ed. London, New York: Verso.

Law, John. 2009. "Actor Network Theory and Material Semiotics." In *The New Blackwell Companion to Social Theory*, edited by Bryan S. Turner, 141–58. Chichester, West Sussex, Malden: Wiley-Blackwell.

Lundborg, Tom, and Nick Vaughan-Williams. 2015. "New Materialisms, Discourse Analysis, and International Relations: A Radical Intertextual Approach." *Review of International Studies* 41 (01): 3–25.

Maldidier, Denise. 1990. "(Re)lire Michel Pêcheux aujourd'hui." In *L'inquiétude du discours: Textes de Michel Pêcheux*, 7–91. Archives du commentaire. Paris: Éditions des Cendres.

Marx, Karl. 2002. "The Eighteenth Brumaire of Louis Bonaparte." In *Marx's Eighteenth Brumaire: (Post)Modern Interpretations*, edited by Karl Marx, Mark Cowling, and James Martin, 19–109. London, Sterling, VA: Pluto Press.

———. 2010. "Theses on Feuerbach." In *Karl Marx and Frederick Engels Works*, Vol. 5, April 1845-April 1847, 3–5. London: Lawrence & Wishart.

Miller, Daniel. 2005. *Materiality.* Durham, NC: Duke University Press.

Noys, Benjamin. 2015. "Matter against Materialism: Bruno Latour and the Turn to Objects." University of Warwick, October 27. Accessed February 09, 2016. https://www.academia.edu/21686931/Matter_against_Materialism_Bruno_Latour_and_the_Turn_to_Objects

Parker, Ian, and David Pavón-Cuéllar, eds. 2014. *Lacan, Discourse, Event: New Psychoanalytic Approaches to Textual Indeterminacy.* London, New York: Routledge.

Paveau, Marie-Anne. 2007. "Discours et matérialisme. Quelques points d'articulation entre la pensée althussérienne et l'analyse du discours dite 'française.'" Accessed April 27, 2016. http://www.europhilosophie.eu/recherche/IMG/pdf/Disc_et_mat_MAP.pdf

Pêcheux, Michel. 1982. *Language, Semantics and Ideology: Stating the Obvious.* London: Macmillan.

———. 1995. *Automatic Discourse Analysis.* Edited by Tony Hak and Niels Helsloot. Amsterdam, Atlanta, GA: Rodopi.

Pink, Sarah, Elisenda Ardévol, and Débora Lanzeni. 2016. *Digital Materialities: Design and Anthropology.* London: Bloomsbury.

Richardson, John, and John Flowerdew, eds. 2017. *The Routledge Handbook of Critical Discourse Studies.* Routledge Handbooks in Applied Linguistics. Basingstoke: Routledge.

Rossi-Landi, Ferruccio. 1983. *Language as Work & Trade: A Semiotic Homology for Linguistics & Economics.* Massachusetts: Bergin & Garvey Publishers.

Sacks, Harvey. 1992. *Lectures on Conversation.* Oxford, Cambridge, MA: Blackwell.

Stavrakakis, Yannis. 1999. *Lacan & the Political.* London, New York: Routledge.

———. 2007. *The Lacanian Left: Psychoanalysis, Theory, Politics.* Edinburgh: Edinburgh University Press.

Sum, Ngai-Ling, and Bob Jessop. 2014. *Towards a Cultural Political Economy: Putting Culture in its Place in Political Economy.* Northampton: Edward Elgar Publishing Inc.

Torfing, Jacob. 1999. *New Theories of Discourse: Laclau, Mouffe, and Žižek.* Oxford, UK, Malden, MA: Blackwell Publishers.

Vološinov, Valentin. 1973. *Marxism and the Philosophy of Language.* London: Seminar Press.

Williams, Glyn. 1999. *French Discourse Analysis: The Method of Post-Structuralism.* London: Routledge.

Wodak, Ruth, and Michael Meyer, eds. 2001. *Methods of Critical Discourse Analysis.* London: Sage.

Woodward, Ian. 2007. *Understanding Material Culture.* Los Angeles: Sage.

Chapter 1

Materialist Discourse Analysis as Social Critique

Combining Critical Theory with Discourse Studies

Benno Herzog

In the Marxist tradition, materialism is a theory of materiality or matter as well as the relation between the material and symbolic worlds.[1] Materialism in the Marxist tradition is fundamentally anchored in historical and dialectical thinking. An awareness of the embeddedness of the work of the intellectual and historical social worlds leads intellectual enquiry to take a conscious stance toward social change. Historical and dialectical materialism is therefore engrained in the concept of *social critique*, which is understood as a practice of fundamental social change. However, narrow deterministic perceptions of materialism, doubts concerning the normative scope of social critique, and the struggle regarding the definition of matter, especially since the linguistic turn in the Social Sciences and Humanities in the 1970s, present serious objections to classic Marxist materialism. In particular, the last critique requires a close examination of Discourse Studies because it also developed from a critique of traditional Marxism that originated from the Marxist tradition itself.

In this chapter, I combine materialism and empirical research to develop a general critique of the processes of social reproduction. Here, discourse theory and discourse analysis come into play. Considering the "discursive production of realities," it seems reasonable to suppose that discourse analysis can be used to understand the processes of social reproduction. Although discourse analysts often conceive of their work as critical, there is little theoretical discussion regarding the possibility of a normative critique in the scientific community of discourse analysis. Rarely are the normative grounds and normative scope of such a critique clear. Often, one's own critical perspective is nothing more than an external positing.

The main aim of this chapter is to show how materialism can be used to develop a normative social critique and how discourse analysis can provide useful tools for that predominantly practical task. This approach can help Critical Theory to overcome its sociological deficit and can provide discourse analysis with specific research questions and a coherent normative foundation for its own position.

To achieve this objective, I first develop the notion of a theoretically informed and normative foundation for a critique in empirical discourse analysis by presenting the logic of immanent critique as found in the tradition of left Hegelianism, especially Marxism and the traditions of the Frankfurt School. These theories agree on the need to empirically ground the normative perspective in pre-scientific practices (a practice-based immanent critique). Thus far, however, all the theories show an empirical deficit that impedes a coherent social analysis.

In a second step, I explain how discourse analysis, as a broad, interdisciplinary field, can be used to combine the analysis of diverse elements to develop a social critique. Discourse analysis can help to extract the normativity that is inherent in language, practices, and structured material dispositions, which can be analyzed as meaningful, normative elements. Discourse analysis can be used as a social critique by considering the implicit normative claims of diverse practices against the social reality of discursive social reproduction.

Finally, I present the methodological procedure for a discourse analysis as social critique. In eight steps, a procedure is developed between sociological discourse analysis and macro-sociological theory. A comprehensive practical example on the topic of meritocracy will help to clarify the procedure and the relevance of the approach.

THE NORMATIVE FOUNDATIONS OF MATERIALIST SOCIAL CRITIQUE

As is well known, Marx develops his notion of materialism based on a critique of Feuerbach (Marx 1970) and outlines the nexus between materialism and critique. For Marx, material reality must be the starting point for critique (first thesis on Feuerbach). Marx does not refer to a stable, given, or objective materiality but to a process toward a "sensuous human activity, practice." For Marx, material reality must prove critique to be true (second thesis), which also refers to the normative "truth." The question of truth is, for Marx, "a practical question." Thinking must be embedded in the real world. Finally, critique must effectively change material reality (eleventh thesis).

Here, we obtain a first look at the dialectical character of materialism. Materiality refers not only to a substance-based idea but also, fundamentally, to processes and practices. To understand this approach to processes instead of fixed matter, it is useful to recall some of the points that David Harvey

(2016) makes to explain dialectics. I present five aspects. First, as already indicated, "dialectical thinking prioritizes the understanding of processes, flows, fluxes and relations over the analysis of elements, things, structures and organized systems. The latter do not exist outside of the processes that support, give rise to or create them" (ibid., 196). Second, for dialectics, parts and wholes are mutually constitutive of one another. Every part consists of other elements, and their relations and elements can be combined. Third, the subjects and objects of analysis can be interchanged. Subjects can be treated as the objects of analysis, and objects can act as subjects (e.g., a structure can cause the process of structuring). Fourth, change is fundamental to all systems. All systems are the result of change, and if they are to persist in the future, they will undergo processes of change. Finally, "dialectical enquiry is not itself outside of its own form of argumentation but subject to it" (ibid., 199). Our "observation" intervenes in the world. As observers or critics, we are the object of a process of formation by the social world, but we are also subjects who shape the social world as an "object."

The processes and practices in which Marx was most interested were the complex processes of social reproduction and, mainly, the practice of work. Marxist materialism attempts to develop a fundamental critique of the processes of social reproduction. Based on a broad notion of the social division of labor, materialism aims to theoretically understand the praxis of society, economy, politics, and culture in its relations. Society and every social phenomenon are viewed as the specific historical results of constitutive human practices.

The Marxian *mode* of critique is often called immanent critique or immanent transcendence (Browne 2008, Herzog 2016a, Romero 2013, Stahl 2013a). The idea of *immanence* and the notion of *critique* or *transcendence* can be divided into the two aspects of norms and methods. Norms originate from the normative potential of existing society (i.e., immanence) but point simultaneously toward a future society (i.e., transcendence and critique). As a method, the results should be developed completely from the empirical material (i.e., immanence) and should simultaneously indicate a practical path or otherwise be a powerful tool to change society (i.e., transcendence and critique).

Currently, the theoretical problem for immanent social critique is the source of this normative potential of societies. In classic Marxist analysis, work was viewed as the specific moral experience that enables the working class to effectively (i.e., practically) criticize and overcome a given society. However, confidence in the emancipatory capacity of this class has diminished significantly in the first half of the last century. In the 1980s, Jürgen Habermas believed that he found in language and its use the moral experience that aims for understanding and emancipation (1984). Through the very fact that people use language, they implicitly accept normative claims of understanding and emancipation. However, since Foucault's critique of the power in language and the multiple mechanisms of exclusion in its use (see, e.g., Foucault 1981), the public sphere can no longer be imagined as a space of free deliberation. Instead, the public sphere must be viewed as a space filled with mechanisms of exclusion, marginalization, and conscious and unconscious rules of participation—that is, *a sphere of heteronomous orders of (in)visibilization.*

Axel Honneth, a disciple of Habermas, uses Foucault's critique but maintains Habermas's communicative approach. Although Honneth's theory is internationally known as Recognition Theory, for Honneth, the practices that are used to ground a normative critique are those of misrecognition or disrespect (Honneth 1995). Misrecognition produces a social form of suffering. Every individual, not only individuals with certain social capital, can suffer from disrespect. Because we can empathically understand the suffering of others, we can speak here of a form of silent communicative action. For Honneth, this suffering can be used as a normative starting point for social critique. For our approach to materialism and social critique, we take our normative standpoint from the social suffering of individuals because this suffering ultimately points toward a social order in which suffering is abolished.

When discussing social suffering here, I am referring to a second-order phenomenon (i.e., a form of evaluation of a first-order phenomenon). It is a suffering that stems from the fact that certain socially accepted norms are not fulfilled in practice or that they have a normative surplus that is not yet realized. Suffering is thus an affective reaction due to the difference between (socially accepted) normative claims and reality. It becomes immediately clear that social suffering does not refer to suffering from natural phenomena but only to suffering that is made or changeable by human beings. Only this suffering can contradict the normative expectations of the participants.

It is important to understand that we are not just adopting another external standpoint; in this case, we are not just taking the avoidance of social suffering as new external perspective from which we criticize society, instead of taking competing norms like freedom or equality. When we accept that people can suffer when normative claims are not realized, we can say that although this capacity is universal, it does not point to a universal norm. In different social situations, there are different normative expectations. A boxer who receives hard punches as part of his work does not claim that he should not be punched. In other words, although he is suffering, it is not a social suffering in the Honnethian sense of suffering due to disrespect. The situation would be different in the case of someone forced to fight in the ring for the amusement of others. In this case, the boxer would suffer from the disrespect received. His normative claim that he should not be forced against his will to fight in the ring would then collide with the reality of disrespect.

At the same time, this approach shows the limits of critique: at the very moment at which people no longer suffer under their conditions, immanent critique is no longer possible. Taking hunger as another example, we can see that it has accompanied humanity throughout its history. Historically, suffering from famine has not been social suffering. This has changed only in the last centuries, in which humanity has theoretically had the means of production to abolish malnutrition. From that point on, hunger is *social* suffering. Thus, at the moment the approximately 800 million undernourished people and the rest of humanity understand hunger as natural or divine and not socially created, which pushes us to action (i.e., in a world of "total delusion"), critique is no longer possible.

This "practice-based" type of immanent critique is identified by Stahl (2013b) as belonging to the Marxist tradition that was developed in the tradition of the Frankfurt School. Thus, the critic "must not only draw on the cultural meaning or the rules accepted in a given community but also on his or her knowledge about the community's *objective practices and institutions*" (ibid., 535). This type of immanent critique always presupposes the existence of normative elements in social practices that are beyond the conscious understanding of the participants and upon which immanent critique can draw.

For an empirical analysis, this theoretical framework requires specific attention to the norms that are contained in practices and in affective reactions to misrecognition. Although practices are always discursively created, shaped, and interpreted by social actors, the primary focus of the analysis that is required for this type of critique must be practices, not more or less conscious language use. However, this type of materialist analysis must simultaneously consider the role of these norms in the reproduction of society and the systemic obstacles to overcoming the existing form of social reproduction. As I argue in the next section, in the toolbox of sociological discourse analysis, we can find all the necessary elements for this materialist social critique.

DISCOURSE ANALYSIS AS SOCIAL CRITIQUE

For empirical social research, the idea of immanent critique means that social researchers must analyze and reconstruct the normative basis of society. As long as this reconstruction refers to the official and explicit normative points of reference, it seems not to be too complicated for discourse analysis. Nonetheless, if we accept the important thesis that socially accepted normativity is immanent in *social practices*, the analysis becomes more difficult. In addition, when analyzing the normative content of practices (or the institutionalized,

Benno Herzog

material social order), the critical approach requires *simultaneous* research on the development potential, obstacles, and systemic or structural limitations that impede the unfolding of these normative claims. We can differentiate real, transcending immanent critique from mere corrective critique only through this second element.

However, we face at least three major problems. First, how should such an analysis proceed? How can we analyze the silent elements of the practices of and affective reactions to misrecognition or the "silenced discourses" that are the result of silent or silenced suffering? When discourses do not appear, when they are reduced to silence before they are even articulated, how can the social researcher access the normative content of this silence? A second issue involves the possibility that the expression of social suffering is pre-structured and that suffering itself is not an immediate experience. Suffering is always already mediated. We can imagine how a white supremacist suffers from having to share public transport with other racial groups. In the same way that Honneth discusses the ideology of recognition (Honneth 2004), we can understand this example as ideological misrecognition or ideological suffering. Therefore, when we accept that the normative content of affective reactions, practices, and institutional orders, for example, can be ideological, then the second problem becomes clearer. How can we differentiate ideologically normative content from the content that the critic wants to use as a foundation for an immanent critique? The problem is how to determine the normative status of a practice or an affective reaction. Finally, there is a third problem, which references the previously discussed relation between immanence and transcendence in a double sense and involves the question of how to effectively transcend society with actual immanent norms. The norms must identify other (better) social relations, and the analysis of these norms must contribute to effective social change.

All of these problems refer to the "sociological deficit" of immanent critique. Presenting the possibility of immanent norms in social phenomena requires an epistemic and methodological approach to these norms. This approach can be found in what I call "sociological discourse analysis." In the last decade, several promising and sociological approaches toward discourses have emerged (e.g., Bührmann and Schneider 2007, Keller 2005) and have broadened the vision of discourse analysis with respect to the analysis of practices, material realities, power relations, social structures, and even affective reactions to disrespect (Guitiérrez-Rodríguez 2007). Although these aspects also inhere in the more linguistic forms of discourse analysis, they have now achieved the status of an independent field of systematic analysis.

Following a more sociological discourse analysis, we can understand the (implicit) interpretations that social actors elaborate in specific situations.

Discourse analysis can perform controlled interpretation, can use reflexive methods, and can analyze the sociohistoric context of these interpretations. For Foucault, individuals are permanently involved in social struggles (i.e., in discursive struggles) that are primarily struggles for truth or resources, and they often have normative effects. These struggles (or the participation in discursive practices) are often unconscious. Therefore, when individuals engage in practices, whether practices of discourse production (e.g., speaking) or practices that are produced by discourses (e.g., taking up cycling because of a discourse on health and well-being), they are frequently unaware of the normative implications of their practices.

The more sociological approaches *simultaneously* focus on texts and the non-textual aspects of social life, such as practices or materialities. With these approaches, we can make explicit the normative pretensions of the individuals who engage in all types of interaction. Concurrently, we can reveal the normative implications of their (often unconscious) struggles. Therefore, we can differentiate justified normative claims from unjustified, ideological, normative claims. Unjustified and therefore ideological normative claims are claims that contravene their own implicit normative ground. In this sense, the analysis of discursive and extra-discursive realities cannot offer normative criteria for immanent critique but can reveal the social effects of possible criteria. Consequently, discourse analysis offers the possibility of adopting a reflexive and informed position regarding different normative claims and their respective discursive and extra-discursive expressions.

The broader sociological discourse-analytical approaches can help us to better understand the normative content of discursive and nondiscursive practices and struggles. More sociologically based approaches help us not only to perform internal critiques on discourses but also to use immanent critique to better understand discourses and material realities. These approaches help us to analyze the differences between (implicit) normative claims and realities. Although we can evaluate the consequences of these differences, it does not necessarily follow that discourse analysis is the empirical research method for materialist critique. To combine both strands, it is important to note three aspects that are frequently omitted in contemporary immanent critique and discourse studies.

1. Contrary to the notion that immanent critique means revealing the contradiction between socially accepted claims and reality, in the materialist tradition, these contradictions have always been *necessary* (Browne 2008). "Necessary" refers to the contradictions that inevitably arise from the social order. Thus, immanent critique is not a matter of holding a mirror to criticized individuals and showing them their own contradictions so that

they can deliberately change their behaviour. This type of critique would surely have a transformative effect, but its transcending character would be limited. Materialist critique is interested in structural and/or systemic conditions that impede the resolution of the mentioned contradictions. Therefore, discourse analysis that seeks to follow the insights of Critical Theory must not only compare claims with (symbolic and material) reality but also reveal the (symbolic and material) obstacles that prevent these claims from becoming reality. As it extends toward the analysis of material resources, sociological discourse analysis has prepared the ground for the merging of immanent critique, as found in Critical Theory, with discourse analysis. Immanent critique can find practical tools for analysis in the discourse-analytical toolbox. For discourse analysts, in contrast, this merging yields clear research questions, such as what the differences are between claims and reality and whether these differences are necessary (i.e., structural or systemic) contradictions.

When we are not referring to contradictions that can be directly influenced by individual, collective, or institutional acts of will, *immanent critique is always social critique.* Immanent critique is never limited to criticizing single social actors and always refers to systemic inadequacies.

2. Regarding the dialectics of the idea of immanent critique, we can clarify the problem of the transcending normative viewpoint. Foucault seems to take his critical stance from the outside by referring to the "art of not being governed like that" (Foucault 2007). However, Critical Theory seems to insist that the immanence of institutions is so overwhelming that a transcending position is no longer visible. Nonetheless, as Zamora affirms, dialectical immanent critique also means that "the total immanence of the system—even through mediation—ultimately is external and forceful to the individual" (Zamora 2011). This clarification suggests that there can be spaces of exteriority even in a totally administered world. According to diverse representatives of Critical Theory (Adorno 1970, Honneth 1995), these spaces can be understood as suffering. Thus, individual and collective human-made suffering is the engine for normative progress. That humans can suffer from social relations indicates the existence of this ultimate normative point of reference.

By merging immanent critique and discourse analysis, we can hypothesize that it is exactly this individual suffering that leads Foucault to his attitude of refusal. The reason Foucault refuses "to be governed like that" is the social suffering that is described in Critical Theory, such as experiences of disrespect as described by Honneth (1995). Foucault experienced this disrespect himself to a degree and was partially able to empathically understand other people who suffered disrespect. Therefore, the capacity to suffer as proof of the existence of a normative perspective that is alien to the system may represent the socially immanent anchor that refers transcendently to this position outside a given society.

Thus, theoretically informed discourse analysis must uncover social suffering and reveal the degree to which this suffering is human-made. Individuals do not necessarily verbally express their suffering. Their affective reactions are frequently silent or expressed nonverbally. Here, the methodological toolbox of sociological discourse analysis can be helpful due to its capacity to analyze not only text and talk but also nonverbal practices and affects (see also Renout 2012, Gutiérrez-Rodríguez 2007). In addition, merging Critical Theory and discourse analysis offers a methodological approach for researchers interested in immanent critique and provides theoretically informed research questions for discourse analysts.

3. When performing immanent critique, we must be aware of yet another aspect that is alien to poststructuralist discourse analysis or of which poststructuralists are often highly suspicious. As clarified by Gregor Sauerwald's (2008) description of immanent critique as "context-bound universalism," the notion of normative transcendence refers to a type of universal norm. However, the idea of universal norms is sharply criticized by Foucault and other poststructuralists. For example, Foucault demonstrates that apparently universal norms are historically contingent and extremely particular and "rare" constellations (e.g., Foucault 1981). Here, too, discourse analysis can help to reveal the particularity of apparently universal norms.

My hypothesis is that, ultimately, there is only one universal social norm: (human-made) suffering should be avoided. This norm can be used as a superlative norm by which to measure all other norms. By considering the norm of the avoidance of suffering superior to all other norms, we may solve the conundrum of ideological norms: if a norm (e.g., the specific recognition of white identities) is not reconcilable with the superlative norm of avoiding human-made suffering, it must be rejected. Similarly, we can demonstrate that implicit or explicit norms of liberty, equality, solidarity, and autonomy are principally compatible with the superlative norm. However, as we have seen above, avoiding second-order suffering is not *one* norm but refers to a *multiplicity* of *historically changing* norms and to the suffering produced when these norms are not realized.

Again, this merging means a methodologization for materialism and the possibility of theoretically informed research questions for discourse analysis. Researchers may then ask which norms are immanent in a society and the extent to which these norms are reconcilable with the (superior, universal) norm of the avoidance of suffering.

EIGHT STEPS FOR DISCOURSE ANALYSIS AS SOCIAL CRITIQUE IN THE MATERIALIST TRADITION

At the beginning of the approach described here, there is a decision to attempt to develop a critique that points toward the core of social reproduction. This decision is usually based on the hypothesis that there is something pathological in our society that is not a surface phenomenon; instead, social pathologies have underlying structural or systematic reasons. Researchers should be acutely aware of these assumptions along with their other prejudices or biases. Awareness of this individual starting point should allow one to eventually distance oneself from the ideas that are being defended. Under no circumstances should the starting point determine the results of the research.

Seriously considering the materialist approach to immanent critique means that it should not be the investigator's norms that lead to social critique but rather the norms of the criticized society itself. Thus, it is the researcher's task to uncover these socially accepted norms and bring them to light by unfolding them and showing a (perhaps systemic) difference between socially accepted normative claims and reality. In general, we can distinguish eight steps for elaborating such a discourse-analytical approach.

1. Finding appropriate research objects and research questions

At the beginning of our research, we must find an object of research that seems to fulfill two conditions. First, it must be related to human suffering. In this sense, discourse analysis as social critique is always problem-oriented and never merely contemplative research that attempts to "simply" broaden our knowledge. We must be aware that human suffering can occur silently and can sometimes be "read" empathically. Second, our object must enable us to see "the rupture of the world" (Adorno) through it; that is, it must allow the reasonable hypothesis that there is a structure that causes suffering and that this structure is indispensable to social reproduction.

Research questions must be asked regarding the relation of human suffering to the structure of social reproduction. Furthermore, questions must be asked about the norms that are at stake and whether these norms can emerge or unfold completely within a given society. A fundamental part of this first step is to review the literature on the possible objects of research.

Example: The ideology of merit

The example that I propose is the valuation of our merits in the labor market and in the educational system. This example seems to fulfill the two basic conditions. First, it points toward social suffering. In the labor market and in the educational system, we can find many people who suffer under a current evaluation. The frustration seems often to be related to the form or the results of the evaluation. Second, social valuation that is based on the merit principle seems fundamentally related to our way of distributing material and immaterial goods. Certainly, this hypothesis concerning the embeddedness of the merit principle in our society is the result of prior research in the literature regarding the "myth" or "ideology" of merit.

The research questions here could be as follows. What relations exist between suffering and the fact that we value certain social characteristics and capacities? Is there a conflict (or a contradiction) of norms? What are these norms? Does it seem possible to overcome the tensions that are produced by these norms?

2. Exploring the object

In this exploratory phase, we must gather the most relevant information regarding our object of analysis. Which discourses seem to exist around the object? Who is involved in the (hegemonic) discourse production, and who is excluded? How does the discourse seem to be expressed? Are there popular discourses, media discourses, and expert discourses, and what seems to be the relation among them? At this stage, we are not yet engaged in a discourse analysis, but we should have a sense of the discourses and dynamics that are involved.

Furthermore, we should gather information concerning the nondiscursive realities that surround social suffering. Is there economic need or a lack of access to basic goods? Are there power inequalities, denigrating identities or some type of exclusion that is legal, material, or ideal? Can we name practices that at first seem inappropriate or exclusive? At this stage, we must also ask for the significant silences. Who does not speak? Which affects or "psychological gaps" seem to have been produced?

For our example of merit, we must now explore how the idea of merit is produced socially. Are there specific discourses on merit? Which social actors stand out in these discourses, and which social actors are not heard in the public sphere? Are there relevant nonverbal practices? In this step, we may see that there are important discourses regarding individual merit in the public sphere, labor relations, and the field of education. There are even legal norms that obligate an evaluation by merit. Furthermore, we see that the most important social actors are the actors with relatively high social status—actors who have been benefiting from the evaluation system. Actors who have rarely been evaluated positively have little access to these discourses.

Moreover, there is a considerable amount of nonverbal social valuations. A smile or open ignoring can be acts of positive or negative valuation to which actors can react nonverbally, such as by smiling back or displaying a suffering face.

3. Elaborating a corpus and a method

Next, we must create a provisional corpus and define our research methods. Because we do not yet know the results of the concrete analysis, we must be open to the possibility of broadening or changing our initial corpus or to adapting our procedure during research. What material do we need to collect? Do we want to analyze institutional or private documents and conduct interviews with experts or with the people who are suffering the most? These techniques of data gathering are very similar to that of traditional Discourse Studies. It is also possible to use empathic communication for discourse analysis. Are there practices, pictures, spatial arrangements, emotions, or body language to read and analyze? These aspects can also form part of the corpus. Furthermore, we must ask questions concerning the relation that we believe may exist between discursive and nondiscursive realities. While collecting the material, we must elaborate an initial approach to analyze this material. For this purpose, there is considerable literature on how to perform discourse analysis or even an analysis of nondiscursive material.

> *The corpus for our research on merit could consist of highly influential texts, such as legal norms or political and social debates. We could also consider conducting interviews with experts and with the "losers" in the system of evaluation. In all of these cases, we are still pointing toward classical discourse analysis, but we can also include in our corpus practices of subtle valuations or corporal reactions that are collected through observation.*

4. Descriptive analysis

The analysis can be logically divided into two parts, a descriptive and an interpretative analysis, although in research practice, both parts are often executed in parallel. During the descriptive analysis, we work closely with the material. It is important to show outsiders at every point of the analysis the relation between what we do and the empirical material that is included in the corpus. Working closely with the empirical material is important not only for transparency and comprehensibility for outsiders but also to guarantee the intersubjective validity of our analysis. It is also important to control our own biases. All too often, researchers are too eager to confirm their hypothesis or prejudices.

For this type of analysis, we can use the entire range of research techniques in the Social Sciences and Humanities. Quantitative data analysis can bring us a step closer. However, at some point, qualitative analysis seems indispensable. Most of the literature on qualitative analysis uses categorizations, codings or heuristic questions to become acquainted with the material.

Researchers usually go a step further to reduce the complexity of the material by synthesizing or grouping the information through metacategories, metacodes, or the like. It is important to emphasize that although we use the toolbox of sociological discourse analysis in most cases, it is possible that our material will result from observation, aesthetic material, or material documents. In these cases, we can proceed logically in a similar way by using coding, categorization, or heuristic questions that are equally adapted to the empirical material.

5. Interpretative analysis

Regardless of whether we started with quantitative or qualitative data analysis or a mixture of the two, at this stage, we must begin to interpret the data. This means that discourse analysis as social critique ultimately follows a critical interpretative paradigm, although quantitative analysis can play an auxiliary part in this type of research. Initially, the interpretative task must be closely connected to the descriptive analysis to conduct a step-by-step reconstruction, in the sense of a second-order hermeneutics, of the social sense or signification that is enclosed in the data. Typical questions involve the relation of the categories. Are there logical connections, oppositions, or contradictions? Can we find regularities or patterns? Is there a difference in the interpretation of the norms regarding different social actors or different empirical material? Is it possible to sum the findings in general schemes such as narrative structures or plots (Viehöver 2001), interpretative schemes or frames (Oevermann 2001, Lüders and Meuser 1997), or phenomenal structures (Keller 2005)?

The aim of this step is to reconstruct the symbolic order and to find the implicitly or explicitly accepted norms, implications, relations and degree of accomplishment in society's practices and material organization. Considering that we may have worked with nonlinguistic data, we must be prepared to broaden our notion of symbolic order toward an order of meaning that is contained in material dispositions, iconography, practices, or silent affective reactions.

In the case of the analysis of merit, the fourth and fifth steps mean starting with the descriptive analysis to uncover step by step the symbolic order. Here, we probably find a general acceptance concerning the principle of merit but discover differences regarding what should count as merit, how merit should be measured, and in which social fields other principles should substitute for or accompany the merit principle. We will likely find a hegemonic discourse and several alternative discourses.

6. Reflection on a social macroanalysis

We must then elaborate general statements regarding fundamental social structures. Here, we can draw on our literature review from the first step. Realistically, this step will involve theoretical research in which we combine the reflections from social and political philosophy with the findings of macro-sociological analysis. The ideal is to develop our own theoretically sound macro analysis of social structure. In the practice of conducting research with limited resources, however, we must usually rely on other researchers' findings.

This more theoretical analysis must focus on three classical sociological questions concerning statics, dynamics, and praxis. The question of statics is perhaps the most fundamental. This is the question of how society reproduces its fundamental structure. We must elaborate the theoretical elements of social order, integration, or social reproduction. However, the question of practice is also highly relevant to develop *social critique*. How can humans collectively intervene in the processes of social reproduction and social change to transform social development into a deliberate and intentional process?

7. The relation of norms and social structure

In this step, we must relate the results of the sociological discourse analysis in the broad sense, including the analysis of silent and silenced suffering, practices, and material dispositions, to general insights regarding societal reproduction. What is the role of norms in guaranteeing social integration and stability? Is there a potential development of the norms—that is, are they already completely unfolded, or are they realized incompletely in our society? What exactly is the relation among the norms, the material organization of society, and the suffering that was detected in the first step of the proceeding?

It is time to test our initial hypothesis and decide whether our discourse analysis truly leads to social critique, which is understood as a critique of the fundamental social structure. We must now ask about the degree to which differences between normative claims and the social realization of norms are necessary contradictions and the degree to which they are mere surface phenomena. Which logical and material obstacles are encountered by the unfolding of norms, and would overcoming these obstacles require a fundamental social change or only a slight adjustment? Finally, how have the norms themselves changed in the process of analysis and unfolding, and how must they change in the future?

In the sixth and seventh steps, we go a step further than classical discourse analysis to prepare the social critique. With research from the literature, we can, for example, understand that the merit principle is a fundamental justification of our way of social reproduction, for legitimating the distribution of material and immaterial goods and for maintaining inequalities over generations. However, we can also see that a significant amount of goods is not distributed by the merit principle but through inheritances. We can even go a step further and understand that inequality is reproduced socially not only through the inheritance of material wealth but also through the transmission of social or cultural capital. Thus, there is an important systemic gap between the claim of individual merit and the reality of the social distribution of wealth by principles other than merit.

To fulfil the claim and to develop the "normative surplus" (Honneth) of the merit principle, the possibility that every single individual receives her fair share through the merit principle and not through other means would ultimately mean a rupture with capitalism as we know it as a form of accumulating capital (material, social and cultural) and to use it accordingly.

8. Contribution to social change

Depending on the reader's academic tradition, the final step may seem outside the scope of academic research. As Marx says, however, the point is not to merely interpret the world; "the point is to change it." Here, all of the important authors who have been used to develop the described approach, including Marx, Adorno and Horkheimer, Habermas and Honneth for Critical Theory, along with Foucault (as well as Butler, van Dijk, etc.) and the rest of the critical discourse analysts, agree that social research is about making a practical difference. Social critique must therefore give its research results back to society, and the social critic must become a public intellectual. The critic must engage in debates and social struggles, and, most importantly, her interventions must contribute to the empowerment of the people who suffer under the current social conditions. The enormous advantage of the critical approach that is presented here is that the critic can rely on norms that are already shared by the vast majority of people. Therefore, in the worst case (i.e., in the case in which norms are only implicitly shared), the critic must show that the participants in a social interaction share some basic, normative assumptions. She need not convince anyone of the validity of a particular norm that is not shared by other people.

Finally, the critic must explain to those who are suffering how their suffering is socially produced and related to a specific social order. By showing the relation among suffering, the incomplete unfolding of accepted social norms and a particular social order, the critic shows that the suffering is an objective moral wrong that must be abolished. Once suffering is understood as structural disrespect, indignation can occur as a first step toward social change. In the words of Pierre Bourdieu, "As skeptical as one may be about the social efficacy of the sociological message, one has to acknowledge the effect it can have in allowing those who suffer to find out that their suffering can be imputed to social causes and thus to feel exonerated; and in making generally known the social origin, collectively hidden, of unhappiness in all its forms, including the most intimate, the most secret" (Bourdieu 2000, 629).

NOTE

1. This chapter is based on my book *Discourse Analysis as Social Critique* (Herzog 2016a) and includes some insights presented in my article "Discourse Analysis as Immanent Critique" (Herzog 2016b). However, the argument as it is presented here furthers some of the points made in both texts.

BIBLIOGRAPHY

Adorno, Theodor W. 1970. *Negative Dialektik. Jargon der Eigentlichkeit.* Frankfurt/ Main: Suhrkamp.
Bourdieu, Pierre. 2000. *The Weight of the World: Social Suffering in Contemporary Societies.* Stanford: Stanford University Press.
Browne, Craig. 2008. "The End of Immanent Critique?" *European Journal of Social Theory* 11(1): 5–24.
Bührmann, Andrea, and Werner Schneider. 2007. "More Than Just a Discursive Practice? Conceptual Principles and Methodological Aspects of Dispositif Analysis." *Forum: Qualitative Social Research* 8(2). http://nbn-resolving.de/ urn:nbn:de:0114-fqs0702281.
Foucault, Michel. 1981. "The Order of Discourse." In *Untying the Text: A Poststructural Anthology,* edited by Robert Young, 48–78. Boston, MA: Routledge & Kegan Paul.
———. 2007. *The Politics of Truth.* Los Angeles: Semiotext(e).
Gutiérrez-Rodríguez, Encarnación. 2007. "Reading Affect—On the Heterotopian Spaces of Care and Domestic Work in Private Households." *Forum: Qualitative Social Research* 8(2). http://nbn-resolving.de/urn:nbn:de:0114-fqs0702118
Habermas, Jürgen. 1984. *Theory of Communicative Action Volume One: Reason and the Rationalization of Society.* Boston, MA: Beacon Press.
Herzog, Benno. 2016a. *Discourse Analysis as Social Critique. Discursive and Non-Discursive Realities in Critical Social Research.* London: Palgrave.
———. 2016b. "Discourse Analysis as Immanent Critique: Possibilities and Limits of Normative Critique in Empirical Discourse Studies." *Discourse & Society* 27(3): 1–15.
Harvey, David. 2016. *The Ways of the World.* London: Profile.
Honneth, Axel. 1995. *The Struggle for Recognition: The Moral Grammar of Social Conflicts.* Cambridge: Polity Press.

Honneth, Axel. 2004. "Anerkennung als Ideologie." *WestEnd Neue Zeitschrift für Sozialforschung* 1: 51–70.

Keller, Reiner. 2005. "Analysing Discourse. An Approach from the Sociology of Knowledge." *Forum: Qualitative Social Research* 6(3). http://nbn-resolving.de/urn:nbn:de:0114-fqs0503327.

Lüders, Christian, and Michael Meuser. 1997. "Deutungsmusteranalyse." In *Sozialwissenschaftliche Hermeneutik. Eine Einführung*, edited by Ronald Hitzler and Anne Honer, 57–79. Opladen: Leske + Budrich, UTB.

Marx, Karl. 1970. "Thesis on Feuerbach." In *The German Ideology*, edited by Karl Marx and Friedrich Engels, 121–123. New York: International Publishers.

Oevermann, Ulrich. 2001. "Die Struktur sozialer Deutungsmuster—Versuch einer Aktualisierung." *Sozialer Sinn* 1: 35–81.

Renault, Emmanuel. 2009. "The Political Philosophy of Social Suffering." In *New Waves in Political Philosophy*, edited by Boudewijn de Bruin and Christopher Zurn, 158–176. Houndmills: Palgrave Macmillan.

Renout, Gilles. 2012. *Wissen in Arbeit und in Bewegung? Wissenssoziologische Diskursanalyse aktueller Strategien von LebenskünstlerInnen in Kreativarbeit und zeitgenössischem Tanz.* Wiesbaden: VS.

Romero, José Manuel. 2014. *Immanente Kritik heute. Grundlagen und Aktualität eines sozialphiolosophischen Begriffs.* Bielefeld: transcript.

Sauerwald, Gregor. 2009. *Reconocimiento y Liberación: Axel Honneth y el pensamiento latinoamericano. Por un diálogo entre el Sur y el Norte.* Berlin: Lit Verlag.

Stahl, Titus 2013a. *Immanente Kritik. Elemente einer Theorie sozialer Praktiken.* Frankfurt M./New York: Campus.

Stahl, Titus. 2013b. "Habermas and the Project of Immanent Critique." *Constellations* 20(4): 533–552.

Viehöver, Willy. 2001. "Diskurse als Narration." In *Handbuch Sozialwissenschaftliche Diskursanlyse Bd. 1: Theorien und Methoden*, edited by Reiner Keller, Andreas Hirseland, Werner Schneider and Willy Viehöver, 193–224. Opladen: VS-Verlag.

Zamora, José Antonio. 2011. "Lässt sich der Kapitalismus immanent kritisieren? Reflexionen mit und über Theodor W. Adorno," Contribution at the international seminar: *Immanente Kritik. Grundlagen und Aktualität eines sozialphilosophischen Begriffs*, Frankfurt/M.

Chapter 2

The Second Disappearance
of Michel Pêcheux

Jean-Jacques Courtine

In the following, I would like to briefly introduce a text I wrote a decade ago. First of all, let me remind you of the circumstances: The Federal University of Rio Grande do Sul organized a congress in Porto Alegre in November 2003, devoted to the twentieth anniversary of the disappearance of Michel Pêcheux, and asked me to open the debate (Courtine 2003).[1] I had therefore written a text entitled *The Strange Memory of Discourse Analysis* (Courtine 2004), in order to say, with hindsight, one or two relatively simple things about Michel Pêcheux and the role that he played in the establishment of this discipline. Not that I want to restrict to this the contribution to the political life and to the intellectual struggles in the France of that time. Michel Pêcheux was much more than what we remember today, when we associate his name with the history of the hexagonal version of discourse analysis (henceforth DA).

He was a philosopher, immensely cultured, with multiple interests, and a moving, restless, inventive thinking. He was also a philosopher engaged in political struggles, for to him intellectual life was inseparable from the struggles to be fought against inequality, domination, and subjection. He was finally, one could say, a "DIY" philosopher, who loved making machines, and especially machines whose inner workings were both computerized and linguistic: This is how Automatic Discourse Analysis was born in 1969, and it was thanks to this ingenious handiwork that I—who was then beginning a career as a linguist that I was not bound to pursue for a long time—got the chance to meet him, to work with him, to become his friend.

And at the very moment of speaking about him on that day, in Porto Alegre, in front of this crowd for which his work still represented a living thought, and that found in what he had been able to invent the tools that made it possible to understand the powers of discourse and to oppose the discourses of power, I was struck by the contrast of this expectation with the disaffection, oblivion, and indifference from which his work had suffered in his own country. Even more so because I had just discovered a dictionary of DA, published shortly before, which distorted his role in the history of this discipline. That is where I started from in the text that follows, which is the transcription of what I said that day, but which I could repeat in the same terms today. I have simply amended the text here and there, updated certain references, reworked some formulations, but the content remains the same: The work of Michel Pêcheux, after the tragic end of its author, has become subjected to a second disappearance, of which the following paragraphs will recall the forms, circumstances, and actors.

And what strikes me in writing these lines is that what I had pointed out then, the oblivion and the tenacious silence to which the work of Michel Pêcheux, with some rare exceptions, became subjected in France, is still true, probably even more true today. And it is again from another place that the need to recall his name emerges, in another country that the desire is felt to prolong his thought. There is some sort of a tacit agreement, a silent pact in the cultural life in France: that of erasing, beyond the name and work of Pêcheux, all the intellectual life which was deeply and sometimes tragically involved in the paths of research that Marxism had then opened. There is still a lot to say on this silence, these omissions, this erased memory. The initiative taken today by *Décalages* to bring together this set of texts on Michel Pêcheux helps to break this silence. Those who took the initiative should be thanked.

Below can be read what I said, on that day in Porto Alegre, about the second disappearance of Michel Pêcheux.

                                   * * *

Allow me, in order to get to the heart of the matter, to read you a passage from a book that has been published recently. It is a *Dictionary of Discourse Analysis* (Maingueneau and Charaudeau 2004). Those who work in this field, and many of us today have devoted their teaching and research to the existence of DA as a discipline, will maybe regard this as good news. No discipline without a dictionary, no matter without a table, no authors without an index: Doesn't DA, of which some of us have lived the uncertain beginnings, while others have subsequently accompanied its problematic developments, thus receive a deserved consecration, an academic recognition that has long been disputed? Finally, it would have become a discipline in its own right, a discipline with dictionary.

I am afraid it is not good news, and that this publication, when examining its content, sheds a singular light on what unites us here, the place that the thought and work of Michel Pêcheux played in the constitution of DA in France. For is it not paradoxical that at the moment in which a dictionary collects and orders the themes, the objects, the methods, and the actors of this current of research, at the moment in which articles reconstitute its history, at the moment in which, finally, the essential role played by Michel Pêcheux seems to be on the way to being recognized, is it not paradoxical that it is here in Brazil, among you, that his thought is questioned, his texts systematically indexed, analyzed, and discussed, as you propose to do in the course of the four days that will bring us together around him?

I would like to raise here, with you, one of the essential questions that in my view seems to be raised by this meeting: Why is it *here, and not there*, where Michel Pêcheux had worked, published, struggled, why is not it in Paris that this colloquium can take place? Understand me: I for myself have no regrets about it, for reasons I have already had to clarify in the past, and to which I shall return. I am very pleased to be with you today, and I am extremely thankful to you for having organized this meeting and for having invited some of those who, despite their differences and sometimes even their divergences, have accompanied Michel Pêcheux in his intellectual adventure, and whose DA is a legacy which you refuse, it seems to me, to see scattered. I can only support you in this, for it is rather the reverse side of this question that concerns me, as it had been formulated by Denise Maldidier in the only work that has, since the disappearance of the philosopher, been devoted to his work.

> What could represent the discourse in the thought (of Pêcheux) seems lost. Concepts he has forged are erring around: they are trivialized, cut off from the ground where they were elaborated, theoretical traces whose enunciator has been forgotten. (Maldidier 1990, 7; translated by the editors)

No book on Pêcheux in France and none of these congresses that the profession is so fond of otherwise, few references; Denise Maldidier is right: concepts without an enunciator, an orphan or celibate theory. And if I wished today to question, to introduce our debates, the link between memory and discourse, it is first and foremost the memory of DA itself that needs to be investigated. And I come back, to this end, to this work, to this dictionary, one of the aims of which it should be to constitute a memory of the discipline. This book, let me open it on page 201, under the heading "Ecole française d'analyse du discours" [=French school of Discourse Analysis; the editors], and read you a part of this article.

> The label "French School" allows to distinguish the dominant current of DA in France in the 1960s and 1970s. This set of research, which emerged in the mid-1960s, was consecrated in 1969 with the publication of issue 13 of the journal *Langages* entitled "L'analyse de discours," and of the book *Automatic Discourse Analysis* by Michel Pêcheux, the most representative

author of this current. This problematic has not been locked up in the French context, it has spread abroad, especially in countries speaking French and Roman languages. The core of this research was a study of the political discourse carried out by linguists and historians, with a methodology that associated structural linguistics with a 'theory of ideology' both inspired by the re-reading of the work of Karl Marx by the philosopher Louis Althusser, and the psychoanalysis of Jacques Lacan. It was a matter of thinking about the relationship between ideology and linguistics, while simultaneously avoiding to reduce discourse to the analysis of language, and dissolving the discursive in the ideological [...]. From the 1980s onwards, this current has been gradually marginalized. But if we can no longer speak of a 'French school,' there are undoubtedly *French tendencies* (Maingueneau and Charaudeau 2004, 202; translated by the editors), underlining and abandoning the dictionary here; "French tendencies," allow me to add, the inventory of which the volume precisely constitutes.

This long quotation, doesn't it go against my words? Doesn't it illustrate the place that Pêcheux would still occupy in DA, the eminent role that he is granted in the foundation of this discipline? I do not think so, and I would like to try to show it to you, by inviting you to make a brief discourse analysis with me.

First point. Let us begin with the very title of the section: *the French school of discourse analysis.* I would like to say here that neither Michel Pêcheux nor those who were with him at the origin of the DA project have ever used the term, or, if they did, never recognized themselves within it. The expression was generalized afterward by those who, soon after the middle of the seventies, thought it would be necessary to produce the first manuals of DA, of which the dictionary quoted above is only the most recent extension. This invites us to distinguish two projects in the initial phase of constructing an analysis of discourse from the late 1960s to the 1970s, which are in no way superimposable or reducible to one another: that of theoretical elaboration and that of disciplinary territorialization. I would like to recall here that, on the one hand, the work of Michel Pêcheux in the 1970s was entirely invested in theoretical construction and methodological invention, and that the disciplinary and pedagogical preoccupations were entirely foreign to him; on the other, the expression "French school of DA" took no account of the contradictions which then passed through the domain. These divergences were at first conceptual and methodological: Those who had originally invented the term "French school" held a contrastive conception of discourse, of which they thought the universe in terms of typology, to which Pêcheux, myself, and some others opposed the notion of discursive formation, conceived on the basis of contradictions that made discursive formations divided units, which are in no way reducible to a typological frame. Their "French school" was in no way our own: it was rather one of the tendencies against which we endeavored to construct a theory of discourse.

But these divergences were also political: It was that of the confrontation between two conceptions of Marxism, one that could be qualified as "orthodox," and the other, opposing the first, constituting the political translation of the works of Louis Althusser. I am not going to drag you into the field of those quarrels which now seem Byzantine, and which were not exempt from blindness. I shall merely point out that here, one is confronted with one of the forms of erasure of the singularity of the positions of Michel Pêcheux in the development of DA in France: the academic and disciplinary homogenization, which amalgamates, neutralizes, and makes indistinguishable the mutually contradictory theoretical positions under a "consensual" label, and which then cuts the link these positions have with the political and historical reality that gave them a good part of their meaning, making undecipherable the political stakes that these positions came to express. It is at this price that one can make of Pêcheux (I quote), "the most representative author of the French school of DA," that is to say the best representative of a conception in which he never recognized himself, and which he resolutely fought. The section of the dictionary is, on this point, sheer nonsense.

Second point. This set of investigations was inaugurated, tells us the article, by the simultaneous publication of the number 13 of the journal *Langages* ("Discourse analysis"), and Pêcheux' book *Automatic Discourse Analysis*. The equivalence posed here masks, again, the reality of the theoretical development of DA. What could be found in *Langages 13* was the articulation of the basic assumptions of DA, as Jean Dubois had conceived the project. It seems to me that one can recognize afterward, without taking anything away from Dubois or his role or his merits, that this was due to relatively little: Discourse was essentially a chain of statements, thought against the background of Harrissian distributionalism and the conditions of production. The theorization of the latter, as well as the conceptualization of their articulation with the linguistic sequences remained entirely to be done. It is, on the other hand, in the work of Pêcheux, and nowhere else, that DA received its true theoretical foundation, through all the texts he published from 1969 to 1975. A somewhat closer exegesis of the texts of this period would show this easily.

Third point. "The core of this research," continues the section, "was a study of political discourse conducted by linguists and historians." The phrase is weak, for it presents as a simple interdisciplinary collaboration what was the theoretical core of the project: It was not a matter of bringing linguists and historians into an alliance between disciplines, but of thinking discourse as a relation, to quote the formulation of the time, "between the real of language and the real of history." I am not so sure today, if I have ever been so, of the meaning that should be given to this formula. But what I am certain of—and

Pêcheux kept coming back to it—is that the articulation of these historical and linguistic dimensions was an absolute necessity for him: "Taken between the real of language and the real of history, DA cannot yield either way," he repeated in *L'étrange miroir de l'analyse du discours* [=The strange mirror of discourse analysis] (Pêcheux 1981; translated by the editors).

This additional forgetting, the effacement of the historical dimension in DA, has considerable consequences, which explain to a large extent the dis-affection with the work of Pêcheux. I had expressed this feeling a few years ago by observing that, under the label of DA, descriptions of the thread of discourse have been developed from a formal, interactive, or conversational point of view, which in most cases had already abandoned purely and simply the articulation of the discursive sequences with the historical conditions of their production (Courtine 1991).[2] This tendency now almost completely covers the field of DA, and the most eloquent proof that one can advance for that is the simple reading of the different entries of the dictionary. In which context do we find the concepts—discursive formation, interdiscourse, pre-construct, discursive memory, etc.—which gave its theoretical status, I feel like saying its theoretical dignity, to the conception of discourse that had been elaborated Michel Pêcheux? They can be found buried under the ageless figures of old rhetoric, drowned under the recycled remains of Greimassian semiotics, covered by a vague concept of communication and of psychosocial interactions through language. Who will tell me what place the entry "face" has in a dictionary of discourse analysis, why there is an article on "emotion"; and why it reads, I quote: "In DA, the question on the relationship between 'emotion' and 'reason' arises. From this point of view, the positions adopted by discourse analysts consist in describing and explaining the functioning of emotional events in persuasive discourse." (Maingueneau and Charaudeau 2004, 219; translated by the editors.) "Analysts of discourse"? Who exactly is this? Are we actually talking about the same thing? For this is strange: In the discourse analysis that I have known and contributed with others to found, the only question that ever arose in relation to the emotion/reason pair is why such questions should never appear within its scope, at least not in this form.

It is unnecessary to dwell on that: In the survey offered by the most recent dictionary of the discipline, one can find almost everything, or *anything* to be more exact. I would indeed like to suggest the following operation: It would consist in putting next to each other this dictionary of discourse analysis, a recent dictionary of semiotics, a compilation presenting the state of the sciences of communication, and, let's say, a handbook of rhetoric brought up to date. One would realize that these are only variants of the same work. The reason for this is simple: the domain of DA covered by the dictionary is none other than one of the possible institutional responses to the disciplinary solicitations created by the existence of an empirical and practical field as vast as it is badly defined, as vague as little delimited, that of communication and the media. If one took the trouble to re-read the founding texts of DA, it would immediately become apparent to what extent such a project turns its back on the theoretical demands expressed there.

Last point. We can better understand the distortion and the forgetting that the work of Michel Pêcheux suffers from, which the dictionary section summarizes with the formula: "From the 1980s, this current has been progressively marginalized." The discourse analysts that you are will not have failed to spot here the erasure of the agent. The formulation is ripe for nominalization ("the gradual marginalization of this current from the 1980s"), and thus ready for reuse, in the form of a preconstructed object of discourse, by other manuals, compilations, abstracts, and various academic works, the production of which the dictionary will not fail to intensify. It is a strange story, of course, the one produced by the book: This current was not "progressively marginalized," but brutally interrupted by the tragic end of Michel Pêcheux. The historical reasons, political causes, and personal factors which could account for this interruption and then for the disaffection with which the philosopher's thought was going to be victimized are numerous and complex.[3] Any interrogation that seeks to restore meaning to these abandoned texts today must, in my opinion, begin here, by questioning this end, by bringing forward these causes, by identifying this conveniently erased agent.

For there is no reason to consider that the project of discourse analysis that inspired the work of Michel Pêcheux must be purely and simply buried, and your presence in numbers, your interest, clearly shows it today. This project, however, had its demands, which still fix the conditions of labor which might prolong it. In the first place, it is necessary to reintroduce the historical dimension into the field of discourse: in its absence, the concepts on which relied the theorization of discursive processes that Pêcheux tried—particularly that of the discursive formation—have no meaning.

This is also true of the "dehistoricization" of the notion of *discursive memory*. Its treatment, moreover, gives a fairly good idea of the way in which some of the articles in the dictionary operate. Those who know the history of DA also know that the notion was introduced for the first time in June 1981 in no. 62 of the journal *Langages*,[4] and that the question of memory became one of the great advances of historical work during the 1980s with the publication of *Lieux de mémoire* by Pierre Nora. One would search in vain for a trace of this initial occurrence in the field of the DA in the corresponding section of the dictionary. This vanishing is all the more strange, as this first appearance constituted the only reference to discursive memory by the same author in one of his DA manuals dating from 1987 (Maingueneau 1987). Curious amnesia, accompanied by the truly astonishing absence of any reference to *Lieux de mémoire* and the innumerable discursive projects that this endeavor has opened (on this point see Courtine 1994), precisely at the point where the author of the article, in his previous manual and still on the topic of discursive memory, chose to add: "Non-psychological memory, which supposes the enunciated insofar as it is inscribed in history" (Maingueneau 1987, 84). Unfathomable mysteries of the second hand.

I feel sorry to insist: For my part, it is in order to keep me aloof from these forms of *analysis without memory*, that is to say, *without discourse*, that I have, for more than twenty years, enrolled my work in the field of cultural history, whether it be that of the field of public speech (see in particular Courtine 2006), or that of the practices and representations of the body, gender or emotions (see, among others, Courtine 2011, Corbin et al. 2005–2006, 2011, 2016–2017). For discourses remain an essential material, and their interpretation a crucial stake in the work of a historian. I contend, for my part, that the notions of discursive formation and memory such as they can still be apprehended from the works of Pêcheux but also Foucault, and without necessarily having to oppose these perspectives to one another, have lost nothing of their pertinence. If I have technically ceased to do DA, it is in particular because of the extreme scale, heterogeneity and dissemination of the corpus that make necessary historical work on long periods. The documentary and interpretative requirements of the latter make an exploration of materials that is essentially based on formal linguistic criteria untenable. But I have never stopped paying close attention to the transformations of discursive processes in historical work, and in this respect, I have learned enormously from my close collaboration with Michel Pêcheux.

It is therefore necessary to give back a memory to DA, where the work of Pêcheux would resume its meaning and its place. This will only happen, and I say this here particularly for the younger ones of you, those who follow this path on which I once embarked myself, by making the choices and distinctions that must be made. Thus, one cannot at the same time want to prolong the perspective opened by Pêcheux, and grant any credit to the sum of omissions and approximations that dedicates his thought to effacement. But here we have a procedure to follow. Michel Pêcheux had to make these choices himself, in order to tear from the academic pressures and disciplinary grids of that time the field of reflection which is today called discourse analysis. They remain the means to hear his voice and to feel his presence among us.

NOTES

1. *Remark by the editors:* This article is based on a presentation given at a conference on the legacy of Michel Pêcheux, which took place in 2003 in Porto Algre, Brazil (Courtine 2003). A French version has previously been published in a special issue of the open access journal *Décalages*, which also contains some previously

unpublished writings of Michel Pêcheux (see http://scholar.oxy.edu/decalages/vol1/iss4/). For the present volume, the French original has been translated into English, and complemented with some references to English translations of the work of Michel Pêcheux by us. We are grateful to Jean-Jacques Courtine and Warren Montag at *Décalages* for kindly granting us the permission to translate and publish this contribution.

2. The constancy with which Jacques Guilhaumou maintained this requirement merits all the more to be emphasized.

3. I have sketched a beginning of analysis in Courtine (1991).

4. See pages 51–53 and 122–123.

BIBLIOGRAPHY

Corbin, Alain, Jean-Jacques Courtine and Georges Vigarello, eds. 2005–2006. *Histoire du corps, XVI-XXème siècle*, 3 volumes. Paris: Le Seuil.

———. 2011. *Histoire de la virilité, de l'Antiquité au XXIème siècle*. 3 volumes, Paris: Le Seuil. US Translation: *History of Virility*, 1 volume, New York: Columbia University Press, 2016.

———. 2011. *Histoire des émotions, de l'Antiquité au XXIème siècle*. 3 volumes, Paris: Le Seuil.

Courtine, Jean-Jacques. 1991. "Le discours introuvable. Marxisme et linguistique, 1965–198." *Histoire, Epistémologie, Langage* 13(II): 154–171.

———. 1994. "Le tissu de la mémoire : quelques perspectives de travail historique dans les sciences du langage." In *Mémoire, histoire, langage*, edited by Jean-Jacques Courtine. *Langages* 114: 5–12.

———. 2003. "Michel Pêcheux i Anàlise do Discurso," Presentation given in a colloquium at Universidade Federal do Rio Grande do Sul, Porto Alegre, 10–13 November 2003.

———. 2004. *A estranha memoria da analise do discurso, Michel Pêcheux e a Anàlise do discurso*, São Carlos: Editora Claraluz, 25–32.

———. 2006. *Metamorfoses do discurso polìtico. Derivas da fala pùblica*. São Carlos: Editora Claraluz.

———. 2011. *Déchiffrer le corps. Penser avec Foucault*. Grenoble: J. Million.

———. 2014. "La seconde disparition de Michel Pêcheux." *Décalages* 1(4). Available at: http://scholar.oxy.edu/decalages/vol1/iss4/19 [Last accessed on 03/05/2017].

Maingueneau, Dominique. 1987. *Nouvelles tendances en analyse du discours*, Paris: Hachette.

Maingueneau, Dominique, and Patrick Charaudeau, eds. 2004. *Dictionnaire d'analyse du discours*, Paris: Le Seuil.

Maldidier, Denise. 1990. *L'inquiétude du discours*. Paris: Editions des cendres.

Pêcheux, Michel. 1669. *Analyse automatique du discours*. Paris: Dunod.

———. 1981. "L'étrange miroir de l'analyse du discours." *Langages* 62: 5–8.

———. 1995. *Automatic discourse analysis*. Edited by Tony Hak and Niels Helsloot. Amsterdam, Atlanta, GA: Rodopi.

Chapter 3

Materialist Discourse Analysis

Three Moments and Some Criteria

Johannes Beetz and Veit Schwab

Discourse Studies started out as materialist and political endeavor. Many aspects of this heritage, however, seem to have gotten lost in contemporary approaches to discourse, or live on as a spectral undercurrent that remains implicit. Although Critical Discourse Analysis (CDA), the Essex School, enunciative pragmatics as well as other strands avail themselves to materialist theories and could be dubbed materialist, we believe that the relationship between discourse analysis and materialism has not been explored enough with regard to the methodological and conceptual consequences a materialist conception of discourse entails.

In this chapter, we propose to explore the entanglement of materialism and discourse analysis before and in Discourse Studies across three *moments* of materialist discourse analysis. This will allow drafting some criteria for a materialist study of discourse.

Our argument resonates within a broader research agenda that aims at promoting a genuinely materialist take on discourse by focusing on the relation between discourse, ideology, and political economy (DIPE[1]). We briefly introduce this perspective in the first section of this chapter.

In the second section, we claim that viable theoretical and methodological elements of a genuinely materialist approach to discourse can be found before and in what is called "French" Discourse Analysis (FDA).[2] More specifically, we argue that a materialist understanding of language and discourse is present in Marxian materialism as well as other early theorists of language and discourse, such as Bakhtin and Vološinov, who help understand discourses in their material and effective reality, as well as in relation to social conditions of power and exploitation—a first moment of materialist discourse analysis. Furthermore, we suggest that parts of Louis Althusser's work do not merely constitute a theoretical source on which discourse analysts drew and draw, but a *discourse analysis avant la lettre*—and thus represents *a second moment* of materialist discourse analysis. We then propose to locate *a third moment* in the materialist political project of a group of researchers around Michel Pêcheux.

Against this background, the chapter closes with a brief discussion of four criteria that for us characterize a materialist approach to discourse. We will also point to some tensions between them, which can and need to be made productive within a materialist methodological framework.

DISCOURSE*IDEOLOGY*POLITICAL ECONOMY: A MATERIALIST PERSPECTIVE ON LANGUAGE, POLITICS, AND SOCIETY

The materialist approaches to discourse we will be concerned with below operate under different epistemological and ontological horizons. What unites them, however, is a common concern for three crucial dimensions of analysis: discourse, ideology, and political economy. While special emphasis is often put on one of these dimensions, we argue that it is their productive entanglement that provides a genuinely materialist approach to discourse.

In our view, Discourse*Ideology*Political Economy is not a mere calculation or tick box exercise that magically allows to create the possibilities for a materialist discourse analysis to come. Instead, it points to a longstanding intellectual and political challenge concerning the ontological and epistemological relation of these three dimensions. It reaches beyond the limits of Discourse Studies as a field, and simultaneously constitutes one of its most important points of emergence.

Instead of replicating a habitus of demarcation that is, unfortunately, widespread in academic settings, we believe that the discussion on materialist discourse analysis needs to be opened (again), to explore commonalities, gaps, and blind spots *across* the intersecting dimensions of discourse, ideology, and political economy. While this chapter certainly does not furnish a definite answer to the problematic at stake, it hopefully shows a possible way for getting to grips with it.

THREE MOMENTS OF MATERIALIST DISCOURSE ANALYSIS

If we speak of materialism and discourse analysis before and in (and potentially also beyond[3]) Discourse Studies, we are not referring to an aleatory encounter of two perspectives that are discrete from the outset. Thus, what will be characterized as materialist discourse analysis below is an articulation of the always-already existing entwinement of the two. A *differentialist* view which conceptualizes the two as essentially distinct is most common on the level of theory. Here, claiming an incompatibility between "poststructuralist" or "postmodernist" paradigms and "materialism" serves to deny "discourse analysis" any grasp of what is beyond "language," "speech," or "text." Unfortunately, such reasoning has resulted in a barrier of reception that invites ritualized performances of delimitation rather than a careful scrutiny of methods and, more importantly, common political trajectories and possible alliances.

Instead of presenting discrete and linear histories, we are thus interested in how their uneasy, often contradictory entanglement forms an undercurrent in what came to be distinguished as "materialism" and "Discourse Studies." True to a materialist conception of history (Benjamin 1968), our argument refutes a nostalgic or historicist understanding of the matter at stake. Challenging the boundaries even further, we are convinced that the workings of the pair go beyond these two "fields," and (re)emerge in discussions across the Social Sciences and Humanities.

A (PRE-) HISTORY OF MATERIALIST DISCOURSE ANALYSIS

The conjugation of discursive phenomena and materialism did not constitute a prominent current in materialist theory and philosophy from which a linear historical account of materialist discourse analysis could be constructed. Rather, it can be maintained that in early materialism, discursive and symbolic phenomena were somewhat degraded to a *shadow existence*. Nevertheless, it is possible to find *traces* of this conjugation before the advent of Discourse Studies "proper." Marx's writings (e.g., Marx and Engels 1965; Marx 1990; 2002) as well as Bakhtin's (1981) and Vološinov's (1973) work to an extent, it will be argued, can serve as examples of such traces of materialist conceptions of discourse. Justifying this claim calls for a preliminary delineation of what we are concerned with.

On a very basic level, whether an approach to discourse qualifies as *materialist* could be said to hinge on two interrelated criteria. The first touches on the relation between the discursive and the material conditions in a social formation. The second concerns the materiality of discourse and language. The discursive should not be seen as something immaterial or merely ideational that is determined by the material world. In short, discourse, understood as a set of symbolic social processes and practices related to the production of meaning and social order, must be conceptualized as a *material* and productive element of the Social (Beetz 2016, 82ff; Hennessy 2013, 38ff; Kristeva and Menke 1989, 18; Marx and Engels 1965, 41–42).

This entails that material social "reality" is not conceived of as fundamentally distinct from and of a different ontological order than the discursive. Rather, they are coextensive and can only be separated conceptually and methodologically in discourse-analytical work. This further entails that the relation between the discursive and other material instances cannot be understood as mechanical or expressive. Material conditions do neither univocally determine the forms and content of the discursive nor do language and discourse simply express the material conditions they emerge in. Instead, discursive processes and practices reproduce and transform material social (power) relations and conditions.

Materialism and Language

Materialism denotes, first and foremost, the primacy of the *material* over the *ideal* and thus stands opposed to *idealism.* The common paradigm of Cartesian as well as German idealism is that immaterial ideas are primary and the material world is secondary. Classical materialism, in contrast, gives primacy to the material and "posits the primitive unicity of being" and gives the multiplicity that constitutes this unity a name: *matter;* that is, in the narrow sense, "mass, electrons, atoms, energy, waves, various particles, and so on" (Badiou 2013, 190). Persistently juxtaposed to this matter, language, symbolic representation, consciousness, as well as the production of meaning were to a large part seen as the Other of the material world in materialism before Marx. Idealism had given thought (and language) an independent existence. Where the strict dualisms of material/immaterial, mind/body, being/consciousness, etc., were invertedly adopted from this idealism, language and consciousness were seen as secondary and dependent.

It was only with Marx that a new materialism—born from the simultaneous critique of old (Feuerbachian) materialism and (Hegelian) idealism—emerged, which started to dissolve the binary order at the core of old materialism and idealism alike. Here, material reality was not merely composed of passive objects of contemplation or an extra-social force acting on individuals, but seen as intimately related to practical human activity (Marx 2010, 3). Marx and Engels write that "[a]ccording to the Hegelian system, ideas, thoughts, and concepts produced, determined, dominated the real life of men, their material world, their actual relations" (Marx and Engels 1965, 472–73). It is this supposed determination of the material world by immaterial ideas that they set out to "debunk and discredit" as a "philosophic struggle with the shadows of reality" (ibid.). To idealism, they juxtapose a materialism that begins with premises that are not abstract but concrete, namely "the real individuals, their activity and the material conditions under which they live, both those which they find already existing and those produced by their activity" (ibid., 32).

This practical human activity is not exclusively extralinguistic, but *includes* language and discourse as the material exchange of symbolic material between individuals. Furthermore, this practical *linguistic* activity does not belong to the ideational realm. The separation of language and the material production of life "exists only in philosophical illusion" (ibid., 472–73).

As Marx writes in the *German Ideology*, from "the start the 'spirit' is afflicted with the curse of being 'burdened' with matter, which here makes its appearance in the form of agitated layers of air, sounds, in short, of language" (ibid., 41–42). We could add, that the same burden befalls "consciousness" and "spirit" in the form of material markings in texts, etc. And what is more, material language, just like consciousness, cannot be made "into an independent realm" (ibid., 472–73) but has to be seen as in some ways conditioned by the conditions it emerges in.

Marxian theory and Marxism in general can certainly be seen as an important element in the formation of Discourse Studies (see, e.g., Pêcheux 1988; G. Williams 1999, 44ff; Coward and Ellis 1977; Jameson 1974, 101ff; Fairclough and Graham 2002; Jørgensen and Phillips 2002), but Marx himself never developed full-fledged theories of language or other "superstructural" phenomena, like ideology or subjectivity. Understanding language as a material instance that is productive as well as affected by its conditions of production and other material instances does not constitute a materialist theory of language. But it can be seen as a *precondition* for an approach to the discursive that could be dubbed materialist.

The main problem with making more classical and orthodox interpretations of Marxian theory fruitful for discourse analysis, however, is that language, consciousness, and the symbolic appear as mainly derivative of other "real" material processes. Althusser's accusation, namely that the early Marx inverted the idealist principle of consciousness for "*another simple principle, its opposite: material life, the economy*" (Althusser 1969, 108), points to the fact that in classical Marxism, the idealist dualism of "ideas" and "material reality" is flipped, but with its priorities reversed (R. Williams 1977, 59). This dualism is particularly apparent in a model of *base and superstructure*. In its most orthodox form, it purports that ideology, language, culture, etc., are solely effluences or reflections of the economic, material infrastructure. As an all too simplifying edificial metaphor of the Social, it is partly responsible for the late emergence of materialist theories of language and helps explain why Marxism "failed to provide a really systematic exploration of superstructures" (Jameson 1974, 102) for the longest time. In this simplistic conception, the discursive can hardly be grasped as productive and semi-autonomous.

Ideology and Language in Marx's Eighteenth Brumaire

The strict conceptual separation of base and superstructure—and by the same token of "immaterial" discourse and "material" world—hinders a truly materialist analysis of discursive material. Traces of such materialist irreductionist analyses can be found in those texts where Marx presents his critique of ideology. It is here that we find his implicit theories of ideology and subjectivity, where the ideological and symbolic are not an "imaginary assemblage (*bricolage*), a pure dream, empty and vain, constituted by the 'day's residues' from the only full and positive reality, that of concrete material individuals materially producing their existence" (Althusser 1972, 160) or a "misrecognition or illusion" but gain increasing autonomy from the material "base" narrowly understood.

For brevity's sake, only a few aspects which open up Marx's writing to discourse analysis will be sketched out here. They touch on ideology, symbolic practice, and the discursive constitution of social reality. One point of convergence of these interrelated aspects can be found in Marx's *Eighteenth Brumaire of Louis Bonaparte* (Marx 2002). In many ways, it is a text that can be construed as illustrating "the great extent to which Marx anticipated subsequent discourse-theoretical insights into the performative nature of language, the discursive constitution of identities and interests, and their role in shaping the forms and terms of political struggle." (Jessop 2002, 180). In it, language and the ways in which individuals symbolically represent themselves and others in their social conditions do not only have a "considerable degree of autonomy and independent effect" (Cowling and Martin 2002, 6), but genuinely take part in the constitution of the political situation and social relations. Ideology, as related to the production of meaning, has a relative autonomy.

Language plays a central role in this historiography of Louis-Napoleon Bonaparte's *coup d'état* of 1851, in that it is presented as a material (performative) force in the form of representations of the symbolic positions of the political actors in the political struggle recounted (see also Cowling and Martin 2002). This points to a reconfiguration of the role of ideology, which gives the symbolic a new status. Marx analyses not only the economic conditions of the moment in question to grasp the political upheaval, but also considers the ideological production of the political actors as a factor sui generis, that is, not simply as a distorted reflection of the economic and power relations in the consciousness of individuals. In other words, the ideologically produced *meaning* (of the bourgeoisie and the (lumpen-)proletariat alike) of the social relations subjects find themselves in are materially effective—albeit in the constraints the material conditions impose.[4] What is important to note, however, is that the ideological positions do not necessarily *correlate*, that is, are not *coextensive* with the social positions of subjects (Beetz 2016, 37ff).

The famous quote stating that "[m]en make their own history, but they do not make it just as they please in circumstances they choose for themselves; rather they make it in present circumstances, given and inherited" (Marx 2002, 19) suggests a limitation of subjects by the conditions they find themselves in. This limitation can be described as a *structural limitation* that not only restricts political practice, but is also a limitation to what can be thought and said at a given historical point. Fredric Jameson identifies this notion as a *strategy of containment*, which denotes that the economic broadly understood does not directly determine literary, linguistic, or ideological production, but confines it via an ideological closure (Jameson 2002, 37). Thus, the *conditions of production* of linguistic, ideological material impact the form and content of the latter.

Although the productive and performative role of symbolic representations of social reality and language in this text and Marx's work in general should not be underestimated (see, e.g., Jessop 2002, 182; Carver 2002, 113f; Cowling and Martin 2002; Riquelme 1980, Balibar 2007, 54ff; Fairclough and Graham 2002), it does by no means constitute a theory of discourse or a comprehensive toolbox for a materialist discourse analysis.

Bakhtin's and Vološinov's Impulses

Attempts to give a Marxist-materialist account of language and its role began long before the "linguistic" turn in Social Sciences and Humanities (Rorty 1992) or the rise of "cultural Marxism" (Nelson and Grossberg 1988). In the first half of the twentieth century, for instance, there was an increasing interest within Russian linguistics in a conciliation of Marxism and semiotic and linguistic thought. Such (failed) attempts of transcoding historical materialism to linguistics can be found in Nicolai Marr's work (Thomas 1957), Stalin's response to it in *Marxism and the Problems of Linguistics* (Stalin 1972), and some theories developed within Russian Formalism (see e.g., Jameson 1974, 43ff). Much more pertinent impulses for Discourse Studies came from elsewhere. To mention but two thinkers who developed an approach contributing to the prehistory of materialist discourse analysis, we can highlight some of the points Vološinov and Bakhtin made on the interrelated materialities of discourse and ideology and their relation to social reality. Both worked closely together and saw language as actual material utterances, as discourse, and wanted discourse understood as *ideological* and ideology as fundamentally *symbolic and semiotic*. This implied rejecting the notion of discourse as an exclusively "superstructural" phenomenon.

While Vološinov was not a discourse analyst in the narrow sense, he contributed to a materialist conception of language and discourse. His main theoretical innovation—made several decades before the apex of structuralism—lies in his notion that a Marxist linguistics should see signifi-cation practices and signs more generally as material elements of social real-ity. With a starting point that assumes the intimate entwinement of ideology and the semiotic, he develops a theory of language that conceives of the latter as an inherently ideological, as well as material and practical phenomenon. For him "[e]verything ideological possesses *meaning* [...] it is a *sign. Without signs, there is no ideology"* (Vološinov 1973, 9). As he makes clear in his seminal work on *Marxism and the Philosophy of Language,* written in the late 1920s, these ideological signs are not "reflections" or simply "represen-tations" of some reality, but each sign is "also itself a material segment of that very reality" (ibid. 11). Furthermore, consciousness is moved from an immaterial existence to a material reality relying on processes and practices of semiotic social intercourse that are tied firmly to social conditions and "forms of social communication" (ibid. 13). Signs only emerge in social interaction with others under specific conditions. Critiquing Saussure's syn-chronic model, Vološinov (like Bakhtin) sees the "actual reality of language" not as an abstract structure of linguistic forms but in dialogic interaction "implemented in an utterance or utterances" (ibid. 94). The material character of meaning, consciousness, and ideology derived from this perspective would later take a prominent role in Althusser's and Pêcheux's approaches to dis-course, albeit with a slightly different focus.

Bahkin's "dialogic materialism" (Jordan-Haladyn 2014) has certainly been influential in the field of Discourse Studies and in particular for approaches that conceptualize discourse as dialogic and polyphonic (Angermuller 2014, 27). What is sometimes overlooked, however, is that aspects of his theory of language lay the foundations for a materialist theory of discourse in which language is "not to be seen either as 'expression,' 'reflection' or abstract sys-tem, but rather as a material *means of production,* whereby the material body of the sign was transformed through a process of social conflict and dialogue into meaning" (Eagleton 1996, 102). Discourse as a material, ideological, and social phenomenon—"social throughout its entire range and in each and every of its factors, from the sound image to the furthest reaches of abstract meaning" (Bakhtin 1981, 259)—cannot be analyzed as an abstract system, but as utterances and symbolic practice inserted into social conditions, which they transform and reproduce.

Althusser's Materialist Discourse Analysis

While a concern for discourse has evidently been present in materialist lit-erature, the intimate connection between materialism and discourse analysis, however, is perhaps most pronounced in the work of Louis Althusser. While his theories of ideology and subjectivation (Althusser 1971) and, to a lesser extent, his work on the contradiction and overdetermination of social realities (Althusser 2005) are widely regarded as important points of inspiration for discourse theories (see for example Butler 1997; Laclau and Mouffe 2001; Beetz 2016, 62ff), the beginning of "discourse analysis proper" is commonly located after Althusser (see for example Angermuller and Maingueneau 2007). Acknowledgments of Althusser as a discourse analyst are virtually absent from the contemporary discussion (Kramer 2014 is a notable exception). By contrast, we argue that Althusser's materialist method qualifies as a discourse analysis *avant la lettre:* It did not merely influence "French" Discourse Analysis, but constitutes one of its most important points of emergence.

The key to Althusser's materialist discourse analysis arguably lies in the concept of "symptomal reading." Briefly mentioned in the introduction to *For Marx* (Althusser 1969), its most comprehensive formulation figures in *Reading Capital* (Althusser et al. 2015). In this book, he essentially undertakes a discourse analysis of Marx's *Capital*, with a special focus on concepts in Political Economy. Against empiricist epistemologies that conceive of knowledge as the result of an innocent "abstraction" or "extraction," Althusser shifts the perspective to knowledge *production*. In his anti-substantialist version of materialism, the production of knowledges is embedded in a mode of production, " a structure which combines [...] the type of object (raw material) on which it labours, the theoretical means of production available (its theory, its method and its technique, experimental or otherwise) and the historical relations (both theoretical, ideological, and social) in which it produces" (Althusser et al. 2015, 42). Accordingly, "there are no innocent readings, [...] because every reading merely reflects in its lessons and rules the real culprit: the conception of knowledge underlying the object of knowledge which makes knowledge what it is" (ibid., 34). This means that knowledge is the result of an ongoing process, which is not only infused with ideology, but also characterized by an unequal distribution of the means of knowledge production. Beyond a mere theoretical invention, then, Althusser's arguments were intended as a political intervention in the Marxist cleavages of the Paris of the 1960s (de Ípola 2012; Montag 2013; Althusser 2016).[5]

Less often addressed, however, is the methodological dimension of this in(ter)vention, which complements its epistemological and political outlook. If the epistemology of knowledge production is Althusser's discourse theory, symptomal reading constitutes his version of discourse analysis. Looking for the "visible/invisible, absent/present keystone" of a given text, "it divulges the undivulged event in the text it reads, and in the same movement relates it to *a different text*, present as a necessary absence in the first" and "in the new one the *second text* is articulated with the lapses in the first text" (Althusser et al. 2015, 27–29). We would be mistaken, however, to interpret Althusser's gesture towards a "second text" as a static reference to another *substantial* entity that would serve as a mere contrast or supplement.

Strongly influenced by Freudian psychoanalysis (as the vocabulary suggests; also see Althusser 1999), he rather points to the radical heterogeneity of a text. This means that meaning always depends on the ideological and political conjuncture at stake and, perhaps more importantly, the workings of the unconscious. His assertion that "there is no *pure* discourse" (Althusser 2003, 83) perfectly encapsulates this understanding, and reads like a mission statement for materialist DA.

Only recently made available, Althusser's *Les vaches noires* (2016) arguably constitutes one of his most complete attempts to conduct a materialist discourse analysis. In the form of an imaginary self-interview, Althusser furnishes a discourse analysis of the historical-materialist concept of the "dictatorship of the proletariat" in the political context of the transformation of the French Communist Party. It was, however, not before the collaborative endeavor of a young circle of scholars that materialist discourse analysis would receive a more systematic implementation.

The Political Project of Pêcheux's Discourse Analysis

The materialist strand of FDA came into full swing between the late 1960s and the mid-1980s, nurtured by the collaborative work of a new generation of researchers around Michel Pêcheux.[6] Strongly inspired by the encounter with Althusser and his work, they picked up, as it were, at the point where he had left them off intellectually. Now using the label *discourse analysis,* they tried to come to grips with the methodological implementation by deepening the engagement with linguistics. Using the words of Pêcheux (1982b, 211), they formed a "triple alliance" between Marxist historical materialism, psychoanalysis in the Freudo-Lacanian tradition, and linguistic approaches focusing on syntactic mechanisms and the process of enunciation (Pêcheux and Fuchs 1975). This alliance resulted in an impressive array of analytical approaches that continue to resonate in contemporary Discourse Studies (Angermuller, Maingueneau, and Wodak 2014). Less acknowledged, however, is the fact that discourse analysis also constituted a political project from the outset. Thus, the methodological developments were always driven by an interventionist desire: After all, as Paul Henry recalls, Pêcheux imagined his version of discourse analysis to be nothing less than a "Trojan Horse which could be infiltrated into the social sciences in order to bring about a revolution" (Henry 1995, 40).

The trajectory of materialist FDA as a methodological-political project is perhaps best visible in Pêcheux's short reflection on the *three stages of discourse analysis* (Pêcheux 1995b), in which he describes a series of successive "de-borderings" of DA: The conception of discourse shifts from a closed and clearly delimited textual corpus, which is interpreted as structurally determined by a discursive machine (DA-1), over a concern for the interdiscursive relations between these machines in the guise of relations between different discursive formations (DA-2), to the deconstruction of the cognate ideas of the machine and a stable corpus (DA-3).

The methodological implications of this development can be neatly illustrated with a view to the conditions of production—a concept that is present throughout the different "stages" (see also Courtine 1981, 19–24): In DA-1, the conditions of production provide a stable outside against the background of which a (class-) antagonism can be discerned in homogeneous corpora. Here, differential ideological positions are coextensive with the social positions of discourse participants, and discourse is a mere support of the (class-) contradiction that separates them. In DA-2, this linear mapping is opened by looking at the mobility of discursive sequences between different discursive formations. This means that the antagonism is replicated *within* the different ideological positions that are analyzed: Discursive sequences (and participants) ambivalently contribute to the reproduction or transformation of the conditions of production, no matter where they seem to "stand," and it is the task of the analyst to scrutinize this "vacillation." DA-3 is nothing but the logical continuation of this line of reasoning: What crumbles with the idea of a stable and clearly discernible antagonism is the illusion of a strictly sequential analysis. The discourse unfolds in a "spiraling" movement alongside the practice of analysis, the results of which are re-inscribed into, and reconfigure the "corpus" and its borders. Here, conditions of production are an ongoing concern, and seen as affecting discourse all the way down, from the discursive sequences over the epistemological framework and the practice of analysis to the way its results feed back into the discursive conjuncture in question. To put it succinctly, if there is no outside of discourse, discourse analysis *never* stands outside of the discourse it analyses, and the conditions of production within which it operates.

While Pêcheux's three stages are commonly referred to in terms of a periodization of FDA (for example by Angermuller 2014, 10), this is only half of the story. Contrary to the idea of a linear development with discrete stages,[7] we believe it is more appropriate to read it as a reflection on different dimensions of criticality that make up for discourse analysis as a materialist method. Consequently, we argue that it is more sensible to talk about a process of political ripening and autocritique instead of assuming a series of straightforward recalls. Against this background, it is not a mere coincidence that the text ends with a question that fundamentally challenges the initial optimism with which the project started off: "On what conditions is it possible (or impossible) for an interpretation to make an intervention? Can we (re-)define a 'politics' of discourse analysis?" (Pêcheux 1995a, 241).

What could thus be dubbed the "reflexive moment" of materialist FDA is best visible in a text with the rather cryptic title *The Strange Mirror of Discourse Analysis*[8] (Pêcheux 1981a) and Pêcheux's opening words for a workshop on *Discursive Materialities* (Pêcheux 1981b). Here, he develops an incisive reflexive critique of discourse analysis as a method and discipline that resonates with the perspective of DA-3. What is perhaps most striking about these documents is their timeliness. Indeed, Pêcheux's concerns about a looming analytical arrogance of a "scientifically substantiated partisan position that tends to treat the indigenous of the political sphere like jerks," the fact that that discourse analysis effectively became an attractive product that complies with the laws of supply and demand in academia (Pêcheux 1981a, 5–6; our translation), denying analytical responsibility, or becoming complicit with what he calls "universalitarian emptiness," the realm in which academic discourse analysis becomes "some sort of an orthopedic lecture, forming a prosthesis for a failing political thinking" (Pêcheux 1981b, 17; our translation) are not only still relevant today. In a context in which the neo-liberal transformation of academic institutions advances rapidly, addressing these questions becomes perhaps more pressing than ever. After all,

> Discourse Analysis is no more than a transitory discipline, artefact of the theo-retical conjuncture. If that's its destiny, why construct theoretical objects like we will try to do, that risk to be no more than ephemeral constructions? Such is the destiny of thought: we need to construct sewing machines to rip false totalities. (Courtine and Marandin 1981, 33; our translation)

CHARACTERISTICS OF A MATERIALIST APPROACH TO DISCOURSE

We believe that the border between "materialism" and "discourse," and the way it is policed in theory, methods, and academic debates are *effects of discourse*. Against this background, working against the oblivion of materialist discourse analysis is more than mere nostalgia or antiquarianism. It helps uncovering (and potentially even transcending) some limits of contemporary knowledge production at the intersections of the linguistic, the social, and the political, and questioning the institutional structures within which it operates. Against the background of the three moments of materialist discourse analysis explored above, the following set of criteria offers one possible way to make the combination between discourse, ideology, and political economy matter (again).

Materiality Matters

We suggest that one of the key characteristics of a materialist discourse analysis touches on the status of the discursive and symbolic in a materialist approach to the Social. Thus, determining the role discursive practices are given in a materialist analysis is crucial. Language, discourse, and ideology should not be conceived of as "immaterial" instances juxtaposed to "material" conditions, but as semi-autonomous and productive parts of material reality. As we have seen, this entails a reconfiguration of the edificial metaphor of base and superstructure, in as much as there is no expressive or mechanistic relationship between semiotic material and its context or the material (economic/social/historical) conditions it is produced in. Against this background, the distinction between the planes of "the discursive" and "the material" is only possible in terms of an analytical moment.

Ideology Matters

From the beginning, Marxism conceived of the relation between the discursive and the material in terms of ideology. However, because there is a semi-autonomy of discursive practices, ideology is not to be seen as merely "false consciousness" or a distorted reflection of material reality. Thus, the production of meaning and the way individuals relate to social realities is not *directly* determined by their position within relations of re/production, but refracted through ideological forms of misrecognition. Consequently, the intimate relation between ideological, discursive, and social formations and subject positions needs to be explored analytically without assuming that they neatly map onto each other. In such a conception, it is not possible to stand outside of ideology, which has consequences for materialist discourse analysis. Namely, this means refuting the empiricist illusion it sometimes entails: Never operating outside of the discourse it looks at, the ever so comfortable distinction between theory- and object-discourse collapses. There is no innocent reading—just as much as there is no un-ideological text. Doing discourse analysis is messy, and means getting our hands dirty.

History Matters

Material discourse analysis needs to *historicize*, without relapsing into a teleological or mechanistic *historicism*. Practically, this requires accounting for the historically specific conditions of (knowledge-) production that affect discourse all the way down, from production to analysis. However, history is not a mere sequence of events, but an ongoing process crucially determined by struggles. For us, materialist discourse analysis needs to develop a strong sensibility for the uneven distribution of the means of knowledge production in a given context and conjuncture. A materialist approach always entails taking sides, accounting for our own positionality, and reflecting on how the very results of our analysis can ambivalently feed back into the discursive and ideological formations we are confronted with.

The Object Matters

There is no one-size-fits-all solution for materialist discourse analysis: There is no methodological procedure that could be followed step-by-step in order to arrive at a materialist analysis of a given object. Instead, the object itself should guide what methods are utilized. There is a multitude of discourse-analytical tools at our disposal: For instance, an enunciative-pragmatic analysis of utterances can help scrutinize the different subject positions that are involved in processes of production and reproduction, in and beyond discourse. Such a formalist, praxeological approach can show how the social is ordered through discursive practices by tracing the instructions the linguistic material gives for its own contextualization. In combination with the other criteria just outlined, this allows for a perspective that is highly aware of power dimensions that infuse discursive practices.

A materialist approach does not give all the answers before the fact, but guides practices of analysis, critique, and intervention that acknowledge contradictions instead of trying to tame them. If certain tensions arise, this is not to be seen as a failure of the approach, but a reminder of the stubbornness of the social realities we are confronted with.

For us, being materialists means being open to surprises, unexpected turns, leaving the comfort zone of abstract analysis and static methodology for a critical and collective reflection on how we are bound up with the horrors of late capitalism.

NOTES

1. We are grateful to our friends and colleagues in the discourseanalysis.net research group on *Discourse, Ideology, and Political Economy (DIPE)*, which not only constitutes an intellectually challenging and rewarding, but also highly supportive space to work on the issues presented here. We would also like to thank all participants of the workshops *Materialist_Discourse_Analysis: Methodological entanglements* at the University of Warwick, in July 2016, and *Diskursanalyse nach dem Marxismus. Kritik, Emanzipation und Neuvermessung eines theoretischen Spannungsverhältnisses* at the University of Gießen (Germany) in April 2017 for their highly valuable comments.

2. In the long run, we believe that it is equally important to scrutinize moments of materialist DA beyond Discourse Studies: First, this would allow highlighting the transcendence of (materialist) Discourse Studies vis-à-vis the borders that demarcate it in terms of an analytical paradigm or "discipline." And second, it would allow widening its political quality by reincorporating critical arguments that have been formulated "elsewhere." In a concomitant move to the first step, this would uncover that materialist discourse analysis has always been and continues to be performed inside and outside of what is regarded the principal domain of Discourse Studies.

3. Paradoxically, the materialist tradition of "French" DA seems to be more alive outside of France, as illustrated by Marie-Anne Paveau (2007) and Jean-Jacques Courtine (in this volume). Courtine also points to the disciplinary politics behind the label of FDA.

4. It should still be mentioned that the *meaning* and the force of utterances and "phrases" depends on the positions individuals hold in the present social relations. This point will be important for Pêcheux's discourse analysis and theory.

5. It is beyond the scope of our article to reconstruct this unique political climate. Roughly speaking, Althusser had hoped to challenge two Marxist tendencies: The specter of Stalinism and the economist orthodoxies that went with it; and humanist versions of Marxism, which he perceived as incapable to critically reflect on the ideological formation of the subject beyond the assertion of ("false") consciousness.

6. Once again, it is hard to do justice to this exceptionally productive period of collaboration. Important moments include the early discussion in the journal *Cahiers pour l'Analyse* (Hallward and Peden 2012a, 2012b), the contributions to the issues 24, 37, and 62 of the linguistic journal *Langages*, Pêcheux's two monographs on discourse analysis (Pêcheux 1995a, 1982a) and his collaboration with Françoise Gadet (Gadet and Pêcheux 1981), as well as the proceedings of a conference on *Discursive Materialities* (Conein et al. 1981). For a comprehensive overview, we recommend the meticulously crafted account by Denise Maldidier (1990), and a shorter piece by Marie-Anne Paveau (2007).

7. Which is arguably evoked by the original title. While Pêcheux is referring to "epochs" [époques] instead of "stages," this doesn't really change the problematic, almost historicist connotation.

8. L'étrange miroir de l'analyse du discours.

BIBLIOGRAPHY

Althusser, Louis. 1969. *For Marx.* New York: Pantheon Books.

———. 1971. "Ideology and Ideological State Apparatuses (Notes Towards an Investigation)." In *Lenin and Philosophy and Other Essays*, edited by Ben Brewster, 127–86. New York, London: Monthly Review Press.

———. 1972. *Lenin and Philosophy, and Other Essays.* New York: Monthly Review Press.

———. 1999. *Writings on Psychoanalysis: Freud and Lacan.* New York: Columbia University Press.

———. 2003. "Three Notes on the Theory of Discourses: (1966)." In *The Humanist Controversy and Other Writings: (1966–67)*, edited by François Matheron, 33–84. London, New York: Verso.

———. 2005. "Contradiction and Overdetermination: Notes for an Investigation." In *For Marx*, 87–128. London, New York: Verso.

———. 2016. *Les vaches noires: Interview imaginaire.* Edited by G. M. Goshgarian. Perspectives critiques. Paris: Puf.

Althusser, Louis, Étienne Balibar, Roger Establet, Pierre Macherey, and Jacques Rancière. 2015. *Reading Capital: The Complete Edition.* London, New York: Verso.

Angermuller, Johannes. 2014. *Poststructuralist Discourse Analysis: Subjectivity in Enunciative Pragmatics.* Houndmills: Palgrave Macmillan.

Angermuller, Johannes, and Dominique Maingueneau. 2007. "Discourse Analysis in France: A Conversation." *Forum Qualitative Sozialforschung* 8 (2). http://nbn-resolving.de/urn:nbn:de:0114-fqs0702218. Accessed September 10, 2015.

Angermuller, Johannes, Dominique Maingueneau, and Ruth Wodak, eds. 2014. *The Discourse Studies Reader: Main Currents in Theory and Analysis.* Amsterdam: John Benjamins Publishing Company.

Badiou, Alain. 2013. *Theory of the Subject.* London: Bloomsbury Academic.

Bakhtin, Michail M. 1981. *The Dialogic Imagination: 4 Essays.* University of Texas Press Slavic series 1. Austin, Texas: University of Texas Press.

Balibar, Etienne. 2007. *The Philosophy of Marx.* London, New York: Verso.

Beetz, Johannes. 2016. *Materiality and Subject in Marxism, Post-Structuralism, and Material Semiotics.* London: Palgrave Macmillan.

Benjamin, Walter. 1968. "Theses on the Philosophy of History." In *Illuminations,* edited by Hannah Arendt, 253–64. New York: Schocken Books.

Butler, Judith. 1997. *The Psychic Life of Power: Theories in Subjection.* Stanford: Stanford University Press.

Carver, Terrell. 2002. "Imagery/Writing, Imagination/Politics: Reading Marx through the Eighteenth Brumaire." In *Marx's Eighteenth Brumaire: (Post)Modern Interpretations,* edited by Marx, Karl, Mark Cowling, and James Martin, 113–28. London, Sterling, Va: Pluto Press.

Conein, Bernard, Jean-Jacques Courtine, Françoise Gadet, Jean-Marie Marandin, and Michel Pêcheux, eds. 1981. *Materialités Discursives: Colloque des 24, 25, 26 avril 1980, Université Paris X - Nanterre.* Lille: Presses Universitaires de Lille.

Courtine, Jean-Jacques. 1981. "Quelques problèmes théoriques et méthodologiques en analyse du discours, à propos du discours communiste adressé aux chrétiens." *Langages* 15 (62): 9–128.

Courtine, Jean-Jacques, and Jean-Marie Marandin. 1981. "Quel objet pour l'analyse du discours?" In *Materialités Discursives: Colloque des 24, 25, 26 avril 1980, Université Paris X - Nanterre,* edited by Bernard Conein, Jean-Jacques Courtine, Françoise Gadet, Jean-Marie Marandin, and Michel Pêcheux, 21–33. Lille: Presses Universitaires de Lille.

Coward, Rosalind, and John Ellis. 1977. *Language and Materialism: Developments in Semiology and the Theory of the Subject.* London, Boston: Routledge and Paul.

Cowling, Mark, and James Martin. 2002. "Introduction." In *Marx's Eighteenth Brumaire: (Post)Modern Interpretations,* edited by Marx, Karl, Mark Cowling, and James Martin, 1–15. London, Sterling, VA: Pluto Press.

de Ípola, Emilio. 2012. *Althusser, l'adieu infini.* Pratiques théoriques. Paris: Puf.

Eagleton, Terry. 1996. *Literary Theory: An Introduction.* Minneapolis, MN: University of Minnesota Press.

Fairclough, Norman, and Peter Graham. 2002. "Marx as Critical Discourse Analysis: The genesis of a critical method and its relevance to the critique of global capital." *Estudios de Sociolinguistica* 3 (1): 185–229.

Gadet, Françoise, and Michel Pêcheux. 1981. *La langue introuvable.* Théorie. Paris: F. Maspero.

Hallward, Peter, and Knox Peden, eds. 2012a. *Concept and Form: Volume 1. Selections from Cahiers pour l'Analyse.* London, New York: Verso.

———, eds. 2012b. *Concept and Form: Volume 2. Interviews and Essays on the Cahiers Pour L'Analyse.* London, New York: Verso.

Hennessy, Rosemary. 2013. *Materialist Feminism and the Politics of Discourse.* London: Routledge.

Henry, Paul. 1995. "Theoretical Issues in Pecheux's Automatic Discourse Analysis (1969)." In *Automatic Discourse Analysis,* edited by Tony Hak and Niels Helsloot, 21–40. Amsterdam, Atlanta, GA: Rodopi.

Jameson, Fredric. 1974. *The Prison-House of Language: A Critical Account of Structuralism and Russian Formalism.* Princeton, NJ: Princeton University Press.

———. 2002. *The Political Unconscious: Narrative as a Socially Symbolic Act.* London: Routledge.

Jessop, Bob. 2002. "The Political Scene and the Politics of Representation: Periodising Class Struggle and the State in the Eighteenth Brumaire." In *Marx's Eighteenth Brumaire: (Post)Modern Interpretations,* Marx, Karl, Mark Cowling, and James Martin, eds, 179–94. London, Sterling, Va: Pluto Press.

Jordan-Haladyn, Miriam. 2014. *Dialogic Materialism: Bakhtin, Embodiment, and Moving Image Art.* New York: Peter Lang.

Jørgensen, Marianne, and Louise Phillips. 2002. *Discourse Analysis as Theory and Method.* London: SAGE.

Kramer, Ingo. 2014. *Symptomale Lektüre: Louis Althussers Beitrag zu einer Theorie des Diskurses.* Wien: Passagen.

Kristeva, Julia, and Anne M. Menke. op. 1989. *Language, the Unknown: An Initiation into Linguistics.* New York: Columbia University Press.

Laclau, Ernesto, and Chantal Mouffe. 2001. *Hegemony and Socialist Strategy: Towards a Radical Democratic Politics.* 2nd ed. London, New York: Verso.

Maldidier, Denise. 1990. *L'inquiétude du discours: Textes de Michel Pêcheux.* Archives du commentaire. Paris: Éditions des Cendres.

Marx, Karl. 1990. *Capital: A Critique of Political Economy.* London: Penguin in association with New Left Review.

———. 2002. "The Eighteenth Brumaire of Louis Bonaparte." In *Marx's Eighteenth Brumaire: (Post)Modern Interpretations,* edited by Marx, Karl, Mark Cowling, and James Martin, 19–109. London, Sterling, VA: Pluto Press.

———. 2010. "Theses on Feuerbach." In *Karl Marx and Frederick Engels Works, Vol. 5, April 1845-April 1847,* 3–5. London: Lawrence & Wishart Electric Book.

Marx, Karl, and Frederick Engels. 1965. *The German Ideology.* London: Lawrence & Wishart.

Marx, Karl, Mark Cowling, and James Martin, eds. 2002. *Marx's Eighteenth Brumaire: (Post)Modern Interpretations.* London, Sterling, VA: Pluto Press.

Montag, Warren. 2013. *Althusser and His Contemporaries: Philosophy's Perpetual War.* Durham, London: Duke University Press.

Nelson, Cary, and Lawrence Grossberg, eds. 1988. *Marxism and the Interpretation of Culture.* Urbana: University of Illinois Press.

Paveau, Marie-Anne. 2007. "Discours et matérialisme. Quelques points d'articulation entre la pensée althussérienne et l'analyse du discours dite 'française.'" Accessed

April 27, 2016. http://www.europhilosophie.eu/recherche/IMG/pdf/Disc_et_mat_MAP.pdf

Pêcheux, Michel. 1981a. "L'étrange miroir de l'analyse de discours." *Langages* 15 (62): 5–8.

———. 1981b. "Ouverture du colloque." In *Materialités Discursives: Colloque des 24, 25, 26 avril 1980, Université Paris X - Nanterre*, edited by Bernard Conein, Jean-Jacques Courtine, Françoise Gadet, Jean-Marie Marandin, and Michel Pêcheux, 15–18. Lille: Presses Universitaires de Lille.

———. 1982a. *Language, Semantics and Ideology: Stating the Obvious*. London: Macmillan.

———. 1982b. "The French Political Winter: Beginning of a Rectification: (Postscript for English Readers) [1978–1979]." In *Language, Semantics and Ideology: Stating the Obvious*, 211–20. London: Macmillan.

———. 1988. "Discourse: Structure or Event?" In *Marxism and the Interpretation of Culture: International Conference : Selected Papers*, edited by Cary Nelson and Lawrence Grossberg, 633–650. Urbana: University of Illinois Press.

———. 1995a. *Automatic Discourse Analysis*. Edited by Tony Hak and Niels Helsloot. Amsterdam, Atlanta, GA: Rodopi.

———. 1995b. "Three stages of discourse analysis [1983]." In *Automatic Discourse Analysis*, edited by Tony Hak and Niels Helsloot, 235–41. Amsterdam, Atlanta, GA: Rodopi.

Pêcheux, Michel, and Catherine Fuchs. 1975. "Mises au point et perspectives à propos de l'analyse automatique du discours." *Langages* 9 (37): 7–80.

Riquelme, John P. 1980. "The Eighteenth Brumaire of Karl Marx as Symbolic Action." *History and Theory* 19 (1): 58.

Rorty, Richard. 1992. *The Linguistic Turn: Essays in Philosophical Method: with Two Retrospective Essays*. Chicago: University of Chicago Press.

Stalin, Iosif V. 1972. *Marxism and the Problems of Linguistics*. Peking: Foreign Language Press.

Thomas, Lawrence L. 1957. *The Linguistic Theories of N. Ja. Marr*. Berkeley: University of California Press.

Vološinov, Valentin. 1973. *Marxism and the Philosophy of Language*. London: Seminar Press.

Williams, Glyn. 1999. *French Discourse Analysis: The Method of Post-Structuralism*. London: Routledge.

Williams, Raymond. 1977. *Marxism and Literature*. Oxford: Oxford University Press.

Chapter 4

The Black Consciousness Movement in Brazil

A Materialist-Enunciative Approach to Discourse Analysis

Helio Oliveira

This chapter aims to combine materialist and enunciative approaches in the field of discourse analysis to scrutinize the discursive formula "*consciência negra*"[1] (hereafter, "Black consciousness") in Brazil. By analyzing the circulation of this formula in contemporary Brazilian public space, my objective is to examine the relation between social inequality and racism (usually conceived in terms of cause and consequence, respectively) as well as other discursive positions, and eventually contrast it with the conception that socioeconomic inequality is caused by racism. While some discursive positions present themselves as supporting the Black Consciousness Movement, they do not represent the issues that are important to Black activists. Similarly, others present themselves as neutral, but this assertion of neutrality cannot be sustained against the background of the discourse at stake.

To elucidate this discursive operation, I propose a discourse-analytical methodology that moves between enunciative and materialist perspectives, starting from the assumption that these approaches combine, rather than being mutually exclusive. The main interest is to analyze how the formula "Black consciousness"—by its nature as a social referent, as a "place" of confrontational positions and a focus of discursivations—constitutes itself as an essential participant in the debate on racism. In this way, it contributes to the emergence of a discourse that represents the demands of the Brazilian Black Movement in terms of "Black discourse."

The notion of discursive formula, as proposed by Krieg-Planque (2009), considers the enunciative dimension of language together with the discursive process of meaning production. At the same time, it allows the analyst to become aware of issues pertaining to the reproduction and transformation of discursive and ideological formations, as developed by Pêcheux (1975) in the tradition of Althusserian Marxism (1984). Every formula has a crystallized

47

linguistic structure (syntactic and morphologic), works as a social referent within a specific social historical limit, and produces various controversies, to name just a few main features. These properties are closely related to disputes of power and opinion in the public space, and consequently cannot be separated from their historical conditions of production. This assertion is a core feature that qualifies an approach to discourse as materialist. A materialist discourse analysis not only looks at the processes of interpellation and subjugation (*assujettissement*), but mainly focuses on resistance movements as well as transformations of subjects and contexts. In contrast to research that insists on separating materialist and enunciative approaches, my contribution maintains that there is no obstacle to the coexistence of two types of analysis in the same framework. The notion of the discursive formula is mobilized as a theoretical base in research areas as diverse as sustainable development (Krieg-Planque 2010), selective immigration (Brilliant 2014), fair trade and fair commerce (Masasa 2014), digital democracy (Amadori 2014), as well as Black consciousness, which is my focus in this chapter. The corpus[2] consists of texts from various media genres, namely the largest newspapers in Brazil (*Folha de S. Paulo, O Estado de S. Paulo*), news magazines, and blogs of journalists who represent the Brazilian Black Movement. The notion of "discursive formula" itself implies a corpora-composing methodology: texts are collected and selected from criteria involving the occurrences of the formula in question, for example, functioning as a social referent, lexical relative crystallization, controversial character, etc. (Krieg-Planque 2009).

THE MYTH OF RACIAL DEMOCRACY IN BRAZIL

"The country of samba" and "the land of Carnival" are two well-known Brazilian stereotypes in which Black people occupy a prominent place—for instance the samba musician with his tambourine, or the beautiful Black women known as the "musician's queens" who are ubiquitous in the Carnival parade. The strong presence of Black people[3] since the time of colonization and their wide influence on the Brazilian language, cuisine, music and festivals have led to the false belief that there is no racism in Brazil. A recent example of the materialization of this discourse is the publication of the book *Nós não somos racistas* (*We are not racists*) by Ali Kamel, head of journalism at Globo TV. According to many anthropologists, the myth of Brazilian "racial democracy" is a founding element of national identity (Freire 1933, Azevedo 1953, Skidmore 1974). With regard to the stereotypes, it is important to note the fact that Black culture often appears in folkloric and popular contexts, but rarely in the academic, intellectual, and political fields, for example.

Although they are widely denied, cases of racist discrimination are daily events and range from taxi drivers refusing to stop for Black passengers (an experience reported by the rapper Emicida[4]) to murder (the torture and execution of the mason Amarildo de Souza[5] at the hands of police in Rio de Janeiro). These latter cases figure prominently in statistics indicating that more than 77% of homicide victims in Brazil are Black.[6]

Some achievements point to a less frightening (but no less complex) scenario; these include the establishment of quotas for African descendants to access public bids and attend public universities, "Black beauty" events (including the largest African fair in Latin America, *Feira Preta* in São Paulo), contests featuring "Black culture and Black art" (such as the *FUN-ARTE* Black Art Prize), a federal department for racial equality policy, as well as various associations related to the Black Movement. Since 2003, São Paulo has also been home to Zumbi dos Palmares University, which bills itself as a "Black university" and is the first in Latin America and one of only a few worldwide created by, managed by, and made available to the Black public. Brazil has also passed Code 7437/1985 which criminal-ized acts motivated by racial prejudice, the 2010 Racial Equality Statute, and Code 12519/2011 through which the ex-president Dilma Rousseff established the National Day of Black Consciousness, also called "Black Pride Day."

Although there is this wide discursivation around the conditions of Blacks in the Brazilian social space, their demands continue to be invisible. Accord-ing to contemporary sociologists (Guimarães 2009 and Schwarcz 2012, for example), making racism a crime does not solve the problem, but only moves it to some other place by diluting it among everyday interactions. Van Dijk supports this point of view, in a stance closer to Discourse Studies, stating that inequalities in daily interaction with indigenous and Black people in many societies today have been attributed to social class and not to race, without extensive investigation of the various roots of class and economic inequality (Van Dijk, 2008, 13). He proposes a definition of racism based on the idea of continuing social inequality:

Racism is essentially a system of domination and social inequality. In Europe, the Americas, and Australia, this means that a "white" majority (and sometimes, a minority) dominates non-European minorities. Domination, in turn, is defined as an abuse of power by one group over another and is represented by two inter-related systems of daily social and cognitive practices: on the one hand, by vari-ous forms of discrimination, marginalization, exclusion or questioning, and on the other by prejudiced ideologies, beliefs, and attitudes based on stereotypes. These latter can be considered, in many ways, "motivation" or "reasons" to explain or justify the former. (2015, 33)

I agree with Van Dijk, for whom "many everyday practices of racism (…) need to be discursively explained, considering the role of the discourse in the reproduction of these practices" (2008, 17). However, Kilomba presents a definition of racism that allows us to scrutinize the complexity of social practices related to this subject by observing it from the perspective of those who face racism every day. Kilomba proposes understanding racism through

> three simultaneous features: first, the construction of difference. [...] One only becomes "different" because one "differs" from a group who has the power to define itself as the norm—the white norm. [...] Second, these constructed differences are inseparably linked to hierarchical values. Not only is the individual seen as "different," but also this difference is articulated through stigma, dishonor and inferiority. [...] Finally, both processes are accompanied by power—historical, political, social and economic power. It is the combinations of both prejudice and power that form racism. (2008, 42)

From this perspective, which is articulated here within the theoretical framework of discourse analysis, it is a fundamentally discursive relationship that updates racism, even when racism is cloaked in a new appearance. This relationship derives from the operation of an interdiscursive memory in combination with practices of historical conditioning.

In this sense, the notion of the formula appears as a productive input for research that aims to cover the discursive dimension of complex social phenomena, such as the functioning of racism. This is at the same time a theoretical and methodological framework: by using the theoretical principles to characterize, isolate, and describe the functioning of a formula, discourse analysis can process very large and heterogeneous corpora, since the formula condenses discourses. Demands for the specificities of a particular formula lead to successive downscaling and filtering of the material, which in turn helps to build the corpus by organizing the data for the analysis stage (which I describe here in subsequent steps, but in practice this frequently consists of movements back and forth between the corpus and the theoretical texts, including constant reorganization of the corpus). This promotes a typical discourse-analytical approach, which Angermuller describes as a formal-qualitative method or a quasi-qualitative approach (2005, 2014). The goal of this approach is to break down a complex object into smaller constituent elements and expose its organizing mechanisms. According to Angermuller, the multiplicity of empirical phenomena must at least ideally be reduced to a few fundamental rules of production. Thus, he continues, instead of seeking to reconstruct the stock of socially shared knowledge ("what?"), discursive research is interested in the rules and mechanisms of the discursive process ("how?"). In other words, the analyst must examine the enunciation device that connects a certain textual organization with a particular social place, without forgetting historical injunctions. Furthermore, work based on this type of method seems to be another example of analysis (in addition to works related to the notion of discursive formula) which can also straddle the enunciative and materialist approaches.

ONE FORMULA FOR DISCUSSING RACISM

In presenting a dossier about formulas, Motta and Salgado (2011) explain that all discursive formulas contain historical density that becomes apparent in their circulation, and are supported by what has previously been constructed and focused on new constructions. They add that

> [e]ven thinking in terms of crystallization, it would not be the case to see something immobile or immutable there. All speech is movement, and when crystallized, a node is created in a network—not an end, not a single point, but a nerve center, a strategic place in the historical dynamic that establishes and emphasizes. And this "node" has to do with the controversies which are the focus of a given speech community, with the beliefs that sustain them, with the discourse that feeds and can also transform them. (Motta and Salgado 2011, presentation; my translation)

Defined as "a set of formulations used in a time and in a specific public space, crystallizing political and social issues" (Krieg-Planque 2010, 07; my translation), the discursive formula presents a situation in which there is a shared signifier and a disputed signified. Once the formula constitutes itself as a "problem"—once it has a value of description of the political and social facts—it is the object of several controversies. For Krieg-Planque,

> [t]he formula is the bearer of socio-political issues. [...] it involves ways of life, material resources, nature, and decisions by the political regime individuals depend on, their rights, their duties, relations of equality or inequality between citizens, human solidarity, the ideas people form about the nation they feel they belong to. (2010, 100; my translation)

One example of how "Black consciousness" participates in the way of life and "the ideas people form about the nation they feel they belong to" is the controversial opinion that there is no need for a social movement to fight to establish "Black consciousness" in Brazil, since there is no racism or racial segregation in the country, according to the excerpts below (emphasis/italics added):

Excerpt 1:[7] The *problem* with having a day to celebrate "Black consciousness" lies in the fact that it promotes a *distinction* that *separates* people by color.

By this principle it would be natural to have days to celebrate "white consciousness," or "indigenous consciousness," or "nearly Black" or "yellow consciousness" etc. Consciousness has no color. (…) From the collective point of view, we all have patriotism, which is the sense of belonging and *equality* experienced by people who share a historical formation. It is, therefore, a *sum*. In these groups there can't be a *special category*, because *all of us* are *equal* as Brazilians. (…) There are no legal impediments to a Black or Asian person *having access to any property or right*, or any *advantages* for whites that guarantee them *benefits*.

Excerpt 2: In a country where millions of whites are poor and face the *same hardships* as poor Blacks, instituting *racial preference policies*, rather than ensuring quality education for *all poor people* and giving them all the opportunity to overcome poverty according to their own merits, risks placing Brazil on the road to a nightmare: an explosion of racial hatred, which we have not experienced up to this point. When *poor whites, who have always lived alongside poor Blacks* and experienced the *same troubles*, end up neglected simply because they don't have dark skin, this will begin the *racial split* of poverty, with consequences that international experience has shown to be *terrible*.

These two passages refer to the same position, which can be characterized as typical discourse opposing the Black Consciousness Movement (BCM), the holiday, its demands, etc. The same lexical unit, "equality," appears in these statements and acts as a *sema*[8] (a semantic nucleus), which is also common in the pro-BCM discourse. The difference is that in each case (anti-BCM and pro-BCM), "equality" has a very different meaning. As a comparison, the phrase below appears in a Brazilian documentary about the importance of racial quotas in the entrance examination for the University of São Paulo (USP), the country's largest university, and is considered here as Excerpt 3:

E3: "There is no merit without equality."

E3 shows an opposition between equality (in accessing a public university) and the alleged "meritocracy" (in this case, evoking the fallacy that access is free to all through personal merit). These statements in which personal merit does not correspond to equal university access are repeated frequently in the documentary and used as a base for argumentation. The equality that activists in the Black Movement demand would come about through assuming that there is a gap between white and Black access to higher education, a problem that can only be solved through affirmative action in the form of legislation. In this sense, it would first be necessary to recognize the differences (historical, social, and economic, which are not restricted to mere skin color, but do refer to it) and then to propose specific measures and actions. A subsequent aim might include discussing equality, at least ideally. In summarizing the Black Movement's demands in the area of economic inequality, the anti-BCM discourse dissolves the specificity of the BCM, since all poor people would suffer the same impediments. Similarly, in summarizing the differences only with regard to skin color and refusing to even express the formulation "Black consciousness," the same discourse means to erase what essentially defines the BCM, the presence and acceptance of Black people in society. Also noteworthy is the fact that the meanings related to "difference" are in the positive register of BCM discourse, since marking and eventually imposing difference is a major platform of the BCM (here I can refer to some internationally known concepts and movements such as "Black pride," "Black power," and "Black is beautiful").

In order to summarize these two opposing discourses, it can be said that for the opponents of Black Consciousness Day, affirmative action produces racism and racism causes (and exacerbates) social inequality. For those who support Black Consciousness Day, it is racism that causes social inequalities and perpetuates this condition.

DISTINCTIONS WITHIN THE DISCOURSE SUPPORTING THE BLACK CONSCIOUSNESS MOVEMENT

Unlike the two discourses briefly discussed above (for and against Black consciousness), I was able to identify differences within what could initially be classified as the discourse supporting Black Consciousness Day. The absence of texts about the representative demands of the BCM in the major news media (in large-circulation newspapers and magazines with printed and digital versions) led us to the first assumptions. The discursive dimension of the formula, associated with its relatively crystallized structure, allows it to circulate abundantly in the social space, across various discursive fields. However, the press is presented as one of the most important spaces to be occupied by formula in order to reach the public dimension of discussions and constitute itself as a social referent, especially in the case of "Black consciousness" and the issues concerning racism. Van Dijk states that "the role of the press in the reproduction of racism in society can no longer simply be accessed by listing its stereotypical topics or giving examples of obvious bias against minorities." (1991, 253)

When we look at the recent editions of two major Brazilian newspapers on November 20, Black Consciousness Day, they exhibit very few demands related to the group this date is meant to support. The following statements are associated in some way with Black consciousness; they are restricted to the headlines on the cover, the most prominent location in the newspaper (and one of the "preferred places" for the formulas):

E4: *Paladar* [food section]: Points of resistance. In Bahia you can still try authentic African-Brazilian food.

E5: *Ilustrada* [culture section]: Events and books celebrate *favelada*[9] writer on Black Consciousness Day.

In Excerpt 4, the references to Black Consciousness Day are presented as a human-interest story, and are transformed into a culinary theme in the food section. In the first excerpt, the bold subtitle "points of resistance" seems to refer to social struggles and struggles for power according to the current sense of the word "resistance." Yet the actual story describes remote regions of Bahia where traditional dishes with strong African influences can still be found. Next to the text, a picture of raw ingredients (seafood and green onion stalks) in a clay pot sets a rustic scene (few ingredients and a lack of sophistication). The formula is not even mentioned.

In Excerpt 5, "Black consciousness" appears in connection with the work of Carolina Maria de Jesus. The "books and events" celebrate the writer (and no one celebrates the November 20 holiday). In syntactic terms, the writer is not presented as an agent but rather appears in the object position. This inversion of positions, in which inanimate beings occupy the agent/subject position and the human is placed in an object/passive position is a prototypical example of the discursive construction of racist inferiority. A further indication of my claim is the absence of the definite article before the "writer" which follows the adjective *favelada* (as opposed to "the writer"). In Brazilian Portuguese, the absence of this article produces an effect of disqualification, placing the personality in an ordinary position. This inferiority is further exacerbated by the adjective *favelada*, which has largely been abandoned in journalism due to its pejorative connotation. The full story in the newspaper section discusses curiosities about the literature of Carolina Maria de Jesus (who was only widely recognized posthumously, particularly in academic and intellectual circles).

Another aspect related to the verb "celebrate" is the fact that E5 places itself within the same discourse that promotes Black Consciousness Day through publicizing commemorative events, coupled with the fact that November 20 is a holiday in most Brazilian cities. This discourse even circulates in less-traditional journalistic texts that nevertheless have a considerable readership, such as journalistic blogs. Some of these cases feature reformulations such as the "Black Consciousness Party" in Excerpt 6:

E6: The Black Consciousness Party, which takes place on the municipal holiday of November 20 (Friday) in the Cidade Nova district from 2pm to 10pm, will feature concerts by [the singers] MC Gui, Netinhode Paula, and Rick (formerly of the duo Rick &Renner). This information was confirmed by councilman Givanildo Soares (PROS party), who authored the municipal law that established "Black Consciousness Day" in the city of Itu.

Although this text explicitly states the formulation "Black consciousness" (while *Folha de São Paulo* does not) and brings some visibility to the BCM, this kind of text is still criticized by BCM activists as merely "informative" discourse.

> From the activist viewpoint, the commemorative events do not make a concrete contribution to reducing racism or improving living conditions for the Black population, and mask the main reason for the holiday as well as actions creating awareness about the nature of racism. The following are illustrative excerpts from that discourse:

> E7: There are those party animals, and those who feel alienated at the party [...] The media reinforces invisibility, stereotype, and the social and historical distortion of facts about Black culture, transforming it into an appendage of the consumerist spectacle. [...] What is a "Black Consciousness" holiday for?

> E8: I think there should be no celebration, although it is a date related to Zumbi dos Palmares, who represents Blacks. The main point should be to discuss why Black people still live on the margins of society. Since 1888, when slavery was abolished, the situation has changed a little—but only very little. Not talking about racism is drawing the shades on the struggle of my ancestors and many other Blacks who fight every day for a place. What happened to me in March was nothing new [after refereeing a game, the speaker found bananas on the hood and in the exhaust pipe of his car parked at the Montanha dos Vinhedos stadium in Bento Gonçalves]. But this time I decided to express myself, especially because my thinking has changed since I became a father. How can I pass this lesson on to my son if I just give up when faced with this kind of situation? I took legal action and I think that the punishment of those involved will be a milestone in our state. [...] It is not normal for a Black person to be called a monkey. Only a Black person knows just how painful it is.

> E9: There is nothing to celebrate on Black Consciousness Day when 70.8% of the population living in extreme poverty in the country is Black. There is nothing to celebrate on Black Consciousness Day when 60% of the prison population is Black. [...] We do not want a party, we want justice, rights, opportunities, reparations. November 20 is not a day for a party!

In Excerpt 7 (which was published on the blog of the activist group Geledés), the celebrations are considered a source of alienation and seen as transforming the Black cause into an "appendage of the consumerist spectacle," while the media (in the current sense, broad-scale media communication) places Black history and culture in second place, which is confirmed by the minimal importance and small space given to this date in the major newspapers considered in E4 and E5.

Similarly, in the interview in Excerpt 8, which was published on the website of the newspaper *Zero Hora*, a soccer referee and sports commentator for the RBS Group talks about the importance of discussing racism on this date instead of celebrating. He even takes advantage of the space offered by the site to share his personal experience as a victim of a racist act who pursued his rights in court. The report in question is a typical example of the BCM's discourse, because it contains the utterances that highlight issues and themes which are important to Black activism as well as references to Zumbi dos Palmares (who "represents Blacks"), to the era of slavery (the abolition of which, according to the report, did not bring real improvement to living conditions for Black people; note the word "still" comparing extreme violence in slavery times to the current situation faced by the Black population in the statement, "The main point should be to discuss why Black people still live on the margins of society"), the struggle for basic civil rights ("the struggle of my ancestors," "Blacks who fight every day for a place"), the discussion of racism, and punishment for aggressors, among others. Additionally, the highly personal tone of the account brings the readers closer to the theme of racism and makes the description more vivid by exposing the emotional burden involved in the aggression described: the apparent presence of his son when he found his car vandalized, the details of the assault ("it is not normal ... to be called a monkey") and the feelings involved ("Only a Black person knows just how painful it is").

These narrative fragments containing personal vivid experiences allow the Black perspective come to the forefront, as Kilomba showed for the assumptions mentioned previously. This aspect cannot be disregarded in discursive analysis, at the risk of perpetuating ideologies of neutrality and depoliticization. On this subject, Schwab argues that "locating positions that have the power to differentiate, as well as practices of contestation proceeding on the basis, in spite of, and/or against established structures of difference is a first step towards an ethical practice of critique" (2015, 06)—in an expertise which is generally characteristic of the materialist approach to discourse.

The textual-discursive traces of the personal narrative in Excerpt 8 show how the BCM discourse functions, although the text is not a militant pamphlet, for example. Even so, it is unlikely that this text could have been published in a large Brazilian newspaper.

Another assertive example is the text in which Excerpt 9 appeared, a post on the *Blogueiras Feministas* blog that repeats the statement, "There is nothing to celebrate on Black Consciousness Day when" and shares statistics proving the unfair conditions faced by Blacks today. While fighting the manifestations of the "party" on November 20, the text works in a metadiscursive manner as a model of posts and topics that must be prioritized on that date: proposals of a Black agenda (or, at least, providing visibility for these proposals), namely, "justice, rights, opportunities, reparations. November 20 is not a day for a party!" The presence of data and percentages in E9 produces an effect of truth and reliability which activist discourses often turn to.

The opposition between Black activist discourse and Black Consciousness Day festivities can be compared to the feminist discourse that rejects celebrations of International Women's Day, when women are presented with roses and beauty salons offer special promotions. For feminists, Women's Day should be observed with social manifestations and public discussions in favor of women's rights as well as human rights which are frequently denied.

In short, between the discourses that somehow "accept" and contribute to the circulation of the formula "Black consciousness" (here targeted as B), the initial analysis identified two main positions:

(B1) the position that presents this day as a commemorative and somehow folkloric day (a day of festivities, music, fashion shows, Black beauty contests etc.);
(B2) the position that demands political activism (personal engagement, discussions in the public space, protests, marches, etc.);

Table 4.1   Initial Analysis: Pro-BCM Discourse Divided Into Two Positions

(A) Anti-BCM discourse	(B) Pro-BCM discourse	
	(B1)	(B2)
Rejects the formula "Black Consciousness"	Accepts the formula	Accepts the formula
Rejects parties on Black Consciousness Day	Promotes celebrations and parties on Black Consciousness Day	Rejects parties on Black Consciousness Day
Rejects parades and public discussions about racism	Does not promote parades and public discussions about racism	Promotes parades and public discussions about racism
Opposes the Black Consciousness Movement's agenda	Does not correspond to the BCM's agenda in its texts	Highlights the BCM's agenda in its texts

However, instead of considering these two positions within the same pro-BCM discourse, the large disproportion between B1 and B2 in terms of influence and impact in the public space (B1 reaches substantially more people than B2, for instance), as well as the fact that B1 contributes to the reproduction of social differences that support the white elite and its racist practices, leads me to move B1 into A, opposing BCM.[10] Therefore, B1 is reclassified as A2.

Schematically, the final configuration can be represented as shown in Table 4.2:

Although it presents some formal similarity with B, A2 is discursively incompatible with B.

At this point, the materialist approach is essential to the analysis and classification of the media discourse represented in A2. What was stated at

Table 4.2   Final Analysis: Two Discourses Against BCM, One Explicitly Opposed and Other Functioning Covertly, thus Dissimulating the BCM Agenda

(A) Anti-BCM discourse		(B) Pro-BCM discourse
(A1)	(A2)	
Rejects the formula "Black Consciousness"	Accepts the formula	Accepts and spreads the formula
Rejects parties on Black Consciousness Day	Promotes celebrations and parties on Black Consciousness Day supporting some social alienation	Rejects parties on Black Consciousness Day
Rejects parades and public discussions about racism	Does not promote parades and public discussions about racism	Promotes parades and public discussions about racism
Opposes the Black Consciousness Movement's agenda	Does not dialogue with the BCM's agenda in its texts	Highlights the BCM's agenda in its texts, specially by presenting it from a personal perspective

the beginning of this work about the process of reproducing social inequalities should be recalled. Pêcheux conceived discourse against some kind of background of a class society in which what is said is always related to one's social-ideological position (determined by an ideological formation, explained below). Specifically in my work, the ideological position corresponds to the newspaper's editorial line or, on the other hand, to the ideological orientation of the Black Movement, since these positions are never related to empirical individuals, but rather to a discursive construction which is deeply affected by history and class struggle. In their own words, Pêcheux et al. state:

> We will speak of ideological formation to characterize an item (e.g. an aspect of struggle in the apparatuses) capable of acting as a force facing other forces in the ideological conjuncture characteristic of a social formation in a given time; each ideological formation is thus a complex set of attitudes and representations that are neither "individual" nor "universal" but relate more or less directly to positions of classes in conflict against each other. (Haroche et al. 1971: 102)

It was possible to clarify the differences between A2 and B in order to use this theoretical apparatus in the corpus analyzed herein. The major difference comes from the circulations of these discourses, directly related to the relations of power in the journalistic field and in the construction of public opinion. B struggles to expose the injustices committed by white domination, the social inequalities that occur today, everyday cases of racism, and so on.

Its circulation is restricted to personal blogs, activist spaces, and eventually intellectual spaces. On the other hand, A2 contributes to the invisibility of the BCM's demands and erases sensibility about the Black fight against social and historical injustice. It is present in the vast majority of large newspapers, magazines, journalistic TV programs, and websites with large readerships.

Moreover, its "fake similarity" can be the manifestation of one important feature of racism: its *atopy*, related to disguised and even denied forms of racism, which I have partially explored elsewhere (Oliveira 2015).

CONTRIBUTIONS TO A MATERIALIST DISCOURSE ANALYSIS

If I started from the enunciative perspective, we now move to the conclusion with the materialist contribution. This means that my analysis began from the observation of the enunciative phenomenon, considering the formal-qualitative aspects of the utterances such as the lexical and syntactic usages of verbs and adjectives, the relevance of textual support concerning the immediate contexts (position in the headline, color, typography, thematic focus, section of the newspaper where the text appears, etc.), the larger social context (is the newspaper broadly recognized or independent? Does it have a clear political position related to the left wing or right wing?), and further aspects related to the enunciative analysis which I did not explore here, such as ethos and scenography (Maingueneau 1984), the different durations of discourse (Possenti 2015), and questions about discursive memory (Possenti 2011). It also means that the role of materialism in the discourses (even when not stated explicitly) was essential for the analysis and categorization of the discourses considered herein, focusing the analysis on the material conditions in which the racist discourse emerge—always marked by the struggles (the relationship between the discourses examined and the reproduction of inequalities, the dimensions of what can be named as activism and how deeply people are conscious or unconscious of their ideological positions, the role of history and memory in white domination and its effects today, etc.).

The material I analyzed allows us to affirm that the Brazilian media focuses on problems attributed to the Black population (e.g., poverty and social differences) instead of the experiences and perspectives that arise from Black Brazilians themselves. The emphasis that the journalistic texts place on the "historical" socioeconomic inequality of Blacks seems to victimize them and positions them as people who only wait for financial handouts from the government. This scenario which is discursively constructed by the major media limits the discussion of racist practices to social class differences and pushes away acts of racial violence which are reported in some of the excerpts we have seen.

In this sense, the circulation of "Black consciousness" as a formula escapes from the process of naturalizing racism as a product of socioeconomic inequality and makes it possible to deal with the complexity that characterizes the functioning of racism in Brazil. By its very heterogeneous nature—for example, the controversy between its shared signifier and disputed signified—a discursive formula reveals itself as an object of great interest for studies in the fields of social science, linguistics, history, communication, and journalism, among others.

Favoring such an enunciative and materialist approach allows us to contemplate the heterogeneity of a branched and fragmented discourse, which is typical of the modern experience. Once formulas cross different discourses, they raise questions concerning class struggle and struggles for power and opinion, and analysis profits from both discursive approaches.

NOTES

1. Technically, the formula analyzed here is "*consciência negra*," not "Black consciousness." This specification is important because a formula becomes a formula within a specific geographical space and social context, as I hope to make clear throughout this text.

2. The corpus analyzed herein corresponds to a subset of a larger corpus related to my PhD research at the University of Campinas. Some aspects of this corpus have already been partially analyzed, for instance, the genesis of the formula "*consciencia negra*" (Oliveira and Salgado 2017).

3. In this work, "Black people" refers to Afro-Brazilians as a sociological classification. This group comprises Africans who were brought to Brazil as slaves under the Portuguese crown; Brazilian indigenous people and other non-whites are not included in the Black movement.

4. "Dois negros e a recusa de um taxista: aconteceu com Emecida." *Revistaforum. com.br.* Last modified July 23, 2015, http://www.revistaforum.com.br/blog/2015/07/dois-negros-e-a-recusa-de-um-taxista-aconteceu-com-emicida/. Accessed January 28, 2017.

5. "A banalidade do mal." *Observatoriodaimprensa.com.* Last modified October 23, 2013, http://observatoriodaimprensa.com.br/interesse-publico/a_banalidade_do_mal/. Accessed January 28, 2017.

6. "Jovem Negro Vivo." *Anistia.org.br.* Accessed January 28, 2017, https://anistia.org.br/campanhas/jovemnegrovivo/

7. Please note that all endnotes are listed in a separate section of the bibliography.

8. As proposed by Maingueneau (1984), a "sema" corresponds to the systematic exploration of the same semantic nucleus that characterizes the identity (the global semantic grid) of a discourse. From its semes, a discourse constantly produces a simulacrum of the discourse that is taken as its antagonist (empirical or virtually).

9. *Favelada* refers to someone who lives in the *favela,* a poor urban community with high levels of violence; similar terms are *slum* (English) and *bidonville* (French).

10. Here I would like to express my gratitude to the DISCONEX group at the University of Warwick for their valuables discussions and considerations about my work, especially Johannes Angermuller and Veit Schwab.

EXCERPT BIBLIOGRAPHY

E1

Wanderley Filho. 2012. "Consciência não Tem Cor," *Blog do Wanfil,* November 20. http://www.jangadeiroonline.com.br/blogs/wanderley-filho/cultura/consciencia-nao-tem-cor/. Accessed January 28, 2017.

E2

Kamel, Ali. 2006. *Não Somos Racistas* Rio de Janeiro: Nova Fronteira.

E3

Gonçalves, Gabriela. 2015. "'Só há Mérito com Igualdade,' diz diretor de filme sobre o negro na USP," *G1*, November 4, http://g1.globo.com/educacao/noticia/2015/04/so-ha-merito-com-igualdade-diz-diretor-de-filme-sobre-o-negro-na-usp.html. Accessed January 28, 2017.

E4

Marques, Daniel Telles. "A Cozinha Negra que Resiste," *O Estado de São Paulo*, November 20, 2015, D4.

E5

Monteiro, Karla. "Luz Negra," *Folha de São Paulo*, November 20, 2015, E1.

E6

"Festa da Consciência Negra terá Shows de MC Gui, Netinho de Paula e Rick," *Jornalperiscópio.com.br.* November 14, 2015, http://jornalperiscopio.com.br/site/index.php/festa-da-consciencia-negra-tera-shows-de-mc-gui-netinho-de-paula-e-rick/. Accessed January 28, 2017.

E7

D'Ameida, José Ricardo. 2013. "Para que Serve o 20 de Novembro?" *Geledes.org. br.* November 17, http://www.geledes.org.br/para-que-serve-o-20-de-novembro. Accessed January 28, 2017.

E8

Martins, Luisa and Felipe Martini. 2014. "Dia da Consciência Negra é uma Data para Comemorar ou Para Reivindicar?" *Zhclicrbs.com.br,* Accessed January 28, 2017.

http://zh.clicrbs.com.br/rs/noticias/noticia/2014/11/o-dia-da-consciencia-negra-e-uma-data-para-comemorar-ou-para-reivindicar-4646206.html. Accessed January 28, 2017.

E9

Sousa, Fernanda. 2013. "Sobre o Esquenta, da Rede Globo, Festejando o Dia da Consciência Negra," *Blogueiras Feministas Blog,* November 22, http://blogueirasfeministas.com/2013/11/sobre-o-esquenta-da-rede-globo-festejando-o-dia-da-consciencia-negra/. Accessed January 28, 2017.

BIBLIOGRAPHY

Althusser, Louis. 1985. *Essays on Ideology.* London: Verso.
Amadori, Sara. 2014. "'Democrazia Digitale': Usages Politiques et Rhétoriques d'une Formule dans le Cadre des Elections Politiques Italiennes de 2013." *Revue Repères DoRiF* 5 - La Formule en Discours. Dorif-Università.
Angermuller, Johannes. 2014. *Poststructuralist Discourse Analysis: Subjectivity in Enunciative Pragmatics.* Houndmills: Palgrave Macmillan.
Angermuller, Johannes. 2005. "'Qualitative' Methods of Social Research in France: Reconstructing the Actor, Deconstructing the Subject." *Forum Qualitative Qualitative Social Research* 6(3): Art. 19.
Angermuller, J., D. Maingueneau, and R. Wodak. 2014. *The Discourse Studies Reader: Main Currents in Theory and Analysis.* Amsterdam, Philadelphia: John Benjamins.
Azevedo, Thales. 1953. *Les Elites de Couleur dans une Ville Brésilienne.* Paris: UNESCO.
Brilliant, Maria. 2014. "'Immigration Choisie': l'Expert Contre le Politique. Analyse d'une Correspondence Publique (2005–2006)." *Revue RepèresDoRiF* n. 5 - La Formule en Discours. Dorif-Università.
Freyre, Gilberto. 1933. *Casa-Grande e Senzala: Formação da Família Brasileira sob o Regime da Economia Patriarcal.* Rio de Janeiro: Maia & Schimidt.
Guimarães, António Sérgio. 2009. *Racismo e Antirracismo no Brasil.* São Paulo: Editora 34.
Haroche, Claudine, Henry, Paul, and Michel Pêcheux. 1971. 'La Sémantique et la Courpure Saussurienne: Langue, Langage, Discours.' *Langages* 6 (24): 93–106.
Kilomba, Grada. 2008. *Plantation Memories: Episodes of Everyday Racism.* 3rd ed. Münster: Unrast.
Krieg-Planque, Alice. 2009. *La Notion de « Formule » en Analyse du Discours. Cadre Théorique Et Méthodologique.* Besançon: Presses Universitaires de Franche-Comté.
Krieg-Planque, Alice. 2010. "La Formule 'Développement Durable': un Opérateur de Neutralisation de la Conflictualité." *Langage & Société.* Paris: Editions de la Maison des Sciences de l'Homme.

Maingueneau, Dominique. 1984. *Genèses du Discours*. Liège: P. Mardaga.

Masasa, Karina. 2014. "'Commerce Equitable': une Formule au Prisme d'une Logique des Valeurs." *Revue Repères DoRiF* n. 5 - La Formule en Discours. Dorif-Università.

Motta, Ana Raquel and Luciana Salgado. 2011. *Fórmulas Discursivas*. São Paulo: Contexto.

Oliveira, Helio. 2015. "Indícios de Atopia Discursiva no Funcionamento do Discurso Racista." *Revista da ABRALIN*, 14 (3): 371–387.

Oliveira, Helio and Salgado, Luciana. 2017. "Consciência negra : une formule pour discuter le racisme au Brésil". *Revue Repères DoRiF*, Dossier Formules et aphorisations dans le discours de presse au Brésil, DoRiF Università. http://www.dorif.it/ezine/ezine_articles.php?id=351 Acessed October 28, 2017.

Pecheux, Michel. 1982. *Language, Semantics and Ideology. Stating the Obvious.* London: Macmillan.

Possenti, Sírio. 2011, "Réflexions sur la Mémoire Discursive." *Argumentation et Analyse du Discours* Vol.07, [online], URL: http://aad.revues.org/1200

Possenti, Sírio. 2015. "Durações Históricas e suas Relações com o Público e o Privado." In: *Discurso e Desigualdade Social*, edited by Lara and Lamberti. São Paulo: Contexto.

Schwab, Veit. 2015. "Analysing and Unsettling Discursive Differentiation and Effects of In-/Exclusion." *Journal of Multicultural Discourses,* 11 (1). DOI: 10.1080/17447143.2015. 1042385.

Skidmore, Thomas. 1974. *Black into White*: *Race and Nationality in Brazilian Thought*. NewYork: Oxford University Press.

Van Dijk, Teun. 1991. *Racism and the Press*. London: Routledge.

Van Dijk, Teun. 2008. *Racismo e Discurso na América Latina.* São Paulo: Contexto.

Chapter 5

Heterogeneous Materialities on YouTube

A Discursive Analysis from a Brazilian Point of View

Ligia Mara Boin Menossi de Araújo, Marco Antonio Almeida Ruiz, and Roberto Leiser Baronas

In the following, we will provide a brief description of the emergence of discourse analysis as a field of knowledge production which is constituted by a number of voices.[1] It has Michel Pêcheux as the figure that marked its origin and produced important theoretical displacements, positioning himself in a context of production which is dominated by a reflection on historical materialism as studied by Louis Althusser under the influence of Marx. In doing this, we hope to show that this field has undergone changes in terms of theory generation that have been influenced, above all, by new technologies that enable (re-) thinking its heuristics. Thus, we want to show that, based on the concepts put forward by Pêcheux in 1969, it is possible to envisage new theoretical developments and trends in discourse analysis, which are not only related to the materiality of language, but also to multimodality, sound, and picture.

We begin by tracing the irruption of discourse analysis (DA), its changes and, particularly, how it has developed in Brazil in the face of new discursive materialities. Next, we briefly share some theoretical assumptions ventured by Jaqueline Authier-Revuz—a contemporary of Pêcheux—concerning enunciative heterogeneity, formulated at the time to promote and discuss the notion of discourse. Following this short review of Authier-Revuz's theory, we resort to the notion of *ruled interincomprehension* used by Dominique Maingueneau, which enables us to delineate the derisory discursive construction[2] in humorous video montages on YouTube. That way, we will explain the origin and then try to show how Pêcheux's theory has been taken up and made to interact with current theories dealing with multimodal discourses.

In the case of Brazil, for instance, it is difficult to support the idea that a single view on discourse ever emerged. As in other contexts throughout the world, it is necessary to work with the thesis of countless irruptions of Discourse Studies in distinct academic contexts. Accordingly, we understand Discourse Studies as a set of approaches that have language, imbricated in its different domains (linguistic, enunciative, historical) and made manifest in distinct materialities (verbal, visual, verbo-visual), as the object of study. Although those different approaches have discourse as the object of attention, they construct quite different theoretical objects.

Discourse analysis emerged at the end of the 1960s, particularly in the United States, France, and England. However, it was only after the 1980s that discourse analysis constituted itself as a truly global research arena, beginning to integrate theoretical strands that had developed independently of one another in distinct disciplinary contexts and countries. The 1985 publication of Teun van Dijk's four-volume *Handbook of Discourse Analysis* (van Dijk 1985) bears witness to such an evolution. It must be noted that an extremely heterogeneous set of works has indeed appeared under the same label (*discourse analysis*) on either side of the Atlantic. Like "post-structuralism," with which it has close relations, discourse analysis is a participant in an intellectual wave whose "center is placed on top of the globalization of theoretical knowledge" and in which "formerly separated theoretical traditions give birth to hybrid scientific cultures"[3] (Angermuller 2013a, 72–3, our translation).

In a broader sense, reflections on discourse have drawn from sources in philosophy, sociology, and linguistics. Throughout the entire twentieth century, and arguably before, philosophy has dealt with language. There has been talk of a *linguistic turn* toward the ideas advocated particularly by Wittgenstein, whose conceptual work in philosophy presumes a previous analysis of language. The work of J. Austin on speech acts is consistent with this perspective. In turn, linguistics has been gradually imbued by pragmatic strands, which approached speech as an activity and focused on the radically contextual character of meaning-making.

France was one of the main places where discourse analysis developed. It was there that DA was first denoted as such and defined as a specific theoretical and methodological enterprise somewhat polemically grounded on structuralism.[4] Thus, in 1969, the journal *Languages* devoted a special issue (number 13) to a new domain called "discourse analysis." In the same year, Michel Pêcheux published a book titled *Automatic Discourse Analysis* steering an entirely new object: discourse. According to the author, this new "discursive machine"[5] played the role of an almost mythical moment of foundation and prototype, ceaselessly redesigned, criticized, corrected, finally abandoned, but always present.

Louis Althusser was an important influence for Pêcheux's theoretical considerations and his epistemological project of discourse analysis. Conversely, discourse analytical thinking is at work in Althusser's texts, giving it both philosophical and political support. In this sense, Pêcheux's writing is placed within historical materialism based on Althusser's reading of Marx. In a coauthored paper that appeared in Langages 24,[6] he underscores the necessity of change in the domain of linguistics. It was necessary to move from the study of language toward the study of discourse at the level of historical materialism. In his words, it was imperative

> to get rid of the subjective conflict centered on the individual [...] and understand that the type of concrete with which we deal and in relation to which it is necessary to think, it is precisely what historical materialism designates by the expression *social relations*, which results from class relations that are typical of a given social formation (through the means of production that dominates it, the hierarchy of practices required by this form of production, the apparatus through which such practices take place, the positions that correspond to them, and the ideological-theoretical and ideological-political representations that depend on them). (Pêcheux 1971, 127, our translation)

Thus, in his proposal for a materialist theory in the field of linguistics, Pêcheux brings forward the Althusserian notion of ideology. In his view, ideology is defined as "a functioning structure that dissimulates its existence in the very interior of its functioning, thus producing a tissue of 'subjective' evidence, [...] 'in which the subject is constituted'" (Pêcheux 1997, 152–153, our translation). Through Althusser's central thesis on ideology, namely that ideology interpellates individuals as subjects (Pêcheux 1997, 148), the French philosopher reflects man as an "ideological animal."

Not restricting himself to Althusser's contributions, Pêcheux puts forward new theoretical considerations in which the object is *discourse* and whose epistemological project critically brings together historical materialism, psychoanalysis, and linguistics. This conceptual framework becomes the analytical raw material marked by a relevant triad: language, subject, and history in its constitution. Pêcheux argues that an essentially political rupture of the term, which would consider language in its relation to ideology, is necessary. That is, discourse produces meanings that are evidenced by history, based on conditions for its emergence in a given event,[7] through ideological effects produced by subjects. In this manner, the theory advanced by this notion shows that we can go beyond this idea. Thus, according to Pêcheux (1997), discourse is the *effect of meanings* among interlocutors. In this process of interlocution, subjects are being constituted, affected by history in the functioning of language.

Automatic Discourse Analysis was developed to raise questions rather than provide answers. It was necessary to think more deeply the machine's soul itself and simultaneously review details of its analysis. Thus, his previous experience in information technology made Pêcheux feel the need for linguistics. We realize that Discourse Studies are grounded in historical materialism and the theory of ideology. The 1971 text *La sémantique et la coupure saussurienne: langue, langage, discours* (Haroche et al. 1971) is a case in point here. At the time, there is the indication of a new object of discourse, which is framed in relation to ideology, thus contributing to its first formulation. Historical materialism became the explicit position from which the epistemological intervention took place against a double threat: that of empiricism, which according to Maldidier (2003) would be a subjective problem centered on the individual, and that of formalism, which would confuse language as the object with the field of language.

Thus, with Althusser's influence and particularly his essay on *Ideology and Ideological State Apparatuses,* it became possible to conceive of the notion of the *pre-constructed.* Stripped of any logical sense, the *pre-constructed* constituted the reformulation of the concept of "presumption" in the new domain of discourse. With this notion, it was possible to think and apprehend interdiscourse, the key concept for the theoretical construction of Pêcheux. The year 1975 is marked by a great breach in the theoretical terrain that led to the establishment of a new research agenda.[8] A time of feelings opened up for Pêcheux's ideas. His approach is at the same time political and scientific, and aims to reveal the umbilical relations between language and ideology. In other words, linguistic functioning is determined, in his opinion, not only by immanent relations but, above all, by history.

In the context of scientific production at the time, discourse analysis gained significant momentum among language scholars who committed themselves to understanding the different social relations by means of production and circulation of discourses. A few decades after Pêcheux, it is possible to consider that this outlook has changed. Conceivably due to the shape its object of study took, we can now think of a *theory of discourses*—or Discourse Studies—which concern not only an idea or contour, but also brings together a number of new trends and approaches generated from different—Brazilian—perspectives, constant developments, and theoretical variations.

In other words, we can see that our society is currently organized around new multimedia technologies in which there is a multitude of discursivities (oral, written, visual and multimodal) in the field of politics as well as in other forms of meaning production, which have radically changed subjects' enunciative processes. These changes do not only take place at the level of language but especially at the level of what can be enunciated. These developments construct a new form of speaking of the other about that same other, changing the effects of primary meanings and causing, very often, humor and ridicule as a result. This is related to the growing importance of phenomena that are not strictly linguistic, but pertain to material sounds, images, and gestures that corroborate to produce meanings and the crystallization of certain images in a given society.

YouTube, to give just one example, has become an interesting virtual environment for the verification of the (de-)construction of discourses and of different themes and characters. This is especially true if we consider some political video montages that focus on the (de)characterization of political subjects during their election campaigns, causing, in turn, the effect of ridicule. In Pêcheux's work, we can see an endeavor to establish a new conceptualization of the notion of discourse. Nowadays, most of the manifold discursive materialities are seeing an increase resulting from different and novel technological supports. The video platform YouTube, for instance, is a technological vehicle through which we can observe different meanings produced by linguistic materiality through multiple social materialities.

In what follows, our corpus of analysis is composed of a multimodal video montage that circulated in this virtual environment at the time of the Brazilian presidential campaign in 2010. Titled *Cut to the Chase: Episode #02 - Literature (Direto ao assunto: Episódio #02—Literatura,* in Portuguese*)*, it represents a growing share of discourses that simultaneously aggregate different verbal, visual, and sonic materialities which become indissociable (Maingueneau 2015). Because they are stored websites such as YouTube, these discourses are often the result of drawing from genres originating in other media such as television and, aggregating other creative possibilities, come to be seen also as a means to promote reflection on social and political issues.

In face of this possibility of expression, we come across a derisive humorous discourses in the video montages selected for our analysis. They aim at questioning and looking down on certain values or a given social order by means of satire. In our case, the video montage questions Dilma Rousseff, the presidential candidate at the time and a constant figure of jokes, because of the way she speaks and reverberates the image of ex-president Lula. We understand that this genre (humorous video montages) are outside of the restraint imposed by legislation and the order of what is seen as politically correct due to its use to challenge someone by means of aggressive attempts at incapacitation (Baronas 2005).

The subject-producer of the video montage takes responsibility for what is said, but the effects of what is said can be softened by mockery or the mobilization of a discourse that is already crystallized in society (ibid.). Thus, we understand that derisive discourse makes the Other (the subject-producer of derision) explicit as a satirical Other, different from Lacan's Other and the dialogical Other in Authier-Revuz (2004). It manifests itself as a jester when it shows presumed flaws in the person it attempts to denigrate through the insertion of multisemiotic elements, and constructs a simulacrum of the first discourse.

We would say that, when it has to do with a satirical Other[9] that is brought to the thread of one's discourse, this satirical discourse presents itself in dissimulation in the traces of interdiscourse. That way, we aim at demonstrating that in order to think about political derision in supports such as YouTube, the notion of heterogeneity can be expanded and thought of as *dissimulated heterogeneity* (Baronas 2005).

We believe the notion of constituted heterogeneity and revealed heterogeneity formulated by Authier-Revuz (2004), though very pertinent when dealing with serious political corpora that circulate in traditional textual supports (e.g., books, newspapers and print magazines) is in need of a reconfiguration when it comes to the treatment of humorous discourses. This expansion of Authier-Revuz's concept (2004) can be seen as one of the evolutions that, according to Maingueneau, "change the gaze that the researcher projects toward the *corpora*, which are progressively less fully verbal. Given that a growing number of discursive productions are multimodal." (2015, 161, our translation)

The video montage *Cut to the Chase: Episode #02—Literature* permits the construction of controversy as ruled interincomprehension (Maingueneau 2007), since it is the subject that builds its discourse as it takes the other's discourse and simultaneously reveals what should be corrected in that other discourse that is not the subject's. That way, it allows for the creation of a *simulacrum* of the self's discourse, which raises a relation of controversy. As Baronas and Kosciureski (2006, 240) explain:

> This is about a dissimulated heterogeneity because the first discourse is constituted out of an *interincomprehension* ruled by the second discourse, i.e., the subject introduces the Other "in its closure, translating its utterances in the Self's categories and, thus, its relation with that Other always occurs in the form of a 'simulacrum' that is built of it" [...] In the specific case of dissimulated heterogeneity the existence can be revealed of an utterance about the simulacrum of an utterance. Such simulacrum is built based on a "non-comprehension" of the Other's utterances. In other words, dissimulated heterogeneity builds the other out of its interdiscourse. (Maingueneau 2007, 22; our translation)

To think about the expansion of a concept like the one put forward by Authier-Revuz is a task that starts with the aim of effectively dealing with new objects and new discursivities—such as multimodal discourses. Her ideas are based on linguistic materiality: From the written utterance there is no gaze toward what is visual, what is multimodal. In our work, we deal with video montages that, in addition to being multimodal, are regarded as humorous. This implies that the Other would be satirical and would make use of the makeup of multimodal elements to support a dissimulation effect, which would then result in a dissimulated heterogeneity in discourse.

ENUNCIATIVE HETEROGENEITY

Authier-Revuz's enunciative heterogeneity (1990, 2004) comes in two types: constitutive and revealed, while the latter can be marked or unmarked. Taken as distinct but not separate processes, constitutive heterogeneity concerns the "real processes that are constitutive of a discourse," whereas revealed heterogeneity refers to "representation processes, in a discourse, of its constitution" (Authier-Revuz 1990, 32, our translation). Both aim at showing how discourse is at times seen as something transparent and at others as something opaque.

Revealed heterogeneity brings the other to the discursive chain and allows itself to be seen more clearly due to its *not hiding*. It is not only characterized by the presence of the other's discourse in the discourse of the announcer, but also the announcer's perception of this presence and the desire for it to be noticed. However, it may not reveal itself with visible marks in a discourse (Authier-Revuz 1990). Even if consciously produced by the subject it may thus be constituted in a *marked* or *unmarked* form.

Marked revealed heterogeneity is in the domain of enunciation. It is visible in linguistic materiality and unequivocally marked. It occurs when the subject, in addition to noticing the other's presence in its speech, is led to make it clear that it is the subject that is talking. This happens by means of *heterogeneity points* that give away the place of one's self and that of the other (Authier-Revuz 2004, 14). Marked revealed heterogeneity is based on two categories: the first explicitly marks the forms that insert the other in the linearity of the discourse thread. This other being the discourse reported as in the direct or indirect speech with syntactic contours that hint at the fact that there is another act in the discursive enunciation.

Unmarked revealed heterogeneity manifests itself in discourses in which there is no readily delimited frontier between the one and the other. Free indirect speech, irony, antiphrasis, imitation, allusion, pastiche, reminiscence, and stereotype can serve as examples here. This form of revealed heterogeneity is characterized by establishing the other's presence as something more diluted in discourse. Thus, it is not possible to apprehend it in the thread of discourse. It is only possible to recognize and interpret it "based on the *irrecoverable indexes* because of its exterior" (Authier-Revuz 2004, 18). It should be stressed that if the frontier between the discourse of one and that of the other presents itself more subtly, it is necessary to resort to a linguistic exterior, different contexts, and to activate the knowledge that engenders us in order to understand these discourses in which we find unmarked revealed heterogeneity.

Considering the historical and epistemological conditions of discourse analysis throughout the last decades, it is possible to note how much it has pushed new and exciting reflections about the notion of discourse and fostered new ideas and trends in research. In this spirit, we present our material of analysis so that we can produce such reflections and associate them with the new materialities that have appeared throughout the twenty-first century.

CUT TO THE CHASE: EPISODE #02—LITERATURE

Cut to the Chase: Episode #02—Literature is part of a six-episode series posted by the subject-producer who uses the alias *Exiles on the Web*. It is made up of slides that convey the discourse of the producer in the video montage, excerpts of an interview with Dilma Rouseff in her blog during the pre-campaign[10] and, simultaneously, inserted pictures and sounds that construct certain meaning effects on the candidate's discourse.

In the first slide that is repeated in the other video montages in the series, we find the utterance: *"Cut to the chase with President Lula's former minister."* While we see it, we hear a kind of jingle in which the viewer hears a whistle and some instruments; in short, we can infer that the music is produced by someone whistling casually and leisurely. Next, another picture is inserted, in which we can see a blackboard, typical of classrooms, with the following question written in white chalk: "President Lula's former minister, what are your favorite books?"

The producer then presents the excerpt from Rouseff's live interview broadcasted on her blog during the pre-campaign. The questions were asked live, and Dilma "answered" them simultaneously: "Well … ,[11] books, you know … , I have been reading a book whose name escapes me … I tried talking a little bit about the soap opera to see if I could remember the name of the book … ." While Dilma is talking, the camera shows the people next to her and how one of them moves from behind the camera and approaches another woman, in glasses, who is next to the candidate, as we can see in Figure 5.1. Because this woman gets very close to the woman sitting next to Dilma, she is presumably whispering something in her ear. The subject-producer inserts a flashing red arrow that pointing to the woman in glasses sitting next to the candidate and we hear the sound of a siren.

The candidate goes on (Figure 5.2): "I can't remember … by Sándor Márai,[12] the book is called, the, the, the embers, yes, that's it, the embers … ." In this part of the video montage, three pictures are inserted at the bottom like those that are normally displayed in quiz shows (Figures 5.2 and 5.3), in

Figure 5.1 Dilma and her allies.

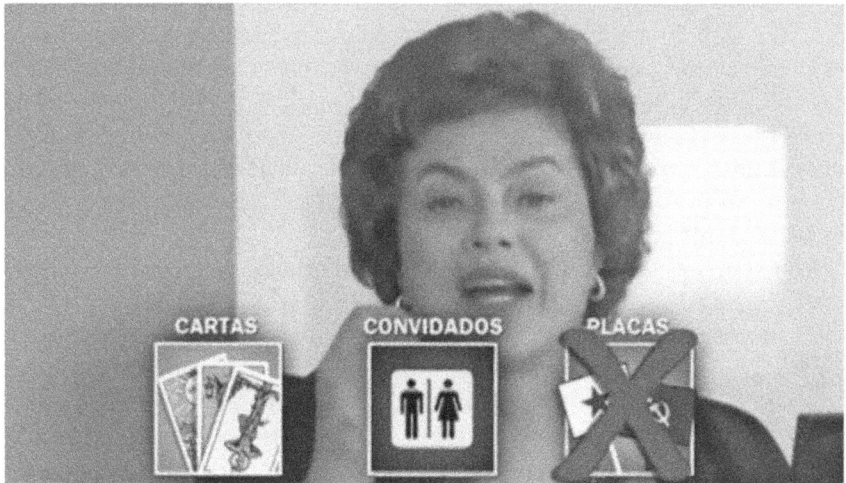

Figure 5.2 The help.

which the contestant has to answer questions correctly to win prizes and is aided by little hints throughout the show in order to be able to answer. The three icons, shown in Figures 5.2 and 5.3, represent the help that a contestant can ask for: help from "cards, guests, or placards." More specifically, this is the format of *Who wants to be a millionaire?*[13]

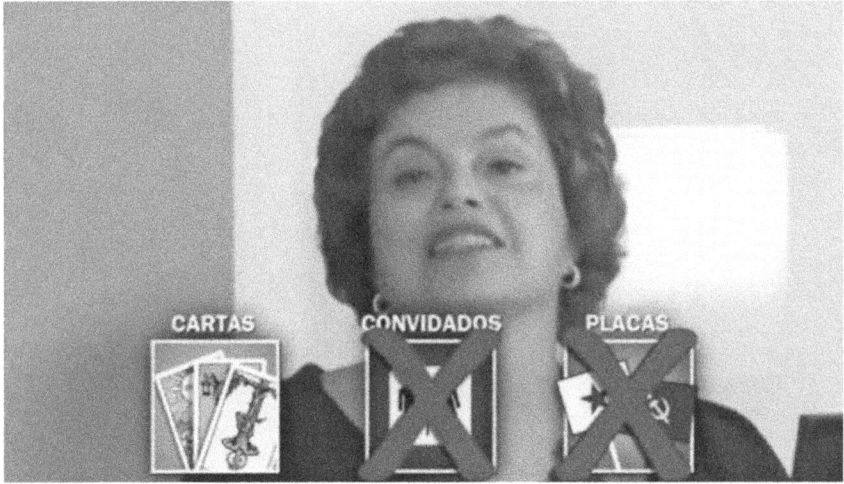

Figure 5.3 Multiple choices.

We notice that the third icon—the placard—is marked with an X (Figure 5.2), as if Dilma had used the audience's help (through the placards) to "remember" the name of the book's author. We can infer that this is about a meaning effect created by the insertion of the marked placard because Dilma looked at the audience attentively a moment before the subject-producer marked the third option. This allows us to guess that the option is marked because, in this game, Dilma has already used of one of the three options when she turns her gaze toward the audience.

The three icons disappear before they are displayed again and the second icon is marked with an X (Figure 5.3). It is the icon of the guests, that is, Dilma presumably asked for help from the guests. This idea is substantiated by the candidate's action of turning to her left, where the woman in glasses is sitting (Helena), who talks to another person who has approached them, as indicated by the red arrow in Figure 5.1. It is possible to suppose that this third person passes information on to Helena, who then delivers it to Dilma. This supposition is confirmed when we can hear Helena say "embers" (therefore, Helena and the third person are the guests who "whisper" the name of the book to Dilma) and the candidate goes on: "the, the ... the embers ... that's right, the embers (*the three options for help are removed*) ... it is maybe one of ... (*there is a four-second pause in the speech accompanied by a clock's tic-tac and when the picture "comes back," we hear the sound of a bell*) thus, it's had a strong impact on me, I finished it quickly last night because I can read it on Sunday."

After watching the video montage, we can note that a humorous discourse permits the construction of meaning around the idea that the presidential candidate has not read the book she mentions in the interview because a third person has presumably approached her "to whisper" the name of a specific book to Dilma, a fact that is supported by a *social imaginary* (Charaudeau 2008) about reading, according to which the true reader remembers (or must remember) what they have read.

Thus, by bringing to his discourse the other's discourse, the subject-producer allows for that discourse to be demarcated, that is, translated from the other's categories, as interdiscourse. For that dissimulated heterogeneity construction mechanism to take place, the producer deploys multimodal resources such as the insertion of three pictures, the clock's sound, the bell and the pause. We are faced with the emergence of a discourse that certifies that, if she does not remember, Dilma therefore has not read (thus, she lies during the interview; like every politician, she is a liar). This allows for the appearance of some implicit ideas, such as the notion that "who does not read is not intelligent, is not an intellectual and, therefore, does not have the competence to govern the country well." Dilma, as well as Lula, would be illiterate because she is not reading a book, she would therefore be a non-reader, and voting for a nonreader would mean promoting stupidity because someone who does not read is stupid. However, reading in itself does not make a person better and does not imply values such as wisdom, competence, or honesty. Thus, associating reading with intelligence, competence, or a high level of education is a mistake (Britto 2003).

Reading, therefore, can be synonymous with a number of attributes such as intellectuality and intelligence. Being in the process of reading a book all the time and making reading a daily habit in which one must read many—and good—books is part of what we find in the social imaginary about reading in Brazil. True to the extent that someone can never say that "they are not reading a book," it is possible to deduce that candidate Dilma would not be "allowed" to say that she is not reading anything. This is because there is an educational and academic discourse that posits that reading must become customary, that children and young people today do not have the habit of reading, and the habit is translated simply, according to this discourse, as an interruption of reading, of always being in the process of reading something.

Just as Dilma would not be allowed to say that she is not reading a book, she would also not be allowed to read "any" book, since some types of reading are valued more than others (Abreu 2006). Thus, the conventional discourses about reading disseminate the notion that there are second-class readers who do not use educated language and do not read prescribed books, so they can even be considered second-class citizens (Abreu 2001).

Another interpretative possibility that is grounded on the interdiscourse of the subject-producer is that we should always remember the books we have read. However, reading, according to Bayard (2007), is constitutively linked to forgetting. When we begin to read we also begin to forget what we are reading, it keeps disappearing while we read it and, thus, we gradually become nonreaders. As a result, this forgetting is the process of "unreading" which can affect all the components of the book. The reader, as seen by the *social imaginary*, must be an example since they are already considered as a symbol of intelligence and culture. Besides, they should always remember what they have read, especially when they wish to take the top leading role in the country, that of President of the Republic.

CONCLUDING REMARKS

When we portray politics derisively we are inverting a preestablished political order. The president of the republic should be the one with the most distinguished authority and, in the *social imaginary*, also the one with the greatest power. However, when the president is derisively translated, the Internet user and the video montage producer enjoy a superior position in relation to them.

We understand humorous political discourse in terms of a multimodal text. These are considered to be nonofficial, though opinionated, and establish a location for the circulation of meaning in which Internet users can access and inscribe themselves in the discourses engendered by video montages that dissimulate the Other/other based on their historical, political, and ideological affiliations. This is possible because the video montages analyzed construct new forms of discursive representing a social phenomenon—the political discourse—since they mobilize technical resources for disseminating relatively new discourses that enhance social communication and construct a simulacrum of political discourse. This perspective is rendered possible by new materialities emerging in technological supports such as YouTube. In order to understand the ramifications of discourse analysis in Brazil, it is necessary to apprehend Pêcheux's discourse theory. Pêcheux's theory is immensely valuable because it provides new ways of conceptualizing the notion of discourse. But with the rise of new technologies, his theory needs to be extended. We thus constructed our perspective and the subsequent interpretation based on Maingueneau's and Authier-Revuz's theory. It should go without saying that there are more perspectives present in the Brazilian context. Our objective here was to scrutinize some of the ramifications of a materialist theory of discourse associated with Pêcheux's notion of discourse. Today, different authors are utilizing a number of different and not always compatible notions of discourse. In our contribution, we aimed at establishing a critical stance based on the confluence of discursive memories that provide cohesion to a community.

New media, and YouTube in particular, play a role in the production and circulation of discourses that engender a form of *spectacularization* and a resulting *depoliticization of politics*. Such is the social role as mediator and builder of discourses that are likely to be the legitimate ones in their time and space, as well as elements that put together a multitude of meanings toward a single direction often marked by a strong ideological tint. Therefore, every multimodal resource in use that is shown would represent a presumed voice of democracy, from a section (or not) of the population that can express and share ideas together with the subject-producer of the video montages.

We can only think about such injunctions because we can rely on new developments in Discourse Studies, which allow thinking—in the Brazilian scenario—about different trends and approaches that resume and circum-scribe it from a particular point of view. We do not claim that one approach is better than another—that would even be outside the scope of science construction. Instead, we hope to show that, based on heuristics of 1969—a number of others, originating in new contexts, from new resources and—above all—new points of view, allow discourse analysis to open up toward a broader research domain which aims at looking at it from new angles.

NOTES

1. We are grateful to The São Paulo Research Foundation—FAPESP (Process number 2015/20984–0)—for the support to publish this paper. It has been conceived and developed from reflections during a research internship (cotutelle internationale de thèse) in France (Paris) in 2016–2017.

2. According to Simone Bonnafous' argumentative perspective (2003, p. 35), derision is "the association of humor with aggressiveness which characterizes it and distinguishes it from pure insult."

3. For this article, we translated all citations into English when using the French version.

4. We can say, based on the relevant literature, that there is still no detailed history of the emergence of discourse analysis in France. Notwithstanding, we have found a suggestive introduction in Angermuller (2013) that highlights the post-structuralist trends in these strands.

5. Denise Maldidier (2003), a contemporary of Michel Pêcheux, points to an important division in the theoretical developments achieved by the scholar after 1969. According to her, there are three great stages in Pêcheux's work: i) one called DA-1, also known as theoretical venture, in which a model is constructed for the discursive machine, closed around itself, subjects "believe that 'they use their discourses when they are in fact subjugated 'servants,' its 'supports'" (Pêcheux 1983); ii) DA-2 is characterized by a move toward heterogeneity, the Other in discourse. For Maldidier (2003), it is *the time of feeling*, which coincides with major reformulations and dis-placements in theory. The notion of discursive machine begins to undergo (re)adjust-ments due to the fact that it was no longer able to support a set of closed utterances,

homogeneous among themselves and, finally; iii) DA-3, the time of *directed decon-struction*. According to Pêcheux, it was the time to work with the construction of dis-cursive objects and resume certain events, in addition to dealing with points of view and enunciative places in intradiscourse. In this sense, we see that in this, third-stage interdiscourse is paramount and the notion of discursive machine is deconstructed. In addition, discourse homogeneity is abandoned, and the need to look at heterogeneity from the different conditions of production in which discourses are brought forward and resignification is reaffirmed.

6. See Haroche et al. 2007.

7. Pêcheux (1997) considers the event as a constitutive dimension of the object discourse and states that it is the meeting point of what is current and a memory.

8. Lakatos argues that there should always be a methodological rationality in the process of developing scientific knowledge. In his work, he defines a reconstruction of the history of sciences that emerge in a scenario that is very different from that coined by Thomas Kuhn. Instead of paradigms in succession based on scientific revolutions, there are research programs in "competition," that is, there may be different research strains "competing" at a certain time in history. Such "competition" may be easier to notice at times of hegemony of one or another program, for reasons that tend to be rational in the medium or long term.

9. Other: Refers to the unconscious, to manifestations of desire and inunctions of the unconscious in the form of language and; other: refers to the outside that consti-tutes the subject, other voices, other subjects, sociohistorical discourses constructed ideologically and culturally, before and outside the subject.

10. Available at: <http://www.youtube.com/watch?v=eapKzN9LZWc> Last accessed on August 24, 2017.

11. Ellipsis marks in the transcription represent pauses in speech.

12. Márai, S. As Brasas. Trad. Rosa Freire de Aguiar. 1st. ed. São Paulo: Com-panhia das Letras, 1999. 176 p. Do húngaro Sandro Márai, "é um romance sobre a amizade, a paixão amorosa e a honra." Available at:< http://www.companhiadasletras. com.br/detalhe.php?codigo=11148>. Access May 5, 2016.

13. *Who wants to be a millionaire?* was a Brazilian television show with questions and answers, which awarded a top prize of 1 million Brazilian Real.

BIBLIOGRAPHY

Angermuller, Johannes. 2013. *Analyse du discours poststructuraliste. Les voix du sujet dans le langage chez Lacan, Althusser, Foucault, Derrida, Sollers.* Limoges: Lambert Lucas.
Abreu, Márcia. 2006. "Literatura, leitura, cultura." In: *Cultura Letrada: literatura e leitura.* São Paulo: Editora Unesp, 9–41.
Araujo, Ligia Mara Boin Menossi. 2011. *Política e derrisão no YouTube: uma leitura discursiva*, 120f. PhD diss., Universidade Federal de São Carlos.
Authier-Revuz, Jacqueline. 2004. *Entre a transparência e a opacidade: um estudo enunciativo do sentido.* Porto Alegre: EDIPUCRS.

————. 1990. "Heterogeneidades enunciativas." In: *Cadernos de estudos linguísticos*, 19. Campinas: IEL.

Bayard, Pierre. 2007. *Como falar dos livros que não lemos?* Rio de Janeiro: Objetiva.

Baronas, Roberto Leiser. 2005. "Derrisão: um caso de heterogeneidade dissimulada." In: *Polifonia,* 99–111. Cuiabá: EDUFMT.

Baronas, Roberto Leiser, and Kosciureski, Mônica Barbosa Silva. 2006. "Observações sobre a textualização do "sic" no discurso político: marcas de derrisão." In: *Estudos do Texto e do Discurso,* edited by Pedro Navarro. São Carlos, Claraluz.

Bonnafous, Simone. 2003. "Sobre o bom uso da derrisão em J. M. Le Pen." In: *Discurso e Mídia: a cultura do espetáculo,* edited by Maria do Rosário Gregolin, 35–48. São Carlos: Claraluz.

Britto, Luiz Percival Leme. 2003. "Leitura e Participação." In: *Contra o consenso: cultura escrita, educação e participação,* 99–114. Campinas: Mercado de Letras.

Charadeau, Patrick. 2008. *Discurso Político.* São Paulo: Contexto.

Direto ao assunto. 2010. Episódio #02—Literatura. (2010) Available at: http://www.youtube.com/watch?v=qWgol6I-YpY&feature=relmfu

Haroche, Claudine, Paul Henry, and Michel Pêcheux. 1971. "La sémantique et la coupure saussurienne: Langue, langage, discours." *Langages* 6 (24): 93–106.

————. 2007. "A semântica e o corte saussuriano: língua, linguagem, discurso." In: *Análise do Discurso: apontamentos para uma história da noção-conceito de formação discursiva,* edited by Roberto Leiser Baronas, 13–31, 2nd. edição. São Carlos, Pedro & João Editores.

Lakatos, Imre. 1979. "O falseamento e a metodologia dos programas de pesquisa científica." In: *A crítica e o desenvolvimento do conhecimento,* edited by Lakatos, and Alan Musgrave. São Paulo: Cultrix.

Maingueneau, Dominique, and Johannes Angermuller. 2007. "Discourse analysis in France: a conversation." [48 paragraphs]. *Forum Qualitative Sozialforschung/ Forum: Qualitative Social Research*, 8 (2), Art. 21. Available at: http://www.qualitative-research.net/index.php/fqs/article/view/254/559. Accessed February 25, 2016.

Mainguenau, Dominique. 2007. *Gênese dos Discursos.* Curitiba: Criar.

————. 2015. *Discurso e Análise do Discurso.* São Paulo: Parábola.

Maldidier, Denise. 2003. *A inquietação do discurso.* Campinas: Pontes.

Márai, Sándor. 1999. *As Brasas,* trans. Rosa Freire de Aguiar. 1st ed. São Paulo: Companhia das Letras.

Pêcheux, Michel. 1969. *Analyse automatique du discours.* Sciences du comportement 11. Paris: Dunod.

————. 1997. *Semântica e Discurso*: uma crítica à afirmação do óbvio. 3º edição, Campinas, SP: Editora da Unicamp.

————. 1990a. *L'inquiétude du discours*, Paris, Éditions des Cendres.

————. 2011. *Análise de Discurso. Michel Pêcheux. Textos escolhidos por Eni Orlandi.* Campinas: Pontes.

van Dijk, Teun A., ed. 1985. *Handbook of discourse analysis.* 4 volumes. London: Academic Press.

Chapter 6

Unspeakable Articulations

Steps Toward a Materialist Discourse Theory

Benjamin Glasson

If, as discourse analysts, we accept that nothing can be known except through discourse, even though there are things that exist outside of the social, we open an analytical space to observe politics being waged at the level of signs. Yet we face a conundrum when we start to consider how the extra-discursive might itself be doing politics on the level of the text. To what extent do the economy and physical nature such as bodies and the environment constitute discursive actors? It is in considering the discourse theory of Laclau and Mouffe that we can view the problem in sharp relief. Laclau and Mouffe profess to be materialists, claiming their discourse theory is not a closed system purely composed of signs. However, on the question of what else there might be, they appear to have it both ways. On the one hand, they reject the "discursive/extra-discursive dichotomy" and the "thought/reality" dichotomy in favor of the "relational totality" of discourse (Laclau and Mouffe 1985, 110). On the other hand, they split reality into two distinct ontological zones. In a well-known example, they insist that an earthquake occurs independently of its social interpretation (as natural disaster or divine vengeance, for example).

Part of the power of Laclau and Mouffe's approach is its eschewal of essentialism. Against Marxist notions of class positing an essential relation between the social and the economy, Laclau and Mouffe contend that everything comes into being through contingent (i.e., contestable) articulation. But how is their claim that "natural facts" are always "discursive facts" (Laclau and Mouffe 1987, 83–4) consistent with their professed materialism? I will argue that Laclau and Mouffe have done little more than displace the semiotic/material binary onto a symbolized/unsymbolized binary that they call being/existence. While I do not believe that, in itself, this warrants the endless attacks on Laclau and Mouffe as postmodern idealists, the charge could have been avoided had they dealt more carefully with the paradoxes inherent

81

in their notion of discursive *totality*—most particularly, with the paradoxical but ultimately unavoidable notion that the totality is not all. My strategy here is to show that Badiou's reformulations of Marx's Hegelian inversion and Engels's notion of reflection provide a theoretical basis for matter in discursive articulation that can address this weakness of discourse theory. Although my focus is on Laclau and Mouffe, this issue has implications for all materialist theories of discourse.

I will not provide an exposition of the major tenets of discourse theory, which are well known. In fact, I depart sometimes from a literal reading of the theory, on account of my different aim. Laclau and Mouffe's discourse theory is oriented toward the broader project of their radical-democratic political theory. My interest, on the other hand, is in reconciling discourse theory's very useful concepts[1] with a genuinely materialist outlook.

Unusually for a materialist perspective, I do not begin with matter but with discourse. This is an intentional move designed to avoid the essentialist leap distinguishing speculative realism and new materialism. Instead, I approach the problem of the extra-discursive from within discourse, exercising vigilance against any positing of matter as pre-given. Recasting the problem of discursive totality into the dialectical terms pursued by Badiou, I show that while social discourse has no foundation beyond itself, neither is it purely the result of political struggle. Badiou reminds us that knowledge of the world, far from the subjective seizing of the object, is a two-way process, a double "crossing," fully one half of which—the material action of the object upon, and formation of, the subject—is constitutively unknowable within any discursive totality. Discourse theory's ontology of lack already provides a space for the beyond of discourse, but only in an undifferentiated void. My final section demonstrates that Badiou's theory of the dialectical process of knowledge helps resolve the paradox of the discursive totality, and offers discourse theory a method for approaching those material relations and forces beyond articulation.

THE OUTSIDE OF DISCOURSE, FROM THE INSIDE

For Laclau and Mouffe, discourses are comprised of arrangements of signifiers. But these are not just signifiers, sounds or words that have no meaning; they produce signifieds (concepts) through relations of difference without positive terms, as in a Saussurean system. In a given discourse, one signifier tends to take on a specialized role in stabilizing that discourse. The empty signifier—so named because the price of its elevation is the hollowing out of its particular meaning—stabilizes the system *qua* system, governing the regularity in dispersion of the other signifiers. As signifier without a signified, the empty signifier is not just one difference among others.

As with Lacan's notion of the *point de capiton* (quilting point), the empty signifier appears to be attached to some substrate that we cannot signify. But it does not *appear* to be so much as *performs* this substrate, it *performs* the Thing out of reach, the bedrock of reality. As a place-holder of the void—the void being that part of discourse that is not articulated and cannot be articulated—the empty signifier assumes "the role of representing the pure being of the system—or, rather, the system as pure Being" (Laclau 1996, 39). Laclau explains that the empty signifier

> is not just a signifier without a signified—which, as such, would be outside sig-
> nification—but one signifying the blind spot inherent to signification, the point
> where signification finds its own limits, but which, if it is going to be possible at
> all, has to be represented as the meaningless precondition of meaning. (Laclau
> 2014, 64)

Thus, the present absence of the empty signifier is the condition of the full presence of meaning. By evacuating the absences between alternative discursive renderings of the social—absences *between* the articulations that comprise the system of signification—the articulations are positivized. It is only through this marking out, "articulating" the unpresentable thing-in-itself, that signs can, ultimately, satisfy subjects that they do what they profess to do: to stand for reality. In ideological discourses, this "bedrock of reality," this supposed thing, signifiable only through the failure of signification as such, is Society. In religious discourses, it is God. In certain environmental discourses and, arguably, in post-Enlightenment discourse in general, it is Nature.

To paraphrase Durkheim, we might say that the extra-discursive (or pre-discursive, if you prefer) Thing is that towards which we act with a certain reverence. Through our words and deeds we continually, ritualistically appeal to it (it is in fact the *final* authority), but cannot directly invoke it. However, by evacuating and condensing the void within, it lends the space of articulation the appearance of a smooth surface. It enables the discourse to appear as a transparent vehicle for the world beyond itself. The play of signifiers produces the phenomena of representation, with the empty signifier allowing a network of signifiers to produce meaning. New signifiers can be articulated to the network, altering the system of differences and producing new meanings. However, all articulations are between identities that are socially constructed. In order to produce meaning, it is not necessary to have something outside of discourse.

And yet, most vehemently when defending themselves against the charge of postmodern idealism, Laclau and Mouffe appear as staunch defenders of a material world beyond articulation. At the same time, the world beyond discourse enjoys an apparently lower status than the discursive. "Outside of any discursive context," they write, "objects do not have being; they have only existence" (1985, 85). Whether in this formulation or in their straight-out avowals of a reality beyond discourse, Laclau and Mouffe directly contradict their claim to have transcended the thought/reality and discursive/extra-discursive dichotomies. There is no other way to gloss it: they have simply displaced this pair of binaries onto a symbolized/unsymbolized binary which they call being/existence. This raises all sorts of questions. Once the earthquake is articulated as, say, the result of natural geological processes (thus given *being*), what happens to its *existence*? Does it now exist inside and outside of discourse? Is it both part of the "relational totality of discourse" and outside of it? We can highlight the problem from the opposite angle too. Can the unarticulated have any effects in the social? Could there be processes, perhaps, that have deep, abstract effects beyond the level of symbolization, even though these effects "trickle up" and eventually intermingle with the social: structural economic forces, climate change, for example? If so, how do we identify at what point such phenomena have "crossed over"? How exactly do entities cross over from existence into being (or vice versa)? What is the precise status of things that have not yet passed into being, come into symbolization? According to Laclau and Mouffe, all of these things—which could well include historical processes, natural objects not yet discovered—are indeterminate. They are denied any systematicity until they are articulated to social discourses.

Laclau and Mouffe's insistence that the ideal and the material are both relational systems of difference is perhaps what most distinguishes them from mainstream Marxism. For Žižek, capitalism is the (Lacanian) Real: that which "always escapes one's grasp" (Butler, Laclau, and Žižek 2000, 291). For Laclau and Mouffe, contrastingly, capitalism is a system of relations of exchange, production, and so on, that are eminently symbolizable. In this debate, discourse goes all the way down for Laclau and Mouffe. Class identity is not essentially different from any other social or cultural identity. All are socially constructed (i.e., discursively mediated) rather than emanating directly from an individual's relation to, for example, the productive apparatus. Marxists insist that the economy has an effect whether one has symbolized it or not. Laclau and Mouffe's position seems to be that the economy is a system of relations just as is discourse in the typical sense—it can be apprehended through the social, but it can have no internal relations of its own that produce effects in the social (discursive). On the one hand, then, Laclau and Mouffe insist that discourse theory is not just a theory of signification. Signs and material reality exist on the same plane. The economy thus has no special ontological status, being simply one system of relations (i.e., a discourse) among others.

One way to address these problems is to pose the question: *If it is all discourse, then why don't the Laclauian categories all neatly map onto matter?* Some of them possibly do. The logic of difference might apply to material-semiotic articulations, perhaps at the atomic or quantum level, or maybe even at the level of form of life, as illustrated by Wittgenstein's example of the builder talking to his assistant. Asking his assistant for a "block" rather than a "cornice" produces material results isomorphic with the linguistic system of differences. The builder proceeds to build the wall with the pieces handed to him by his assistant. In this example, words and things are not two separate worlds, but are intertwined. But it is far from clear how the logic of difference's counterpart, the logic of equivalence, maps onto matter. Laclau even acknowledges this, observing that a "social antagonism [which necessarily involves a logic of equivalence dichotomizing the social field], unlike the opposition between natural forces, requires a type of negativity that is absent from a purely physical world" (Laclau 2014, 116).

The answer is not to be found in Laclau's deployment of the Lacanian Real, either. For a start, not all new articulations are dislocatory, and if the emergence of something material into discourse was to be the result of dislocatory irruption, the social world would be an exhausting place to be in. In Laclau's more recent iteration of the Real in *On Populist Reason* (2005a), he develops the notion of heterogeneity. While antagonism "presupposes some sort of discursive inscription," heterogeneity "presupposes an exteriority not only to something within a space of representation, but to the space of representation as such" (2005a, 176). Yet, this simply recapitulates the basic problem: either something exists outside of discourse and has no qualities or internal structure (and therefore may as well not exist except as a generalized constitutive outside), or it exists internally and is symbolizable all the way down. There is no way of straddling the divide, because to do so would bring the *existent* into *being* and there would be no need for the exterior realm.

The basic problem remains: there is a dualism between being and existence, the symbolized and the unsymbolized, such that the latter is denied relationality until it is articulated to discourse. Without relationality or systematicity, it is simply the "ineradicable exteriority" that contaminates every discourse (Butler, Laclau, and Žižek 2000, 291), a formless outside that only develops consistency through the agency of discourse. Think of all the as-yet-undiscovered things that must wait patiently to be invited to the discourse fraternity! And even if they are so lucky, it is only then that they learn what they actually are and what relations they can enter into!

This is a little cruel, but it illustrates the core problem. I am not attempting an immanent critique but trying to re-read Laclau and Mouffe in a way that can help us theorize the relation between discourse and (what would normally be called) the extra-discursive. After all it was Laclau himself who suggested that discourse theory (or, specifically, the isomorphism between the *objet a* and hegemony) might reveal something "belonging to the very structure of objectivity" itself (Laclau 2005b, 258).

MATERIALISM WITHOUT ESSENTIALISM OR IDEALISM

Does Laclau and Mouffe's discourse theory really does hold open a place for matter, or is it, as many critics have charged, postmodern idealism? Any attempt to answer this question must scrupulously avoid the lure of naturalism, or naïve realism. The imperative must be to ask, whenever we think we see something beyond discourse, how can we be sure it is not the work of discourse itself? Matter cannot simply be assumed, whereas discourse can, not least because it is the very condition and site of any discussion about matter.

Hegel was well aware of the dangers of materialism collapsing into its opposite (Laclau and Mouffe 1987, 87–88). Allegedly materialist theories whose categories are universal concepts ("atom," for instance) are idealist however strident their protestations. The *sine qua non* of materialism is "the ultimate irreducibility of the real to the concept" (Laclau and Mouffe 1987, 87). For this reason, this inquiry is organized around a hyper-vigilance against the type of naïve realism that posits material foundations that are in fact ideal constructs. If that sounds like postmodern radical skepticism, it probably is. Yet it is the kind of skepticism which, like Descartes', is ultimately *not* skeptical. To pursue doubt to the very end is, in actuality, the sole path to the indubitable (Bartlett, Clemens, and Roffe 2015, 369).

In trying to think the "strange stranger" of the extra-discursive in Laclau and Mouffe, there are good reasons to begin with Alain Badiou's discussion of dialectical materialism in *Theory of the Subject* (2009). Although Laclau and Mouffe's discourse theory and Badiou's philosophy are by no means synthesizable, substantial common strands exist that warrant fruitful cross-fertilization.[2] Moreover, bringing Badiou to bear on discourse theory is justified not least by the passionate contempt in which Badiou holds idealism, which he calls the eternal philosophy of the bourgeoisie. Conveniently for the bourgeoisie's efforts to secure its ideology, idealism posits a transcendental beginning and naturalizes the contingent. It always sides with intellectual over manual labor, city over country, industry over agriculture (2009, 187). By contrast, materialism is an "assault philosophy" and, owing to its task, can be vulgar and disgusting. Laclau and Mouffe, their critics charge, are guilty of the worst kind of idealism that plagued late twentieth-century continental philosophy. Badiou calls "idealinguistery" the notion that *la langue* (linguistic structure) produces language and turns the whole world into discourse. There is no transcendental subject, just as there is no object outside of discourse. Idealinguistery believes it can get the measure of the discursive configurations that comprise an entire era. The chief culprit of this "fixist" thesis is Foucault, "that Cuvier of the archives who with some bookish bones examined with genius gives you the entire brontosaurus of a century" (Badiou 2009, 188).

Against the tide of the discursive turn, Badiou seeks a "materialism centered upon a theory of the subject" (Badiou 2009, 189). Such a theory rejects the notion that meaning emerges from the play of signifiers, and refounds a distinction between truth and ideology (Badiou 2009, 133). Unfashionably, Badiou wants "access to the real" (2009, 133). It is by following Badiou's reasoning here, and thinking Laclau and Mouffe's discourse theory through the issues Badiou raises, that we can try to locate within discourse theory that which is not discursive but material. The first step Badiou takes in seeking the "conceptual black sheep" of materialism is to warn us away from simply inverting idealism. Instead, the kernel of materialism is suspended between "perfectly contradictory theses" (2009, 190). These theses are:

1. There is One.
2. One precedes the Other, therefore there is Two.

Strict materialism is monist, as per the first thesis. So is absolute idealism, and in that sense should be reachable via an idealist inversion. Yet Badiou insists that to properly invert idealism, as Marx promised, we need the Two of the inversion. We need the "head and the feet, the idea and matter. How else could we posit the antecedence of the one over the other?" (Badiou 2009, 192).

The most successful versions of idealism, Badiou points out, actually provide for two modes of being. Platonism has the intelligible and the sensible, Christianity has incarnation, and Judaism has creation (Badiou 2009, 191). And so, Badiou's wager is that materialism must "abdicate its essential axiom," monism, so as to recognize that *naming* the One as matter requires the Two (Badiou 2009, 193). It should adopt dualism, that "thesis of all major idealisms," but only to annul it. To restate somewhat the two theses, then, we have:

1. The thesis of identity: being is exclusively matter
2. The thesis of primacy: matter precedes thought, and not the other way around. (Badiou 2009, 193)

Badiou summarizes it thus: "the thesis of identity names the place (of being), and the thesis of primacy the process (of knowledge) under the rule of the place" (2009, 193). The thesis of primacy, it should be noted, does not refer to an ontological hierarchy in which matter is superior. Matter is, in fact, all. It does recognize, however, that knowledge, thought, *reflects* being, as in Engels's metaphor of the forest being reflected in the lake before it (Engels 1962). But this reflection, as "pure, passive image," cannot be enough for a dialectical materialism (Badiou 2009, 194). It is complemented with a second metaphor, with which it stands in constant tension: the asymptote (2009, 195). Badiou claims that the reflection "throws into a tendential abyss the object which it is its fiction to reduplicate." While structure, if you like, is on the side of reflection, history is on the side of asymptote. It is the "fine sift of gross approximations" (2009, 196). Reflection is the metaphor that fuses thinking to being, but asymptote is what reminds us that there is something left over: "a remainder insubordinate to the concept" (2009, 196–97). Materialism for Badiou "occurs" twice: once as structure and once as history. Its process is that of a "unifying scission of reduplication and an effect of approximation. It posits the Same, plus its remainder" (2009, 197). In a revealing quote, he explains that materialism "dialecticizes the metaphors of reflection and of the asymptote, *thus positing the whole in the exception of its remainder*" (2009, 197, italics mine).

FROM REFLECTION TO MODEL-FOR-ACTION

Reflection theories underlie correspondence theories of truth, which state that a proposition is true if it corresponds to the facts. In seeking recourse to materiality in order to test a proposition, it makes an assumption about the very relationship (between propositions and reality) in question. In effect, it offers a naïve realism, which is by no means Materialist. Would it not be more materialist to recognize that the reflection is "valid" rather than truthful? Valid because its survival was awarded on the basis that it is well suited to action, rather than to knowledge *qua* knowledge?

If "man is an animal suspended in webs of meaning he himself has spun" (Geertz 1975, 5), and man is also a somewhat successful actor, then there must be some *articulation* between the world and the reflection. However, it is an articulation that *works* rather than a correspondence based upon truth in a representationalist sense. The human animal, after all, "is such that it can get by very well without truth" (Bartlett, Clemens, and Roffe 2015, 36).

Could science itself be a model-for-action rather than a reflection of reality? Bruno Latour attacks the tendency of scientific discourse to conceptualize universal thought "as a spirit hovering over the waters" (Latour 1993, 119). Science, he argues

always renews and totalises and fills the gaping holes left by the networks in order to turn them into sleek, unified surfaces that are absolutely universal. Only the idea that we have had of science up to now rendered absolute a dominion that might have remained relative. All the subtle pathways leading continuously from circumstances to universals have been broken off by the epistemologists, and we have found ourselves with pitiful contingencies on one side and necessary Laws on the other—without, of course, being able to conceptualise their relations. (Latour 1993, 118–19)

We know from as far back as Saussure that discourse needs no referent in order to function, to signify. In science's case this is particularly true. It is not hard to show that the concepts of science are quasi-Platonic ideals rather than labels that mark out a priori natural kinds. Descola (2013, 82) reminds us of the Western tendency to view the human body as a "replica of a transcendent model," whether divine creation or the genotype. What are species (or any other taxonomical position), if not ideal-typical representation of the common features of a scientifically (i.e., socially) delimited set of biological variations? It is true that anyone can point to the things referred to by the terms tarantula, mungbean, or *tubercle bacillus*. Nevertheless, there is no natural link between each category and its various instances, each type and its tokens, and thus no guarantee linking the category to its representatives. Taxonomical ordering is not simply given by nature, independent of culture (see Glynos 2002, 69), a point that Engels himself saw as one of the most compelling entailments of evolutionary theory (see Badiou 2009, 195).

If we recognize the key implication of this, that pragmatic rather than contemplative concerns govern the picture of the world we carry around, then we can see that the model is a model for *doing* rather than some "pure" reflection.

THE EMPTY SIGNIFIER AND THE VOID OF BEING

By adopting a skeptical approach to discourse's representational function, we trouble the seemingly "natural," intuitive connection between knowledge and being. Hewing close to the postmodern position for the sake of testing it until it breaks, we can posit the provocative claim that:

> The reflection is a model-for-action. Any resemblance with actual beings is purely ideological.

The human animal may have evolved to survive and thrive in nature, but this fact alone does not tether discourse to matter. The symbolic order is inaugurated through a "cut" in being, to which subjects accede by virtue of a "forced choice" (Lacan 1998, 211). No discourse professing to represent matter has an essential, direct relation with its object. For, if the symbolic order "floats free" of being, cutting subjectivity off from its material dimension, discourse can nevertheless be providing a "rough guide" for getting about in it. It just does not provide a reflection as such.

Or does it?

It is often noted that the signifier-without-signified, by *failing* at signification, by its very emptiness, is also the *fullest* signifier. Its emptiness is a petri dish for the multiplication of social fantasies—indeed, Lacan and Laclau differ on characterizing it either as the empty or the master-signifier. But a different side of this signifier (which from hereon in I will refer to, following Lacanian terminology, as the S_1, a first among equals) is little remarked upon. Insofar as it fails to signify, the S_1 falls short of the transcendence achieved by regular signifiers. Could it be that by its very failure to achieve "escape velocity" from materiality, the S_1 might root discourse in material practice?

The S_1 is the only way for discourse, considered as a system of differences without positive terms, to close itself off and become a fully functioning system. Without this foreclosure, meaning proliferates and signifieds slide indefinitely beneath signifiers. As Žižek explains in reference to the failure of the first, proto-scientific iteration of structuralism:

> formal structure is itself tied by an umbilical cord to some radically contingent material element which, in its pure particularity, "is" the structure, embodies it. Why? Because the big Other, the symbolic order, is always barré, failed, crossed-out, mutilated, and the contingent material element embodies this internal blockage, limit, of the symbolic structure. (Žižek 1989, 183)

Consider the "mindless," tautological S_1 that is, in a crucial sense, *in* the symbolic order but not *of* the symbolic order. Does it not *incant* rather than signify, acting as a switch that opens up an interpretive horizon, that structures the field of signifiers in opposition to something unsymbolizable, something sublime? Think of Nation, Reason, Law, Market, Nature, Reality, or God, for example—remembering that no signifier is absolutely empty at all times, but that signifiers such as these are tendentially empty in certain discourses (Laclau 2005a, 70). As the signifier of senseless repetition, of the "meaningless precondition of meaning" (Laclau 2014, 64), the S_1 is a kind of primordial, material inscription: pure mark. As a signifier among signifiers (used simultaneously in sentences with regular signifiers) and yet radically different, it straddles the cut that elevates language out of expression and into *logos*.

Undoubtedly there is no "divine" link between discourse and being, or between concepts and their objects. And yet, as Laclau insists, discourses do partake of something sacred in a special sense: via the S_1 they partake of something transcendent vis-à-vis the symbolic order, something extra-discursive. This is why, I argue, the very materiality of the S_1 performs a kind of *ostensive definition* of the plane of the real. Literally attached, materially, to this plane, it is an incantation. Its very uttering conjures a space of positivity to which, simultaneously, the other signifying members become articulated (see also Curry 2003, 346).

If the S_1 *performs* positivity then it must, in the very same act, perform negativity. The correlate of its presence, as mark, is its absence. The "space" in which it takes place remains, even when it is not inscribed. It is in this very negativity—or, more precisely, its effacement in the mark of the S_1—that we must look for the material basis of discourse. As Badiou explains, there is a need for an impossible, unknowable object, to make knowledge possible: "[A]ll knowledge demands its position" (Badiou 2009, 202). Badiou is adamant that the process of knowledge—as distinct from knowledge itself—is "unknown to the knowing" (2009, 198). And is this not the appropriate balancing metaphor that idealist-tending discourse theory requires? To recognize that, however well we can grasp the product of knowledge, the process of knowledge eludes us? That the process of knowledge might itself occupy the unknowable, a position that is nevertheless essential for knowledge?

> The real of knowledge is at all times that which is impossible to know. But that is precisely what asymptotically fixates the future of the reflection. This impossible, therefore, will be known all the while being placed in the position of possibility (of reflection) by the new add-on in its field. (Badiou, 2009, p. 202)

In later Badiou, this is called the void, the condition of presentation. "Presentation" implies something being presented, and this something necessarily exists beyond the plane of presentation itself. The void is "just the name of inconsistent multiplicity [Badiou's fundamental ontological category] within the situation" (Hallward 2003, 66). Badiou is in broad agreement here with Laclau's position that there is a "blind spot inherent to signification," a "meaningless precondition of meaning," the place of which is taken up by the empty signifier (Laclau 2014, 64).

Badiou explains how knowledge crosses being and discourse. "Knowledge crosses two processes: the process, in the real, of its conditions, and the process, in the subject-effect, of its seizing" (Badiou 2009, 199). And indeed, the further element that we must insert into this equation, this process of knowledge, is the subject. Because, as Lacan is adamant, the blind spot of discourse, where the extra-discursive must be "located," is also the space of the subject, or at least the part of it that remains after the cut elevating it into the symbolic. Despite retaining a foothold in the real, the subject is forbidden (as condition of its subjectivity) from regaining access to the pre-symbolic. It is *both* the subject and the empty signifier, the S_1, then, that obscure the extra-discursive. And is not the latter, that which exists but has no being (the original paradox of articulation in Laclau and Mouffe), not then a question of obstruction rather than of contradiction? Of course, there is very little difference between the subject and the empty signifier. The signifier (by which Lacan means the S_1) "represents the subject for another signifier" (by which he means the regular signifiers) (Lacan 1998, 207).

To return to the original paradox, it is the knower itself that obscures knowledge. And so the paradox returns, but in a different form. While some things are able to exist without discourse, they remain beyond knowledge not because they are outside of discourse but because the subject, that which stands a chance of knowing them, blocks their way. If the subject were able to step out of the way, as it were—which is exactly the process of knowledge— it would simply produce a new occlusion.

A materialist discourse analysis, then, must locate matter in this space obscured by the empty signifier and by the subject. But obscure, occlude, and obstruct are misleading verbs here if they suggest something coming between subject and object in a Cartesian space. We must try to think the obstruction in a non-visual sense, perhaps in a topological sense—a hydraulic blockage if you will. And while this does not solve the materialist question of discourse theory conclusively, it at least offers numerous guidelines. Foremost, we should dissect each subject and each empty signifier and ask: what material relations, unknowable within this discursive formation, might they be obstructing? What does the emergence of *this* subject, *this* empty signifier, tell us about the forces that work upon (but are inadmissible to) this discursive formation? While these questions might apply in general, their possible answers will be, by definition, particular and, because they lie outside of the settled terms of the situation, speculative. Above all, the question of obstructed matter is a methodological question that can only be solved in the context of specific cases. It follows, then, that the onus is on the analyst to account for what is obstructed by the subject and the empty signifier in terms non-native to the specific set of objects and practices under analysis.

NOTES

1. The list is long: antagonism, hegemony, articulation, empty signifiers, logics of equivalence and difference, subject positions, subjects, undecidability, dislocation, heterogeneity.
2. See Marchart (2007) for a discussion of several of these common strands.

BIBLIOGRAPHY

Badiou, Alain. 2009. *Theory of the Subject.* Translated by Bruno Bosteels. 1st ed. London; New York: Bloomsbury Academic.

Bartlett, A.J., Justin Clemens, and Jon Roffe. 2015. *Lacan Deleuze Badiou.* Edinburgh University Press.

Butler, Judith, Ernesto Laclau, and Slavoj Žižek. 2000. *Contingency, Hegemony, Universality: Contemporary Dialogues on the Left.* Phronesis. London; New York: Verso.

Curry, P. 2003. 'Re-Thinking Nature: Towards an Eco-Pluralism.' *Environmental Values* 12 (3): 337–360.

Descola, Philippe. 2013. *The Ecology of Others.* Translated by Geneviève Godbout and Benjamin P. Luley. University of Chicago Press. http://www.press.uchicago.edu/ucp/books/book/distributed/E/bo14417933.html

Engels, Friedrich. 1962. *Anti-Dühring: Herr Eugen Dühring's Revolution in Science.* 3rd ed. Moscow: Foreign Languages Publishing House.

Geertz, Clifford. 1975. 'Thick Description: Toward an Interpretive Theory of Culture.' In *The Interpretation of Cultures: Selected Essays*, 3–30. London: Hutchinson.

Glynos, Jason. 2002. 'Psychoanalysis Operates upon the Subject of Science: Lacan between Science and Ethics.' In *Lacan and Science*, edited by Yannis Stavrakakis and Jason Glynos. London; New York: Karnac.

Hallward, Peter. 2003. *Badiou: A Subject to Truth.* Minneapolis, MN: University of Minnesota Press.

Hoffman, Donald D. 2016. 'The Interface Theory of Perception.' *Current Directions in Psychological Science* 25 (3): 157–61. doi:10.1177/0963721416639702.

Howarth, David R., Aletta J. Norval, and Yannis Stavrakakis, eds. 2000. *Discourse Theory and Political Analysis: Identities, Hegemonies and Social Change.* Manchester: Manchester University Press.

Jørgensen, Marianne, and Louise Phillips. 2002. *Discourse Analysis as Theory and Method.* London: SAGE Publications Ltd. doi:10.4135/9781849208871.

Lacan, Jacques. 1998. *The Four Fundamental Concepts of Psychoanalysis.* Edited by Jacques-Alain Miller. Translated by Alan Sheridan. London: Hogarth.

Laclau, Ernesto. 1996. *Emancipation(s).* London: Verso.

———. 2005a. *On Populist Reason.* London: Verso.

———. 2005b. 'The Future of Radical Democracy.' In *Radical Democracy: Politics Between Abundance and Lack*, edited by Lars Tønder and Lasse Thomassen, 256–62. Manchester: University Press.

———. 2014. *The Rhetorical Foundations of Society.* London: New York, Verso.

Laclau, Ernesto, and Chantal Mouffe. 1985. *Hegemony and Socialist Strategy: Towards a Radical Democratic Politics.* London; New York: Verso.

———. 1987. 'Post-Marxism without Apologies.' *New Left Review* 166: 79.

Latour, Bruno. 1993. *We Have Never Been Modern.* Cambridge, MA: Harvard University Press.

Marchart, Oliver. 2007. *Post-Foundational Political Thought: Political Difference in Nancy, Lefort, Badiou and Laclau.* Edinburgh: University Press.

Žižek, Slavoj. 1989. *The Sublime Object of Ideology.* London: Verso.

Chapter 7

Contingent Materialities as Sedimented Articulations

Anti-Essentialist Discourse Analysis and Materialism at the Nexus of IR and Political Theory

Laura Pantzerhielm

In contemporary social science research, post-structuralist and post-foundationalist discourse analyses have often come to be understood as amounting to radical critiques of materialism.[1] The focus of scholars committing themselves to the said ordering labels on deconstructing textual representation, on uncovering the historical contingency of knowledge domains and their insistence on the fluidity, and constructedness of social realities has oftentimes been equated with disputing the objective existence of social objects and institutions, or refuting the salience of economic forces and physical coercion. International Relations (IR) provides for an instructive example in this regard, as discourse analysis in this scholarly field has come to be chiefly associated with the analysis of texts and meanings conveyed therein amongst both its critics and prominent proponents (Keohane 1988, Milliken 1999, Hansen 2006). Yet, as the interest in materialism and the material aspects of the social and natural world has seen a veritable renaissance in political theory through the newly usurping New Materialism(s), discourse analysts in IR, and beyond increasingly seek to address the relationship between text, perception, and knowledge on the one hand and material manifestations on the other (van Dyk et al. 2014, Vaughan-Williams/Lundborg 2015, Beetz 2016).

In the present chapter, I contribute to this debate by challenging both the necessity and the desirability of upholding the commonly alleged opposition between materialism and the radically constructivist epistemological stance that characterizes anti-essentialist discourse analysis. Moreover, I sketch out theoretical and methodological routes for engaging concepts drawn from post-structuralist and post-foundationalist understandings of discourse analysis so as to grasp materiality as a productive yet contingent presence structuring the

Social by conceiving of its various forms as sedimented political articulations. The argument proceeds as follows: To locate some of the snares in our theoretical field of engagement, I first seek to disentangle a selected set of the meanings ascribed to "materialism" and related terms through the articulation of conceptual oppositions and equations in theoretical debates at the nexus of IR and political theory. In particular, I point to how such regularities are often accorded with a sense of naturalness through their intertwinement with specific epistemological perspectives and related underlying assumptions. Thereafter, I proceed by disputing the analytical and political usefulness of treating materialism and constructivism as dichotomous propositions and instead argue for a conceptual understanding of social materiality within a post-foundationalist/anti-essentialist discourse-analytical framework that operates in a double opposition to (essentialist, metaphysical) idealism and epistemological realism. In order to address how such an understanding might be translated into more concrete research strategies, I then provide a comparative discussion of how social materiality can be conceptualized by drawing on Foucauldian and post-foundationalist (Essex School) discourse analysis, respectively. Here, I contend that a post-foundationalist account of radical ontological negativity offers a fruitful ground for understanding materiality as contingent, but nonetheless stable and productive sedimented political articulations. In terms of concrete research strategies that would locate inquiries into the becoming and effects of such contingent materialities within an anti-essentialist discourse-analytical framework, I propose to combine a Foucauldian mapping of the outer epistemic borders that delineate the present moment, with a subsequent inquiry into instances of political articulation and sedimentation thereof into more solid social institutions and relations.

THE MANY LIVES OF MATERIALISM: CONTENTIOUS MEANING(S) AND STRUCTURING CONCEPTUAL OPPOSITIONS

In IR as in neighboring disciplines, "materialism" has lead and continues to lead many lives: it has entered into a variety of marriages, it has gotten involved in more sporadic, fragile romances, and it has drawn upon it the animosity of powerful opponents. Before delving into a more in-depth discussion of how and why (IR) anti-essentialist discourse analysis can and ought to engage conceptually with material, sedimented aspects of social reality besides patterns of representation and textuality, I believe that it is necessary to first touch upon the historically grown web of recurring dichotomizations and equations that have come to define the borders of what "materialism" means in the context of IR research and political theory.[2] For the past few decades of IR theory and associated research programs, the term material-ism has led a seemingly hybrid existence. On the one hand, it has been associated with (neo-)Marxist approaches at the disciplinary border between International Political Economy (IPE) and IR, such as world system theory, dependency theory, Political Marxism, and neo-Gramscianism in its domi-nant Coxian form. On the other hand, materialism functions as a dividing line that separates constructivism from (neo)realism and neoliberal institutional-ism as theories of international politics (Jackson/Sørensen 2010, 56, 86, 168, 209–11, 228).

However, despite this apparent fragmentation, a commonality or unify-ing exclusion can be identified in how both of the said recurring oppositions tend to constitute "materialism" first and foremost as an attribute of theories that privilege given, objective, physical factors, or "variables" in explaining outcomes and dynamics in IR. To illustrate this point, let us briefly consider the conceptual oppositions that were articulated in the course of moderate IR constructivism's realignment with positivist epistemologies throughout the late 1990s and early 2000s (Levin 2012, Holzscheiter 2013). As scholars familiar with the discipline's historiography will know, the evolution of IR theory is commonly divided into three or four "great debates" between oppos-ing theoretical paradigms: realism vs. liberalism/idealism, traditionalism vs. scientism (sometimes also "history vs. science"), neorealism vs. neoliberal institutionalism and finally rationalism vs. reflectivism/constructivism (Lapid 1989). If the 1980s and early 1990s saw a proliferation of postpositivist approaches ranging from post-structuralist and critical constructivist to femi-nist and postcolonial perspectives, the end of the decade became the scene of reconciliation and integration of "moderate constructivist" approaches into the IR mainstream. As a part of this hegemonic reconfiguration of the theoretical field, moderate constructivist proposals for a "middle ground" research agenda sought to distance themselves from "radical," "relativist" approaches (Wendt 1995, Adler 1997, Risse 2003). Such proposals were frequently underpinned by the perception that the latter attribute sociopoliti-cal "outcomes" and developments solely and *a priori* to ideational-linguistic "construction" and the power of "ideas"—that in postpositivist discourse analysis and constructivism "*only* ideas matter and can be studied" (Adler 1997: 321, my italics). In other words, radical constructivist positions were understood as privileging ideational and ignoring material forces (Börzel 1997, 130, Adler 1997, 321, 323, Fearon/Wendt 2006). In turn, the promise of middle ground constructivism was located in a willingness to submit such hypotheses to empirical testing, so that the causal influence of material and ideational variables would be decided through empirical research properly disciplined through agreed techniques of variation, non-variation, and infer-ence. As Emanuel Adler writes in his seminal plea for a constructivist middle ground, unlike "relativists" and "postmodernist" who are "condemned to interpret discourses" and "subscribe to the view that if people cannot know that there is an objective reality, they should stop wasting time looking for it. [...] constructivism does not build on the relativist implications of interpretative epistemology" (Adler 1997, 326).

Moderate constructivism thus entered the IR stage as a complementary set of ontological propositions for generating hypotheses, hence establishing—or rather rescuing—a matrix premised on a view of science as a search for laws of cause and consequence by means of approximating the natural experiment. In this context, the meaning of materialism came to be defined within the coordinates of a mechanically causal, variable-based "clockwork universe" and as a consequence materialist propositions appear to be intrinsically at odds with discourse-analytical approaches.

Now, how does this compare to the meanings ascribed to materialism as a trait of neo-Marxism? As such, (neo-)Marxist approaches in IR have developed a range of diverging notions of what materialism entails. For instance, Immanuel Wallerstein's world system theory represents a largely economistic, historically determinist reading of the term as referring to the proposition that the modern world system develops according to an economic, structural logic inherent to capitalism as a "system of production for sale in a market for profit and appropriation of this profit on the basis of individual or collective ownership" (1979, 66, Wallerstein [1974] 2013, 346–57). By contrast, Coxian neo-Gramscianism has sought to distance itself from economist reductionism and the search for underlying laws determining the course of history. Building on his well-known distinction between critical and problem-solving theory, Robert Cox differentiates between "historical materialism" as a critical, historical form of Marxist research and theorizing, and "structural Marxism" which he argues engages in ahistorical abstractions and employs an essentialist epistemology (1981, 132–3). (Neo-)Marxist approaches in IR therefore oscillate between critical historicist and determinist epistemologically realist positions. As a result, they advance diverging understandings of the purpose and conditions under which materialist reasoning operates, of its appropriate form and meaning. In this respect, the epistemological battle within IR (neo-)Marxism mirrors opposing moves in the wider theoretical field of Marxist theorizing toward i) essentialist searches for laws of necessity underlying the course of history, or ii) toward a critical historicist concern with "weakening the boundary of essence" (Laclau 1990, 23, on historicism and scientism in Marxist IR, see also Teschke 2014, 2–4).

Yet, the equation between materialism and "material factors" and the interconnected opposition to "constructivism" reoccurs and assumes a structuring function in the context of dominant contemporary scholarly debates and authoritative textbooks seeking to provide students of IR with ordering oppositions by which to navigate the disciplinary field (see for instance,

Jackson/Sørensen 2010, 165, 206–7, 209, Schimmelfennig 2008, 164–67). Here, neo-Marxist IR and IPE research tend to be painted with a broad brush so as to fit the palette of the overall clockwork motive, as deducing or seeking the origins or causes of inequalities within and between groups of states in the economic-material base—in relations and means of economic production, exploitation of labor, extraction of surplus value or the development of technology and communication. Divergences from this pattern do occur. In particular, neo-Gramscian theorizing is sometimes attributed to the constructivist rather than the materialist camp (e.g., Adler 1997, 331). Yet the pattern as such—that is, the allocation of theories to either side of the juxtaposition, as using either material or ideational variables or a combination thereof—to speak with Foucault appears to constitute an overarching "grid of specification" according to which materialism, and related discursive objects are "divided, contrasted, related, regrouped, classified [and] derived from one another" (Foucault [1970] 2010, 42). In other words, neo-Marxism is seen to differ from social constructivism in the *same way* as neorealism and neoliberal institutionalism, namely through the recourse to different sets of material "variables" that influence actors' behavior, interactions and collective/structural outcomes. At the nexus of IR and political theory, the meaning of "materialism" is thus circumscribed by equations and oppositions that are articulated within the borders of a Popperian, epistemologically realist philosophy of science approach: constructivism and materialism figure as sources of opposing propositions about the influence of variables, whilst materialism becomes equated with and allows for the grouping together of (neo-)Marxism, (IR ontological) realism, and neoliberal institutionalism.

Adding to this set of equations and oppositions, in IR theory and political theory more broadly both realism and materialism are circumscribed oppositions to the term "idealism." Classical and neorealism alike—as ontological theories of international relations that emphasize state power, national interests, relative power dynamics, etc.—consistently figure and articulate themselves in opposition to "idealist" theorizing and its perceived consequences for foreign policy practice. In E.H. Carr, as in Hans Morgenthau and John Mearsheimer, idealism figures as a synonym for "utopianism," conceived as a dangerous attempt to establish international order and conduct foreign policy based on liberal internationalist morality and abstract perceptions of the "good," rather than a realist, grounded-in-reality, assessment of the relevant inter-state power distribution and dynamics (Carr 1936, for instance 17, 28, 34, see also Morgenthau [1948] 1985, Mearsheimer 2005). Here, a regularity that juxtaposes realism and idealism by connecting the terms to a practical concern with either power or ideas/ideals therefore appears to be at work. Idealists, Mearsheimer assures, "neglect the crucial role of power when thinking about international politics" (2005, 139). However, classical realist resistance to idealism also entails a philosophy of history component; the insistence that history unfolds as a result of power struggles rather than as an incarnation of ideational, metaphysical abstractions. To be sure, realism advances a set of more specific ontological propositions that conceive of power in a repressive (rather than productive) sense, places it in close proximity to the state apparatus and locates its unfolding in the capacities of and interactions between unitary state actors in the international realm. Yet, on the level of discursive dichotomizations, this perspective might be seen as a convergence with the articulation and specification within various strands of (neo-)Marxist theory of their materialist commitments in terms of a staunch opposition to idealism (Marx/Engels [1845–6] 1972, Engels [1878] 1947, see also, Lenin 1909, Horkheimer [1933] 1988, Althusser [1965] 2005). For Marx, Engels and the (neo-)Marxist tradition more generally, the idealist adversary is not primarily found in liberal internationalism, but takes on the more specific form of Hegelian metaphysics, including both the old-Hegelian affirmation, as well as young-Hegelian critique of the "Herrschaft der Religion, der Begriffe, des Allgemeinen in der bestehenden Welt" ([1845–6] 1969, 20). In this wider context, materialism therefore also figures as a name for different attempts to resist a view of history as constituted through objective mind or spirit, as evolving according to a correspondence with a universal conceptual form (Laclau 1990, 106–7).

TOWARD AN ANTI-ESSENTIALIST MATERIALIST STANCE: SOME DEMARCATIONS TO NAVIGATE THE FIELD

While one could dwell endlessly on analyses of the multifaceted discursive web of historically grown juxtapositions and conceptual relations where the term "materialism" circulates, I believe that the above, if precarious, mapping of its main contours allows for us to begin sketching a route by which to enter the terrain. If post-foundationalist discourse analysis is to become or to be understood as materialist, or if materialism is to be grounded in post-foundationalism and is to employ discourse-analytical tools, how are we to understand this equivalence? And how could one proceed methodologically to implement such a research program?

A first demarcation I believe must be to refute and go beyond the dichotomization between materialism and constructivism that we touched upon above. Scholars engaging in Foucauldian, Essex School and other strands of post-structuralist and post-Marxist discourse analysis have long and self-consciously rejected the variable-based, clockwork-like framework that sustains this conceptual opposition, yet it needs to be explicitly refuted because of the powerful ordering function which it still assumes. Importantly, breaking up the constructivism/materialism dichotomy necessitates a move toward extending axioms about the constructed, discursively constituted, and contingent nature of social relations onto the social sciences themselves. In the context of IR constructivism, this amounts to a need to leave behind the strange split between constructivist ontological propositions and a positivist, empiricist epistemology that has hampered mainstream middle ground approaches, often leading scholars "to believe that it was no longer necessary to problematize the historicity and contingency of their own historical moment and philosophical horizons" as Daniel Levin and Alexander Barder pointedly underline (2012: 585). A consistently constructivist perspective beyond the realist clockwork universe fares better in adopting a view of scholars as inevitably embedded in their object of study and of knowledge as inextricably political and intertwined with power (Foucault [1970] 2010, 210, 216; see also Carter 2006, Pantzerhielm 2016, 17–22).

Yet, if discourse analysis is to be consistent in embracing an anti-essentialist stance not only with regard to knowledge but also with regard to ontology—that is, just as there is no true, actual, neutral meaning of words, there is no divine origin of social order (Foucault [1970] 2010, 48, Laclau/Mouffe [1985] 2001, 112)—a further point of departure must be an explicit stance of resistance against epistemological realist conceptions of the material aspects of social reality. Instead of treating social objects as something given, pre-societal, the task would be to shed light on how social relations, objects, and identities are (re)produced in meaning-endowed practices and stabilized through sedimentation. This demarcation or clarification seems to me to be of particular importance for two reasons: first, as discussed above using the example of IR research, epistemological realism is alive and well in empirical social science disciplines, powerfully structuring the rules according to which statements about social phenomena acquire the status of truth and authoritative knowledge. This goes for the underlying variable-based framework that structures mainstream IR theory debates, as well as for "scientific" currents of Marxist theorizing which lay claims to the epithet "materialism" (Rancière 1975, Teschke 2014). Secondly, in contemporary philosophy, social, and aesthetic theory, the range of approaches that have recently proliferated under that brand of "New Materialism" oscillate between epistemological realism and anti-essentialist, relational ontologies. To exemplify, Jane Bennett advances seemingly neo-Kantian propositions about matter as having a given, as-such force and existence, as being "vibrant," possessing inherent "vitality" and "agency" (2004, 348, 2007). Contra Adorno and Marx, she negates the claim "that things are always already humanized objects," and instead argues for a "naïve realism" that acknowledges "thing-power" and "the force of matter" (2004, 357). In contrast, Karen Barad articulates notions of ontology and matter as inherently relational, contingent, and performative rather than as fixed substance (2007, 238–9). Drawing on research in quantum physics, she

deems the identity of natural objects to be performative, so that her materialism can be read as extending anti-essentialism to the natural world instead of
reimporting naturalism into the social realm. As Thomas Lemke has shown
in much greater detail, there is therefore a general tension in the expanding
realm of "new materialist" theorizing between seeing matter as produced,
and as having a given quality (Lemke 2014). Without going into any further
detail about the epistemological varieties of new materialist approaches, the
point I would like to make is the following: For an anti-essentialist ontology of discourse, language, and materiality, a conscious resistance toward
a realist imaginary of material things as being "simply there" or as having
unmediated effects on social processes is pivotal in order to avoid a line of
thought in which "contingency is eliminated and radically absorbed by the
necessary." (Laclau 1990, 20) In other words, to anchor materialism in a
post-foundationalist framework implies conceiving of materiality neither as
a sum of pre-social things nor as a determinist force underlying history, but
as politically and historically produced sedimentations of political institution.
Yet the insistence on contingent, political origins should not be confused with
a denial of the real, observable effects that temporally stable materialities
continuously unfold.

This notion of social reality as a historically and politically built environment which takes on productive material forms leads us to a further point
of separation—namely the need to avoid metaphysical, objectivist idealism.
This entails tying in with the classical Marxist critique of any view of history and society as a realization of (God-)given ideas or spirit external to
society's own (re)production. The aim here is not to replace the givenness of
the idea with the givenness of objects or materiality—hence the opposition to
epistemological realism just discussed (see also Laclau 1990: 106). Rather,
the implication would be for discourse analysis to insist on a view of history
as unfolding through contingent performative struggles and to see meaning
and materiality as intertwined and historically produced. In this sense, resisting idealism would not entail ignoring perception and patterns of thought,
but rather to abandon any attempts at rescuing their divine truth or origin, to
emphasizes discontinuity, chance, and the production of truth and objectivity
through power relations, or to speak with Foucault as a product of "a particular stage of forces" (Foucault 1977, 149). Such an understanding, I believe, is
salient for a radically constructivist discourse-analytical stance to go beyond
any simple critique of representation as exclusionary, toward embracing a
concern with the interlocking (re)production of ideational and material structures, their power effects and instabilities. Resisting idealism in this manner
may be seen as a tactic to avoid the trap of young-Hegelian critique that
Marx and Engels describe as follows: "This demand to change consciousness
amounts to a demand to interpret reality in another way, i.e. to recognise it

by means of another interpretation. The Young-Hegelian ideologists, in spite of their allegedly 'world-shattering' statements, are the staunchest conservatives." (Marx/Engels [1845–6] 2004, 41)

Instead of merely directing attention toward the inevitable exclusion entailed in any representation of existent social phenomena, their material-ideational becoming hence enters the stage as the focus of an anti-essentialist materialist discourse-analytical inquiry.

THINKING THE MATERIAL AND THE DISCURSIVE WITH FOUCAULT AND MOUFFE/LACLAU: CONCEPTS AND ROUTES FOR EMPIRICAL RESEARCH

The distinction between the social and the political is thus ontologically constitutive of social relations (Laclau 1990, 35)

How can the theoretical alignments and oppositions outlined above be implemented as a research methodology? This concluding section sketches out routes for concrete research strategies by considering how materiality, language, and discursive constitution can be conceptualized by drawing on Foucauldian and post-foundationalist Essex School discourse analysis. Both provide interesting starting points as they lend themselves to understanding power, knowledge, and language to be inextricably intertwined and productive of social realities (Laclau/Mouffe [1985] 2001, 85–6, 105–7, 109, Mouffe 2007, 27, Foucault [1970] 2010). Yet what more specific conceptual tools do they formulate? If one draws on *The Archeology of Knowledge* as a methodological guide book, Foucauldian discourse analysis lends itself to research strategies that seek to uncover the borders of what is reasonably speak- and thinkable in a given historical context. It provides two main points of attack: "archeology" (or "critique") and "genealogy" (Foucault [1970] 2010). The genealogical technique aims to uncover the contingency and emergence of contemporary perceptions by tracing the historical, discursive emergence of "problems" that pose themselves to the present. In practice this typically entails a diachronic tracing of textualities and the teasing out of contrasts between contemporary discursive regularities with those discernible in historical practices and text material (Foucault 1977, 144–52, Foucault 1977, 148–49, see also 142, Kerchner 2006, 24, Kerchner 2011, Saar 2008; Pantzerhielm 2016). Archeology is the corresponding method for describing regularities that characterize any given discursive formation: to describe the rules governing thought, speech, and practice in a specific society at a specific point in time (Foucault [1970] 2010, 230, 233, Kerchner 2006, 29–30). Now, how can the intertwining of such patterns of perceptions with more solid, material aspects of social reality be conceptualized? On a theoretical level, Foucault's discourse-analytical writings often highlight the instability of objects, by pointing to how discursive practices—for example, patterns in text, speech, and other meaning-endowed performances—"systematically form the objects of which they speak" (Foucault [1970] 2010, 49). In terms of more specific methodological tools, in *The Archeology of Knowledge,* one encounters the term materiality first and foremost in Foucault's discussion of the enunciative function as one aspect of the description of statements and their conditions of existence. Here, Foucault identifies the "repeatable materiality" of a given statement as one such condition, understood as the possibility of a given statement to (re)inscribe itself in non-identical and temporally dispersed physical, sense-perceptible elements whilst still being perceived as one (Foucault [1970] 2010, 100–3). "The rule of materiality that statements necessarily obey," Foucault writes "is therefore of the order of the institution rather than of the spatio-temporal localization" (Foucault [1970] 2010, 103). Yet if such considerations may indeed be helpful in making sense of how it is that statements can keep their identity—for example, be perceived/identified as "same"—across physical places/texts, temporality, and contexts, it offers rather little guidance for inquiries into how discourse brings forth the materiality of social objects, rather than a stability in the way that they are thought about, for example, in their representation. In general, a more thorough inventory of the conceptual toolbox that is developed in *The Archeology of Knowledge* provides for a rich set of proposals that can be used in descriptions of contingent regularities in knowledge and perception (Kerchner 2006, 2011, Pantzerhielm 2016). Yet, it also reveals a lack of methodological specification regarding *how* the intertwining of discourse and materiality, in particular the inscription of knowledge/perceptions into more solid forms and constellations, can be studied concretely and empirically. This limitation can be illustrated by the fact that both Foucault himself and Foucauldians after him have seen a necessity to go *beyond* the concept of discourse and the analytical tools associated with it toward an analysis of "dispositifs" in order to be able to grasp the operation of power in wider societal constellations or "heterogeneous ensemble(s)" that include both language, knowledge, and more solid, non-articulatory forms: "discourse, institutions, architectural forms, regulatory decisions, laws, administrative measures, scientific statements, philosophical, moral, and philanthropic propositions—in short, the said as much as the unsaid" (Foucault 1979, 94, see also Foucault 1976, 92–3, Jäger 2001, Bührmann/Schneider 2007, 2008, Herschinger 2015). The lack of methodological specification in archeological analysis and the conceptual split between the discursive and non-discursive that underpins the concept of the "dispositif" in my mind makes it worthwhile to go beyond the strictly Foucauldian conceptual terrain in seeking to concretize the kind of materialist discourse-analytical alignments that we discussed above. To grasp how regularities in text/speech and knowledge that Foucauldian discourse analysis uncover inscribe themselves into and bring forth more stable, material forms of social reality I therefore suggest to draw on Mouffe and Laclau's understanding of the Social as frozen, habitualized, and materialized political articulations.

If a Foucauldian perspective focuses our attention on the historical becoming and epistemic borders of contemporary discursive objects/regularities and locates their productivity in the delineation of the reasonably speakable, Mouffe, and Laclau put a greater emphasis on the inherent instability and political contingency of contemporary forms of social organization (Dreyer-Hansen 2014). This accentuation is closely connected to a double conceptual distinction which structures Mouffe and Laclau's theorizing: between politics and the Political on the one hand, and the Political and the Social on the other. First, Mouffe and Laclau converge with other post-Marxist accounts (Lefort, Rancière) in distancing themselves from how political science, political philosophy, and public discourse in the (post)modern period have rendered the term "politics" synonymous with the positive phenomena of the state and the political system. Instead of equating politics with this historically specific, ontic sphere of political parties, organized interests, policies, state institutions, etc., and imagine it as a specific societal realm besides the economy, civil society, the legal system etc., Mouffe and Laclau argue that the Political—that is, politics in its proper ontological meaning—must be located in discursive, productive acts which determine the shape of a particular society by transforming or reproducing divisions between social realms and subjects (Laclau/Mouffe [1985] 2001, 152–3, Mouffe 2007, 14–15, 2008, see also Dreyer-Hansen/Sonnichsen 2014). The concept of the Political thus highlights both the contingent, conflict-laden nature of discursive articulations, and their productive inscription into social reality (Laclau/Mouffe [1985] 2001, 153). Second, the concept of the Social comes into play to describe more stable, solidified forms of social relations and institutions, which are the product of previous political articulation and inscription, yet display a greater degree of stability at a given point in time (Laclau/Mouffe [1985] 2001, 152). As Mouffe and Laclau explain: "What we wish to point to is that politics as a practice of creation, reproduction and transformation of social relations [e.g. the Political, LP] cannot be located at the determinate level of the social, as the problem of the political is the problem of the institution of the social." (Laclau/Mouffe [1985] 2001, 153)

Drawing on Husserlian terminology, Mouffe and Laclau conceive of the Social as being established through "sedimentation" of the Political that is the temporal "forgetting" or rendering invisible of contingent origins and the materialization of discursive articulations (Laclau 1990, 34, 160, 2005, 117, 154).

Laura Pantzerhielm

The concept of "reactivation" refers to the opposite process, where an articulation makes visible the contingency of a social phenomenon so as to enable political change. To put it in simple terms: the Political refers to discursive acts of producing and shaping social relations, while the Social denotes sedimented or temporally stable relations and institutions. Social and political institutions, subjectivity, and modes of dividing social reality into discernible sub-realms are thus understood to derive from productive discursive acts of instituting the Social: as sedimented discourses whose principle contingency and historical, discursive origins are temporally concealed, forgotten or naturalized, but might be reactivated through counter-hegemonic rearticulation (Laclau/ Mouffe [1985] 2001, vii, 107, 153, Laclau 1990, 20–3, Laclau 2005, 153–4, see also Martilla 2015). Compared to the Foucauldian interest in uncovering power effects of discursive (re)production, its intertwining with knowledge domains and exclusions produced through limits to meaningful "reasonable" speech, Mouffe/Laclau's theory of discourse highlights the inherently political aspect of articulation under the condition of radical contingency and ontological negativity. At the same time, the distinction between the Social and the Political makes it possible to grasp corresponding inscriptions as bringing forth social institutions and identities as well as to account for reactivation processes through which the contingency of social institutions and practices are made visible. Sedimentation seems particularly useful to account for why—despite the principle contingency and ontological emptiness of social reality—the range of meaningful, effective actions and words available to a specific subject in a given moment within a given constellation is mostly markedly restricted.

Rather than juxtaposing the material-physical and the discursive-ideational, discourse analyses drawing on Mouffe and Laclaus concepts of sedimentation and reactivation can shed light on social phenomena—practices, institutions, markets, identities—by highlighting their position on a spectrum between i) reactivation, where contingency is made visible and dislocation occurs and ii) sedimentation in the form of "forgetting" or naturalization and materialization, where contingency is concealed and sedimented forms place limits, costs, and possibilities on their surroundings. Within such a framework, speech brings forth objects; but not merely in the sense that meaningful speech is contingent on sense-making as a process of perceiving of existent social, material objects. Rather, the emergence of any particular form of social relations can be understood as a result of politico-discursive historical processes of institution (Mouffe/Laclau 1990, 107, Laclau 2005, 117, see also Lefort/Gauchet 1990). Their presence then is at once material and productive in the sense that they unfold observable structuring effects, within which the individual subject is doomed to navigate, and contingent in that their objectivity can never escape the condition of radical ontological negativity: it is "constantly threatened by a constitutive outside" (Laclau 1990, 22).

Mouffe/Laclaudian discourse theory therefore provides fruitful conceptual instruments for investigating how discourses become fixed, material, and productive realities and how those realities, once objectified, restrict the realm of possible, meaningful articulations and practices.

Yet, a thus understood analysis of contingent materialities first has to uncover the specificity of the present before it can engage in understanding the processes of discourses-becoming-material that produced it. In terms of concrete research strategies, I therefore propose to combine Foucauldian mapping of the outer epistemic borders that delineate the present moment, with a subsequent inquiry into instances of political articulation and sedimentation thereof into more solid social materialities. Concretely, such research strategies can proceed in three main steps or—given a more circular research process—along three conceptual axes. First, concepts can be drawn from *The Archeology of Knowledge* and applied to the analysis of diachronic text corpuses so as to uncover discursive regularities and transformations therein over time (for more detailed methodological discussions, see Kerchner 2006, 2011, Pantzerhielm 2016). Second, attention can be directed toward the productive inscription of thus defined regularities in thought and perception into material conditions by asking which social entities have the authority to sustain their status as truth, as well as by addressing how institutions define subjects' roles, limit the access thereto and place material/institutional restrictions and possibilities upon them (Martilla 2015). In an additional third step, empirical analyses can draw on Mouffe and Laclau's distinctions between hegemonic and counter-hegemonic articulations of difference and equivalence so as to address the struggle involved in moments of closure and reactivation (Laclau/Mouffe [1985] 2001, Laclau 2005). In addition, this step or axis bridges the two foregoing by ordering discursive breaches and the emergence of novel sedimented social relations in a sequence. This would involve asking what new institutions and subject roles follow upon hegemonic recomposition and closure of struggle, or in other words, the re-forgetting of contingency (Laclau/Mouffe [1985] 2001, xviii, 105–6, 109, 130–2, Laclau 1990).

From an anti-essentialist position, empirical research operting along these theoretical and methodological lines offers a number of advantages: It promises to transcend the conceptual division between materialism and constructivism that functions as a powerful grid structuring much of IR and political theory, implicitly constraining the understanding of both terms to a realist epistemological horizon and a mechanical, variable-based view of causality. Moreover, empirical analyses of the kind suggested here promise to avoid falling into either i) the idealist trap of imagining the course of history as an incarnation of given (metaphysical) concepts, or ii) the mirror-image naïve realist fallacy of attributing "things" and materiality with an as-such existence and deterministic effects. In a nutshell, the theoretical alliances and method-ological proposals that have been advanced in this chapter thus constitute a plea for a specific form of revived relationship between materialism and dis-course analysis. Namely one that is based on the aspiration to "weak[en] the boundary of essence" (Laclau 1990, 23) in our analytical and political rela-tion to both thoughts and things (or perceptions and materialities) by turning attention to their intertwined emergence and effects in contingent historical processes of societal (re)production.

NOTES

1. I would like to thank Jens Bartelson, Anna Holzscheiter, and Thurid Bahr for their comments on earlier versions of this chapter. Moreover, I am indebted to the editors Veit Schwab and Johannes Beetz, as well as to the other participants at the workshop "Materialist Discourse Analysis" at Warwick University in June 2016 for sharing their thoughts on my argument.

2. I highlight three interconnected oppositions that seem to me to fulfill a par-ticularly powerful structuring function in contemporary research at the crossroads between IR, political theory, and discourse studies: materialism/constructivism, real-ism/idealism, and materialism/idealism. I am therefore bracketing out other histori-cal and contemporary discursive fields within which "materialism" figures with yet other contours, inter alia its historical usage as a synonym for physicalism (as com-monly attributed to Thales of Miletus, Anaxagoras, Epicurus, Thomas Hobbes, Denis Diderot, and others).

BIBLIOGRAPHY

Adler, Emanuel. 1997. "Seizing the Middle Ground: Constructivism in World Poli-tics." *European Journal of International Relations* (3): 319–63.
Althusser, Louis. [1965] 2005. "Introduction." In: *For Marx*. London: Verso: 21–40.
Barad, Karen. 2007. *Meeting the Universe Halfway: Quantum Physics and the Entanglement of Matter*. Durham: Duke University Press.
Beetz, Johannes. 2016. *Materiality and Subject in Marxism, (Post)-Structuralism and Material Semiotics*. Basingstoke: Palgrave.
Bennett, Jane. 2004. "The Force of Things: Steps Toward an Ecology of Matter." *Political Theory* (3): 347–72.
———. 2007. *Vibrant Matter*. Durham: Duke University Press.
Bührmann, Andrea, and Werner Schneider. 2007. "Mehr als nur diskursive Praxis?—Konzeptionelle Grundlagen und methodische Aspekte der Dispositivanalyse." *Forum Qualitative Sozialforschung / Forum Qualitative Social Research* (2). http://www.qualitative-research.net/index.php/fqs/rt/printerFriendly/237/525.

Börzel, Tanja. 1997. "Zur (Ir-)Relevanz der Postmoderne für die Integrationsforsc-hung. Eine Replik auf Thomas Diez' Beitrag 'Postmoderne und europäische Inte-gration." *Zeitschrift für Internationale Beziehungen* (1): 125–37.

Carr, Edward Hallet. 2001 [1939]. *The Twenty Years' Crisis: 1919–1939*. New York: Perennial.

Carter, Rodney. 2006. "Of Things Said and Unsaid: Power, Archivial Silence and Power in Silence." *Archivaria* (61), Special Section on Archives, Space and Power 215–33.

Cox, Robert. 1981. "Social Forces, States and World Orders: Beyond International Relations Theory." *Millenium Journal of International Studies* (2): 126–55.

Dreyer-Hansen, Allan. 2014. "Laclau and Mouffe and the Ontology of Radical Nega-tivity." *Distinktion: Scandinavian Journal of Social Theory* (3): 283–95.

Dreyer-Hansen, Allan and André Sonnichsen. 2014. "Discourse, the Political and the Ontological Dimension: An Interview with Ernesto Laclau." *Distinktion: Scandi-navian Journal of Social Theory* (3): 255–62.

Engels, Friedrich. [1878] 1947. *Anti-Dühring. Herr Eugen Dühring's Revolution in Science*. Moscow: Progress Publishers.

Fearon, James and Alexander Wendt. 2006. "Chapter 3: Rationalism v. Constructiv-ism: A Skeptical View." In: *Handbook of International Relations*, edited by Walter Carlsnaes, Thomas Risse and Beth A. Simmon. London: SAGE: 52–72.

Foucault, Michael. [1970] 2010. *The Archeology of Knowledge*. New York: Vintage.

———. "Nietzsche, Genealogy, History." In: *Language, Counter- Memory, Prac-tice: Selected Essays and Interviews*, edited by D. F. Bouchard. Ithaca: Cornell University Press: 139–64.

———. [1979] 2008. *The Birth of Biopolitics: Lectures at the Collège de France 1978–1979*. Basingstoke: Palgrave Macmillan.

Hansen, Lene. 2006. *Security as Practice: Discourse Analysis and the Bosnian War*. Abingdon and New York: Routledge.

Herschinger, Eva. 2015. "The Drug Dispositif: Ambivalent Materiality and the Addiction of the Global Drug Prohibition Regime." *Security Dialogue* (2): 183–201.

Holzscheiter, Anna. 2013. "Between Communicative Interaction and Structures of Signification: Discourse Theory and Analysis in IR." *International Studies Per-spectives* (2): 142–62.

Horkheimer, Max. [1933] 1988. "Materialismus und Metaphysik." In: *Gesammelte Schriften Band 3*. Frankfurt: Fischer Taschenbuch: 70–105.

Jackson, Robert and Georg Sørensen. 2010. *Introduction to International Relations: Theories and Approaches*. Oxford: Oxford University Press.

Jäger, Siegfried. 2001. "Diskurs und Wissen: Theoretische und methodische Aspekte einer Kritischen Diskurs- und Dispositivanalyse." In: *Handbuch Sozialwissen-schaftliche Diskursanalyse*, edited by Reiner Keller et al. Wiesbaden: VS Verlag für Sozialwissenschaften, 2001: 81–112.

Keohane, Robert. 1988. "International Institutions: Two Approaches." *International Studies Quarterly* (4): 379–96.

Kerchner, Brigitte ed. 2006. *Foucault: Diskursanalyse der Politik. Eine Einführung.* Wiesbaden: VS Verlag für Sozialwissenschaften.

―――. "Diskursanalyse der Intersektionalität." In: *Intersektionalität—Theorien, Methoden und Politiken der Chancengleichheit,* edited by Dagmar Vinz and Sandra Smykalla. Münster: Westphälisches Dampfboot, 2011: 140–57.

Laclau, Ernesto ed. 1990. *New Reflections on the Revolutions of Our Time.* London: Verso.

―――. 2005. *On Populist Reason.* London: Verso.

Laclau, Ernesto and Chantal Mouffe. [1985] 2001. *Hegemony and Socialist Strategy.* London: Verso.

Lapid, Yosef. 1989. "The Third Debate: On the Prospects of International Theory in a Post-Positivist Era." *International Studies Quarterly* (3): 235–54.

Lefort, Claude and Marcel Gauchet, Marcel. 1990. "Über die Demokratie: Das Politische und die Insitutierung des Gesellschaftlichen." In: *Autonome Gesellschaft und libertäre Demokratie,* edited by Ulrich Rödel. Frankfurt am Main: Suhrkamp: 89–120.

Lemke, Thomas. 2014. "New materialisms: Foucault and 'the Government of Things.'" *Theory, Culture & Society* (0): 1–23.

Lenin, Vladimir. [1909] 1972. "Materialism and Empirio-criticism. Critical Comments on a Reactionary Philosophy." In: *Collected Works.* Moscow: Progress Publishers: 317–62.

Levin, Daniel J. 2012. *Recovering International Relations: The Promise of Sustainable Critique.* New York: Oxford University Press.

Levin, Daniel J. and Alexander Barder. 2012. "The World Is Too Much with Us': Reification and the Depoliticising of Via Media Constructivist IR." *Millennium— Journal of International Studies* (3): 585–604.

Marx, Karl and Friedrich Engels. [1845–6] 2004. *The German Ideology.* New York: International Publishers.

Mearsheimer, John. 2015. "E.H. Carr vs. Idealism: The Battle Rages On." *International Relations* 19 (2): 139–52.

Marttila, Tomas. 2015. "Post-Foundational Discourse Analysis: A Suggestion for a Research Program." *Forum Qualitative Sozialforschung/Forum Qualitative Social Research* (3). http://www.qualitative-research.net/index.php/fqs/article/view/2282.

Milliken, Jennifer. 1999. "The Study of Discourse in International Relations: A Critique of Research and Methods." *European Journal of International Relations* (2): 225–54.

Morgenthau, Hans. [1948] (1985). *Politics among Nations: The Struggle for Power and Peace.* New York.

Mouffe, Chantal. 2007. *Uber das Politische—Wider die kosmopolitische Illusion.* Frankfurt am Main: Suhrkamp.

Pantzerhielm, Laura. 2016. "Science and Democracy: Contingent regularities in scholarly discourse on European governance." In: *Forschungsberichte internationale Politik* (45), edited by Ingo Peters. Berlin: LIT-Verlag.

Rancière, Jacques. 1975. "Zur Theorie der Ideologie. Die Politik Althussers." In: *Wider den akademischen Marxismus.* Berlin: Merve Verlag: 5–50.

Risse, Thomas. 2003. "Konstruktivismus, Rationalismus und Theorien Internationaler Beziehungen:– Warum empirisch nichts so heiß gegessen wird, wie es theoretisch gekocht wurde." In: *Die neuen Internationalen Beziehungen. Forschungsstand und Perspektiven in Deutschland*, edited by Gunther Hellmann et al. Baden-Baden: Nomos: 99–132.

Saar, Martin. 2008. "Understanding Genealogy: History, Power, and the Self." *Journal of the Philosophy of History* (2): 295–314.

Schimmelfennig, Frank. 2008. *Internationale Politik*. Paderborn: Schöhingh.

Teschke, Benno. 2014. "IR Theory, Historical Materialism and the False Promise of International Historical Sociology." *Spectrum Journal of Global Studies* (1): 1–66.

van Dyk, Silke et al. 2014. "Discourse and beyond? Zum Verhältnis von Sprache, Materialität und Praxis." In: *Diskursforschung. Ein interdisziplinäres Handbuch. Band 1: Theorien, Methodologien und Kontroversen*, edited by Johannes Angermüller et al. Bielefeld: transcript: 348–63.

Vaughan-Williams, Nick and Tom Lundborg. 2015. "New Materialisms, Discourse Analysis, and International Relations : A Radical Intertextual Approach." *Review of International Studies* (1): 3–25.

Wallerstein, Immanuel. [1974] 2013. *Capitalist Agriculture and the Origins of the European World-Economy in the Sixteenth Century*. Berkeley: University of California Press.

———. 1979. *The Capitalist World-Economy*. Cambridge: Cambridge University Press.

Wendt, Alexander. 1995. "Constructing International Politics." *International Security* (1): 71–81.

Chapter 8

Marxism and Discourse

On the Meta-Theoretical Foundation of a Critical Materialist Discourse Analysis

Manuel Iretzberger

This chapter aims to provide a critique of contemporary approaches to discourse, thereby delineating the basic tenets of a possible alternative "Critical Materialist Discourse Analysis" (CMDA). The main intention is to buttress the central argument that materiality and the totality of social orders are crucial to understanding how society functions and hence need to be systematically incorporated into a discourse theory. Instead of reducing society to discourse, one should adopt a stratified ontology, conceiving discourse as embedded in and interlaced with a broader environment. In order to achieve this, the following paragraphs will first establish the problem at hand: It is argued that none of the existing strands of discourse analysis seem to be able to satisfy all of the functions deemed necessary for a critical theory. The second section then continues with a more thorough examination of constructivist versions of discourse analysis and their shortcomings, mainly focusing on the work of Laclau and Mouffe. After that, it is pointed out that Fairclough's Critical Discourse Analysis attempts to overcome those issues by drawing on Marxist arguments, but in fact remains too close to the aforementioned approaches. Thus, the final part of this chapter tries to follow a different route by reconceptualizing the role of discourse within Marxist thought and utilizing the insights of Critical Realism to outline some basic features of a CMDA which might be able to serve as a fruitful alternative to the existing approaches to discourse.

There exists an abundance of analytical approaches that try to investigate discourses. One might draw a rough line between those which fall under the label "(qualitative) content analysis," and "discourse analysis" proper (Bennett 2015, 989–990). While a broad definition of discourse as "a specific ensemble of ideas, concepts, and categorizations that are produced, reproduced and transformed to give meaning to physical and social relations"

(Hajer 1995, 40) seems to comprise the common denominator of both strands, there are several important aspects in which they differ. What sets discourse analysis in a narrower sense apart is the idea that it is not possible to neatly separate discourse from society and treat it as an isolable, self-contained object of study. Instead, it is understood as exercising a productive function, fundamentally shaping peoples' real-life relations, for it is the intersubjective construction of meaning via discourse that mediates their access to the extra-discursive realm (Jørgensen and Phillips 2002, 12). This has at least two implications: First, it follows that researchers do not stand above discourse. Their activity both has a certain effect on discourse itself, and necessarily presupposes a subjective, ideologically informed standpoint toward the subject matter at hand. Second, since discourse is not detached from real life, it not only produces identities, roles, etc., but it also couples them with access to power and resources (Fairclough 1985, 754–758). From this conception, most discourse analysts derive the need to engage critically with discourse and uncover such mechanisms. In order to achieve this, one has to conceptualize the way how discourse and the extra-discursive are entangled, exactly. This is indeed done in a plethora of ways, including approaches where adhering to this very dichotomy is objected to—instead the boundaries between the two realms are dissolved altogether (Joseph and Roberts 2004, 4). All in all, it can be stated that there is a tendency to start analysis from within discourse and focus on contingency and agency at the expense of taking into account external factors that might structure or even determine discourse itself (Jørgensen and Phillips 2002, 12).

The critical intention of Discourse Analysis as characterized so far certainly is to be welcomed. However, as shall be argued below, the sort of criticism it can offer—despite all its merits—contains some shortcomings. Being able to pinpoint those, necessitates laying open the ideal of criticism advocated here (which is subject to contestation, naturally). The label "critical" tends to be used rather carelessly, which calls for some clarification (Hammersley 1997, 238–240): While Kant's famous "Kritiken" were intended to be an investigation, mainly to evaluate phenomena and fathom their true nature, the term had been increasingly connoted with an explicitly leftist, emancipatory standpoint since at least the Frankfurt School (Billig 2003, 38–40). A further shift occurred with the rise of post-structuralist thought, which abandoned universalist notions of humanism or enlightenment and conceived criticism as questioning all claims of objective truth or essentialism, uncovering the contingencies of the certainties held dear by western thought in particular (Forchtner 2011, 2–3). Arguably, most versions of discourse analysis more or less side with this view. Against this, it shall be argued that critique should hold on to a certain notion of truth, being able to identify ideological claims and states of affairs which inhibit human flourishing, while remaining aware of its own embeddedness in specific historical circumstances and the dangers of metaphysics (Scott and Bhaskar 2015, 73). Rather than a priori viewing everything as contingent, critique has to be grounded in an analysis of the potentiality of things to become different (Adorno 1969, 60–61 and 164). Consequently, critique should neither be an end in itself. Instead of regarding everything as an equally eligible object of critique—a fate that radical epistemic relativism is condemned to in a way (Jones 2006, 29)—it should carefully determine what actually can be discarded. At the very least, this means that while critiquing minor, less "fundamental" issues is certainly important, one should not settle for it (possibly in order to avoid intellectual strains or risking one's social position (Billig 2003, 40–42)). The considerations above are meant to serve as a guiding line, which helps to uncover some problems discourse analysis might contain with regard to facilitating a forceful critique. Yet, the following sections will not narrowly stick to the aspect of critique alone, but will cover all kinds of conceptual shortcomings which can be arrived at from this starting point, so that the conditions of a possible alternative approach to discourse become apparent in a more comprehensive manner.

SHORTCOMINGS OF POST-MARXIST DISCOURSE ANALYSIS

The following discussion will center on Laclau and Mouffe's approach to discourse.

Given the vast number of versions of discourse analysis and the limited amount of space here, it is necessary to focus on one account primarily. It goes without saying that this cannot fully do justice to all the existing facets of discourse analysis, or serve as a substitute for a sufficiently comprehensive examination of Laclau and Mouffe's work in its own right. Even critics of post-positivism admit that there is an important difference, for example, between the post-structuralism of the likes of Foucault, Derrida or Deleuze, and postmodernists such as Baudrillard or Lyotard, and that the reception of individual authors is often too superficial (Callinicos 1991, 4–6). While having to be taken with a grain of salt, my focus on post-Marxist discourse analysis (PMDA) should help illustrating the problems that radically constructivist forms of discourse analysis share to some degree.

Foucault, who can be seen as one central influential figure for Laclau and Mouffe, starts off with the assumption of epistemological relativism. Since knowledge has to be discursively produced, scientific accounts might be regarded as "fictions" in a sense, for we lack the means to determine their validity in an objective manner (Foucault 1984, 72–73). Furthermore, the existence of society is dependent on the construction of meaning, making contingent all societal power relations which are established in discourse. According to Foucault, the uncovering of this nexus of power and knowledge makes his approach superior to Marxism's critical potential (1978, 321). Laclau and Mouffe's discourse theory draws heavily on those ideas. For them, only that what is talked about is considered to have an effect on society—unlike material factors outside of discourse, because as long as those are not made sense of intersubjectively they are essentially nonexistent (1985, 108). More precisely, there is no distinction between inside and outside of discourse at all, and neither is it possible to determine the truth of statements within the discursive realm (Jørgensen and Phillips 2002, 18). Nevertheless, Laclau and Mouffe hold an explicit (leftist) normative position (Curry 2004), proposing a strategy of gaining discursive hegemony by making use of populist arguments (Laclau 2005). They arrive there via a decisionism which can be seen as standing in the Nietzschean-Foucauldian tradition of making one's own truths in face of the absence of real ones (Saar 2007, 59 and 93).

Picking up on the questions of objectivity and normative standpoint, a first problem that can be pointed out is that the exclusive (relativist) "epistemologism" makes the choice of one's normative standpoint (van Dijk 1995, 20–21; Forchtner 2011, 10) arbitrary and less credible to a certain extent, possibly even entailing negative strategic effects. It would certainly be farfetched to claim that Ferraris' witticism that "[t]he postmodernists' dreams were realized by populists" (2014, 3) does apply here. Nevertheless, trying to legitimize arguments derived from an analysis which shies away from claims of validity could run into difficulties. Furthermore, such an approach can be successfully applied by the political right (Worsham and Olson 1999, 2) and there don't seem to be many compelling reasons why this should be all too inconsistent (Poole 2010, 149–151)—provided that the normative content is turned upside down, of course.

A second point that shall be raised here is the overall conception of the discursive.

Since everything is considered discourse-immanent and based on language, notions of structure and influence of material factors become problematic (Flatschart 2016, 43). It will be argued later that—very much in the spirit of this volume in general—the crude dichotomy between language and matter within some strands of orthodox Marxism has to be overcome. Here, the focus should lie on the aspect of structure within PMDA. While there is no need to confine oneself to an analysis of the "messy" micro-social realm, for discourse itself can bring about relatively permanent structures that evolve out of an aggregation of speech acts (Harvey 1996, 7–8), there is an inherent barrier when it comes to including structural influences from outside the discursive field. If one ignores how discourse is embedded in this broader environment, the conception of discursive mechanisms is bound to show some flaws (Sayer 1992, 105). Laclau and Mouffe are drawing on Marxism, but they do not and in fact cannot presume a (relatively) independent economic (or any other extra-discursive) material structure (Phelan and Dahlberg 2014). By equating language analysis with political or economic analysis (Jones 2004, 114), PMDA practically blinds itself to every phenomenon that is not "discourse-shaped." Indeed, there are great merits in demonstrating, for example, that what it means to be a worker, or what goods one desires is discursively mediated. However, those phenomena cannot be reduced to the latter, but have to be explained with regard to the relations of production that constitute capitalism as a social totality (Flatschart 2016, 48–49), even including crude material aspects such as human beings' objective need for survival, which, in a commodity-based society, equals having the ability to purchase goods (Jones 2004, 108–110).

Finally, the issue of emancipation needs to be addressed. Constructivist approaches tend to stress agency and the radical contingency of the status quo (Fairclough and Graham 2002, 18). This does not necessarily entail the naïve notion that "everything is possible and achievable," since discursive power relations can become fairly stable, and it would be unwarranted to suggest that post-structuralists are not painfully aware of this. There is a sort of idealist touch to it however, insofar as any form of (possibly) justified essentialism and material restraints are ruled out in principle (Jones 2006, 30; Sayer 1992, 146–148). Thus, the difficulties in determining what extent of change is reachable or desirable in given circumstances get exacerbated. This also applies to the question of where the potential for change should be situated. Change must not exclusively arise from the actions of agents, but can also stem from or be hindered by developments in the extra-discursive realm (occurring with or without the influence of human action), such as economic crises, or technological shifts (Flatschart 2016, 41). In absence of a different concept of how agency and structure, discursive and nondiscursive realm relate to each other, the ability to develop sound political strategies is severely inhibited. Altogether, approaches in this spirit might end up paving the way for more uncritical positions, which are celebrating any deviation from a status quo, sometimes contending themselves with changes in the discursive domain alone (Greenstone 1984, 444). It should lie within the scope of a critical theory of society to be able to identify promising forms of resistance and make the point that the case of, for example, corporate mascots in amusement parks refusing to act superficially happy in front of customers (Bryman 2004) does not fall under that category, as long as the oppressive structures that make such behavior necessary live on. The arguments against PMDA raised so far have been overly pointed, partly due to restrictions of space, partly to depict the potential weak spots in question in a more clear-cut manner. Thus, they hardly apply to any strand of radical constructivist discourse analysis to their full extent. Yet, assuming that they all at least have the tendency to *partly* fall in some of the traps which were outlined above legitimizes the probing for an alternative take on the study of discourse.

THE PROMISES OF CRITICAL DISCOURSE ANALYSIS

Fairclough's Critical Discourse Analysis (CDA) might prove to be such an alternative, since he too is discontent with conventional forms of discourse analysis (Fairclough 1985, 754–758). Given the variety of approaches that stick close to CDA's central tenets (van Dijk 1995, 17–18), focusing on the former alone might seem problematic. It can be justified by considering Fairclough's central role within CDA approaches and due to his explicit attempts to overcome problems similar to the ones outlined above. In the following, it shall be demonstrated, however, that Fairclough's CDA remains closer to these positions than he might like to admit. Thereby, insights might be gained about what pitfalls are to avoid when trying to create a promising alternative to PMDA. Just as in the section above, this discussion unfortunately has to ignore the many facets of CDA and largely pass over the advantages it undoubtedly has.

Departing from an openly normative standpoint (Jones 2004, 98–99), Fairclough aims at laying open "background knowledge" working as ideology in seemingly neutral discourses (Fairclough 1985, 744). In doing so, he wants to draw on Marxism in a more systematic way than PMDA does. Thus, he differentiates between discourses and factors external to them, conceptualizing both as mutually interdependent (Ibid., 747). He devises a three-level model of discourse in which language comprises firstly a communicative event (i.e., text), secondly a discursive practice that needs to be constantly produced and consumed, and thirdly the social practice the text belongs to (Fairclough 1992, 73). Institutions are considered a central element of analysis, mediating between macro- and microlevel (Fairclough 1985, 748). Thus it becomes possible to examine discourses with regard to the specific setting they are occurring in. Within those settings, ideological-discursive formations are operating, shaping the mode and content of the "sayable," and regulating access to discourses by determining eligible actors (van Dijk 1995, 20; Milliken 1999, 229). Hence, discourses are both the consequence of and enable the pursuit of material interests (Fairclough 1985, 751).

Before examining how exactly CDA attempts to incorporate Marxist arguments into its framework, it is useful to consider some general methodological issues that have been raised against it, for if one seeks to avoid the pitfalls of relativism, questions regarding the validity of a possible CMDA should not be brushed aside too easily. Widdowson, among others, has argued that

Fairclough neglects observing how text is actually received by its audience, instead trying to infer the effects it has directly from semiotic analysis (1996, 58; 2000, 5–10; Breeze 2011, 510). Treating text as an isolated object and deducing its ideological efficacy from mere linguistic-grammatical features (Verschueren 2001, 69) can indeed be seen as problematic. While it appears as if Fairclough is formulating ad-hoc hypotheses based on his analysis of discourse (van Dijk 1995, 24), it might be argued that he already has the results in mind prior to it. Through (possibly unintentional) selective sampling and interpreting (Poole 2010, 146) he is able to draw conclusions about his empirical material which fit his critical aims. The downside of this is, that it makes the whole endeavor somewhat arbitrary so that it falls short of overcoming the problems of relativism, outlined above. Carefully attempting to stay clear of the Scylla of positivism, he gets drawn in by the Charybdis of radical post-positivism.

The way in which Fairclough tries to reconcile his desire to be critical and his reading of Marx is illuminating with regard to CDA's methodological problems. In a peculiar manner, he regards "Marx as a discourse analyst 'avant la lettre'" (Fairclough and Graham 2002, 3), stating that for the latter "language is the only way we have of grasping the diachronics of changing social circumstances" (Ibid., 19), thus downplaying the materialist in Marx. It is Fairclough's understanding of dialectics that seems to inhibit him from following Marx in some central aspects (Flatschart 2016, 27–29). For Marx, material factors (including the social relations between people, of course) largely determine the individual and collective consciousness (Marx 1974, 578; Flatschart 2016, 39). However, agency and structure co-constitute each other (the specific configuration of this interrelation has to be discussed later on), while in Fairclough's CDA two monolithic blocks—a material, interest-based structure, and a realm of discourse—interact quite mechanically (Jones 2004, 107). This conception entails some problems. Fairclough falls back into a sort of idealism (Poole 2010, 142), in the sense that he tries to secure some potential for change within the realm of discourse, since he is not able to identify it elsewhere. Equating semiotic with political analysis (Jones 2006, 24), he assumes that language can fundamentally alter social relations, without accounting for the need of actual transformative practice. The downsides of this conception become apparent when looking at empirical CDA-studies. For example, Fairclough repeatedly tries to demonstrate the oppressive effects of neoliberalism or post-Fordism (Chouliaraki and Fairclough 2001, 2–5). While there isn't necessarily a problem with those concepts as such, and Fairclough manages to generate lots of valuable insights with them, the way in which they are applied is precarious in a way. Not being able to show how they are embedded in and relate to the social totality as a whole exactly, they are taken as a rather isolated given fact which doesn't have to be derived from the former. All that is left to do for Fairclough then, is to identify instances in which language contributes to the creation or perpetuation of those regimes.

This dichotomy between a discursive field where change happens and an extra-discursive field where material interests reside contains several drawbacks. First of all, it results in a tendency to personalize and blame (van Dijk 1995, 22). Since there is no explicit conception of how structure and agency are interrelated and how the entirety of social relations both affects peoples' scope of action and the formation of their interests, the easiest way for Fairclough to bring material interests in and try to overcome the flaws of PMDA (Fairclough 1985, 753, and 759) is to resort to conceiving them as unmediated, rational interests of clichéd villains (Breeze 2011, 515). A second issue that should be mentioned here is that the lack of grounding within a holistic view of the social leads to difficulties in finding and justifying CDA's own standpoint (very similar to the problems of PMDA, seen above) (Hammersley 1997, 242–243). Since the choice of the object of critique doesn't have to be justified and since there are no proper methodological guidelines on how to select and interpret corresponding bodies of text, virtually anything can be demonstrated through CDA. Thus, Poole (2010, 149–151) is able to show how Fairclough's method could be modified and then utilized by the political right, while Jones criticizes Fairclough's political stance itself (2006, 25–26). All in all, it can be argued that CDA suffers from being in a problematic, inclined position between radical constructivist conceptions of discourse and (pseudo-)Marxist arguments (Flatschart 2016, 46; Jones 2004, 116). A materialist alternative, aiming at overcoming some of PMDA's flaws would need to theorize social totality and the dialectical relations between its parts more thoroughly, instead of merely stipulating the existence of some material factors and economic interests and adding them as an additional sphere to the post-structuralist notion of discourse.

TOWARD A CRITICAL MATERIALIST DISCOURSE ANALYSIS

Problems of Combining Marxism and Discourse

Fairclough's difficulties while re-interpreting Marx in order to make his work fruitful for the study of discourse don't come as a surprise when one brings to mind the latter's constant insistence on issues such as the importance of the socio-economic realm, or matter and base outweighing ideas and superstructure, respectively (Bernstein 1981, 436–445). Two conclusions can be drawn here: First, Marxism indeed represents a textbook example for a materialist approach in general, and second, it is highly questionable if discourse analysis might find a central place in it, due to its relative disregard for language.

Nevertheless, the remainder of this chapter is an inquiry into the possibility of a CMDA with Marxism being the guiding theoretical frame. This choice is not made by hearkening back to ad verecundiam arguments, but because Marx' course of action seems promising when it comes to counteracting PMDA's aporiae.

Assuming a Marxist discourse analysis is possible, it would certainly put more emphasis on the constitution of discourses by the nondiscursive than on their own constitutive effects (Jørgensen and Phillips 2002, 20), examining in which material environment ideas are embedded in (Bernstein 1981, 437). Compared to constructivist approaches, the general logic of reasoning would be reversed in a way, always primarily accounting for how discourse is integrated within capitalism before considering possible autonomous contributions discourse might add. Yet, in those instances where Marx dealt with discourses, it was in the form of a critique of ideology or other ways of relating them to some notion of a material base (Jones 2004, 119–121). In order for a Marxist version of discourse analysis to make sense then, discourse would have to be understood in a different way: Granting it a role in the constant reproduction of social relations doesn't seem to be sufficient as long as it is deemed analytically negligible because it is seen as essentially caught within the bounds of a material, nondiscursive base.

Now, very much in the spirit of this volume, revisiting the term "materialism" should indeed be welcomed, because it might not only dispose of the simplistic dichotomies of the orthodox Marxist tradition, but it could also help to clarify things here. It seems sensible to abandon a "crude" materialism (against which Marx himself argued) that juxtaposes matter and language/discourse, and to recognize the material efficacy of ideational structures, instead (Wolf 2008, 47 and 50). A materialist approach then would oppose idealism in a spiritualistic, illusionary, ideological sense only. However, it might be problematic to get rid of any differentiations within the concept of materialism. While matter shouldn't be hypostatized as a self-contained, nonsocial category, one should retain the analytical awareness to identify possible differences between material structures that have to be constantly reproduced via discourse and those who exert their influence without this mediation. The latter are being brought into focus by studies on affect(s), for example (Jameson 2009, 29). Certainly, this whole complex would need more elaborating, but for the purpose of this inquiry the most important implication consists in the observation that a renewed materialism doesn't solve, albeit it shifts, the problem at hand.

One can assert, that while the problem of incompatibility between a Marxist *materialism* and the study of discourse diminishes, there remains an obstacle in the form of some kind of *extra-discursive* material base, or at least a structuring social totality on which discourse by and large depends. There might

be good reasons to abandon conceptions like this altogether, in order to allow
for the uninhibited study of discourse. But at the same time holding on to
them promises being able to avoid the shortcomings of post-Marxist thought
mentioned above—one might also imagine various forms of division of labor
between those approaches. On the other hand, when one does decide to stick
with a closer reading of Marx, there is a need to incorporate the productive
power of discourse more thoroughly (Jones 2006, 30–31). Without that, one
would be in constant danger of ending up in a simplistic material determinism,
which doesn't do justice to the complexity of the world. Thus, the difficult
path toward a CMDA which differs from both orthodox Marxism and post-
structuralism should not—pace Fairclough—end at a mere external combination of both, but has to lead through a careful reformulation of how capitalism
and discourse are interrelated. Such a conception has to ascribe to discourse a
role that is sufficiently autonomous in order to make it more than just material
for a critique of ideology, and at the same time avoid reducing capitalism to
a mere "discursive system" (Dahlberg 2014). Critical Realism (CR) might be
helpful here.

Critical Realism, Marx, and Discourse

CR, being a metatheory for the sciences needs to be supplemented with
substantial theoretical approaches (Fairclough, Jessop and Sayer 2004, 24).
While it is commonly held that is highly compatible with Marxism (Bhaskar
and Callinicos 2007), as well as with moderate constructivist approaches, it
shall become clear below that it is at odds with being combined with the epistemologically oriented approach of post-structuralism, despite the arguments
of some scholars (cf. Joseph and Roberts 2004, 4). CR insists on sorting out
ontological questions before turning to epistemological ones, claiming that
there exists an intransitive realm of the world, operating independently of
our awareness of it (Bhaskar 1998, 12). Reality is conceptualized as being
layered, consisting of the level of the real, where unobservable mechanisms
are causally evoking change (Kurki 2008), the actual level, where events
manifest themselves, and the empirical level, which is phenomenologically
accessible to us (Flatschart 2016, 45). Even though the social is an open system, that is, there are many different mechanisms operating at the same time
and generating emergent effects, CR is relatively optimistic that we can gain
reliable knowledge about it (Scott and Bhaskar 2015, 10 and 22).

What combining CR and Marxism promises on a general level is, on the
one hand, providing access for CR to the formulation of more substantial
claims about the world and opening up the way to empirical research, and
on the other hand, to equip Marxism with a fundamental catalogue of necessary existing features of the world which is systematic and detached from

a specific theoretical lens (Fiaz 2014, 497). In the case at hand, CR might be utilized to devise a basic agent-structure-framework in which interaction entails emergent effects, thus seeing structure as tightly interwoven with agency, but in possession of a distinct substantiality, partly developing a logic of its own (Archer 2010, 245–247). This concept helps to keep in mind the necessary role of discourse in upholding and changing the social structure and thus avoids hastily overlooking anything that might not be immediately visible from a Marxist perspective. Thus, in summary, one starts off with a basic outlook that approaches discourse from the outside (while taking it seriously), in contrast to those different strands of post-structuralism, which are more or less caught within it (Ryner 2006). Only then this model has to be filled with concrete Marxist assumptions about the defining character of the contemporary structure, namely, capitalism, and analyze how it exactly relates to discourse.

It needs to be noted, however, that introducing CR doesn't magically make all the difficulties in bringing together Marxism and discourse go away. The two approaches can't be simply added together, as it is arguably done in Fairclough's more recent engagement with CR (Breeze 2011, 505), but decisions about possible incompatibilities have to be made, in order to arrive at a proper synthesis. One central aspect in this regard is the scope of mechanisms. Brown, Slater, and Spencer (2002) argue that CR tends to focus on middle range phenomena, initially granting every causal mechanism a comparable efficacy. Against this, they argue that it is necessary to search for a fundamental, elementary mechanism, which internally connects phenomena within a given social totality. Ascribing this central role—"as a total history of society, in which all other sectoral histories are convened" (Thompson 1978, 262)—to capitalism might tip the scales in favor of Marxism, seeing discourse as a subordinated phenomenon that nevertheless has to be systematically included in terms of its acting as a causal power.

Toward a Critical Marxist Approach to Discourse Analysis

There is no space for further elaborating on the details of the proposed approach but at least some general conclusions can be laid out in broad strokes. Departing from capitalism as the inner connection of the contemporary social totality, one can begin to examine how it systematically influences the way in which people's consciousness is constantly reconfigured in their social praxis (Flatschart 2016, 29 and 35). Discourse is thus always seen in relation to capitalism, which both structurally inhibits or enhances agents' room for maneuvering, and takes part in the shaping of their believes and interests. This relational view also provides a point of reference against which one can judge to what extent discourse exerts a morphogenetic influence, namely, (partly) alters the extra-discursive conditions. It is important to note that the elements of discourse shouldn't be grasped on a phenomenological level alone, or taken at face value (Joseph and Roberts 2004, 5). Social interaction cannot be reduced to explicitly uttered speech acts (Bhaskar 2009, 127). Instead, the wider context, in which certain discourses arise and to what extent articulated rules or believes are actually internalized and thus function as the basis of actual human practice, has to be constantly kept in mind. In conjunction with this, it also has to be stressed that intra-discursive predications or themes don't have to correspond with the reality outside of the discursive realm, in fact they "may be purely and simply an ephemeral fad" (Jones 2004, 113). Thus, there remains some room for a critique of ideology.

In terms of method, leaving behind any simplistic notion of a mechanistic influence that capitalism is supposed to have on discourse and which would enable predicting the outcome of discourses by deriving it from the former, complicates matters significantly. Following Jones' rather similar understanding of discourse, one can say that CMDA necessitates repeated cross-checking, "[tracing] the logic, that is, the *dialectic*, of the movement through repeated cycles from real practices to 'signifying practices' and back to real practices again" (Ibid., 116), in order to allow for insights about how the different spheres are connected. This also precludes a generalizable

> method or procedure that can be applied to 'discourse' in general which can establish either its ideological function or its causal role in the social process. Only positive and integral knowledge of the historically developing practice of humanity and of the place of the alienated and fractured spheres of political, economic and other forms of activity within that practice will do as the foundation and premise for a concrete understanding of the import and implications of the relevant discourse (Ibid., 122).

One hint that might direct the search for relevant discourses and help to determine their relation with the societal whole comes directly from Marx:

> It is, in reality, much easier to discover by analysis the earthly core of the misty creations of religion, than, conversely, it is, to develop from the actual relations of life the corresponding celestialised forms of those relations. The latter method is the only materialistic, and therefore the only scientific one. (Marx 1887, 330)

Instead of simply assigning certain material interests to the "misty creations" of discourse, and seeing the former being fulfilled by the latter, as it happens in CDA, the aim of CMDA has to consist of analyzing how certain ideologies or discursive formations are constructed precisely while being entangled with the social totality of capitalism. This procedure might leave room for discourse insofar as it can—and probably mostly does—substantially deviate from what one might directly derive from the "necessities" of capitalism. Applying this lens allows identifying those instances where the contingent developments of discourse either bring about (quasi-) autonomous effects, or contribute to the transformation of the structure of social totality.

While there can be no standardized textbook method to CMDA, there remains the task of finding guidelines for conducting research that aim for some degree of rationally determinable validity, and not succumbing to positivist demands at the same time (Adorno 1969, 164). Finally, coming back to the understanding of critique this chapter started out with, it should be said that such an approach can alleviate determining what would constitute real progress in view of the social totality, and in formulating viable strategies for feasible change (Jones 2006, 29). Thus, the emancipatory potential of CMDA lies in being able to identify and "disentangle meaning systems that are historically necessary [...] but still false, as they can (in principle) be deciphered as being systematic misrepresentations of a deeper level of emancipatory possibility" (Flatschart 2016, 38). Until then, there remains a lot of conceptual work to be done. But, at least, what has been attempted to demonstrate is that despite all the difficulties revolving around Marxism and discourse—given the shortcomings of the approaches criticized throughout—the search for an alternative (not necessarily a replacement) seems justified and promising. By asserting the need for a different approach toward discourse and outlining the rough direction which it could lead to, this chapter also sought to contribute to discourse studies in a more general way. It invites other scholars to further work on the desideratum of a CMDA—thereby increasing the variety of critical discourse studies—as well as encourages a fruitful, critical dialogue with post-Marxist and post-structuralist positions.

BIBLIOGRAPHY

Adorno, Theodor W. 1969. *Minima Moralia—Reflexionen aus dem beschädigten Leben.* Frankfurt/Main: Suhrkamp.
Archer, Margaret S. 2010. "Morphogenesis versus Structuration: On Combining Structure and action." *The British Journal of Sociology* 61: 225–252.
Bennett, Andrew. 2015. "Found in Translation: Combining Discourse Analysis with Computer Assisted Content Analysis." *Millennium* 43 (3): 984–997.
Bernstein, Howard R. 1981. "Marxist Historiography and the Methodology of Research Programs." *History and Theory* 20 (4): 424–449.
Bhaskar, Roy. 1998. *The Possibility of Naturalism.* London/New York: Verso.
———. 2009. *Scientific Realism and Human Emancipation.* London: Verso.
Bhaskar, Roy and Alex Callinicos. 2007. "Marxism and Critical Realism: A Debate." *Journal of Critical Realism* 1 (2): 89–114.

Billig, Michael. 2003. "Critical Discourse Analysis and the Rhetoric of Critique." In *Critical Discourse Analysis: Theory and Interdisciplinarity,* edited by Gilbert Weiss und Ruth Wodak, 35–46. Houndmills/Basingstoke/New York: Palgrave.

Breeze, Ruth. 2011. "Critical Discourse Analysis and Its Critics." *Pragmatics* 21 (4): 493–525.

Brown, Andrew, Gary Slater, and David Spencer. 2002. "Driven to abstraction? Critical Realism and the Search for the 'Inner Connection' of Social Phenomena." *Cambridge Journal of Economics* 26 (6): 773–788.

Bryman, Alan. 2004. *The Disneyization of Society.* London/Thousand Oaks/New Delhi: Sage.

Callinicos, Alex. 1991. *Against Postmodernism—A Marxist Critique.* Cambridge: Polity Press.

Chouliaraki, Lilie, and Norman Fairclough. 2001. *Discourse in Late Modernity: Rethinking Critical Discourse Analysis.* Edinburgh: Edinburgh University Press.

Curry, Neil. 2004. "Lost in Transit: Reconceptualising the Real." In *Realism Discourse and Deconstruction,* edited by Jonathan Joseph und John M. Roberts, 137–149. London: Routledge.

Dahlberg, Lincoln. 2014. "Capitalism as a Discursive System? Interrogating Discourse Theory's Contribution to Critical Political Economy." *Critical Discourse Studies* 11 (3): 257–271.

Fairclough, Norman. 1985. "Critical and Descriptive Goals in Discourse Analysis." *Journal of Pragmatics* 9: 739–763.

———. 1992. *Discourse and Social Change.* Cambridge: Polity Press.

———. and Phil Graham. 2002. "Marx as a Critical Discourse Analyst: The genesis of a critical method and its relevance to the critique of global capital." http://eprints.qut.edu.au/29764/1/ graham29764.pdf. Originally published in *Sociolinguistic Studies* 3 (1): 185–229.

———. Bob Jessop, and Andrew Sayer. 2004. "Critical Realism and Semiosis (Revised Vision)." In *Realism Discourse and Deconstruction,* edited by Jonathan Joseph und John M. Roberts, 23–42, London: Routledge.

Ferraris, Maurizio. 2014. *Manifesto of New Realism.* New York: Suny Press.

Fiaz, Nazya. 2014. "Constructivism Meets Critical Realism: Explaining Pakistan's State Practice in the Aftermath of 9/11." *EJIR* 20 (2): 491–515.

Flatschart, Elmar. 2016. "Critical Realist Critical Discourse Analysis: A Necessary Alternative to Post-Marxist Discourse Theory." *Journal of Critical Realism* 15 (1): 21–52.

Forchtner, Bernhard. 2011. "Critique, the Discourse–Historical Approach, and the Frankfurt School." *Critical Discourse Studies* 8 (1): 1–14.

Foucault, Michel. 1978. *Die Ordnung der Dinge—Eine Archäologie der Humanwissenschaften.* Frankfurt/Main: Suhrkamp.

———. 1984. "Truth and Power." In *The Foucault Reader,* edited by Paul Rabinow, 51–75. New York: Pantheon.

Greenstone, David J. 1984. "Reviewed Work: Marx and Wittgenstein: Social Praxis and Social Explanation. By David Rubinstein." *American Journal of Sociology* 90 (2): 443–444.

Hajer, Marten. 1995. *The Politics of Environmental Discourse. Ecological Modernization and the Policy Process.* Oxford: Clarendon Press.

Hammersley, Martyn. 1997. "On the Foundations of Critical Discourse Analysis." *Language & Communication* 17 (3): 237–248.

Harvey, David. 1996. *Justice, Nature and the Geography of Difference.* Cambridge, MA: Blackwell.

Jameson, Fredric. 2009. *The Antinomies of Realism.* London: Verso.

Jones, Peter E. 2004. "Discourse and the Materialist Conception of History: Critical Comments on Critical Discourse Analysis." *Historical Materialism* 12 (1): 97–125.

———. 2006. "Why There is No Such Thing as 'Critical Discourse Analysis.'" *Language & Communication,* 27 (4): 1–32.

Jørgensen, Marianne, and Louise Phillips. 2002. *Discourse Analysis as Theory and Method.* London, Thousand Oaks, and New Delhi: Sage.

Joseph, Jonathan, and John M. Roberts. 2004. "Introduction." In *Realism Discourse and Deconstruction,* 1–19. London: Routledge.

Kurki, Milja. 2008. *Causation in International Relations—Reclaiming Causal Analysis.* Cambridge: Cambridge University Press.

Laclau, Ernesto. 2005. *On Populist Reason.* London: Verso.

Laclau, Ernesto, and Mouffe, Chantal. 1985. *Hegemony and socialist strategy: towards a radical democratic politics.* London: Verso.

Marx, Karl. 1887. *Capital, Volume I,* Moscow: Progress Publishers.

———. 1974. *Marx an Ferdinand Lassalle in Berlin, 16.01. 1861.* MEW 30: 578. Berlin: Dietz.

Milliken, Jennifer. 1999. "The Study of Discourse in International Relations: A Critique of Research and Methods." *EJIR* 5 (2): 225–254.

Phelan, Sean, and Lincoln Dahlberg. 2014. "Introduction." *Critical Discourse Studies* 11 (3): 255–256.

Poole, Brian. 2010. "Commitment and Criticality: Fairclough's Critical Discourse Analysis Evaluated." *International Journal of Applied Linguistics* 20 (2): 137–155.

Ryner, Magnus. 2006. "International Political Economy: Beyond the Poststructuralist/Historical Materialist Dichotomy." In *International Political Economy and Poststructural Politics,* edited by Marieke de Goede, 139–156. London: Palgrave.

Saar, Martin. 2007. *Genealogie als Kritik—Geschichte und Theorie des Subjekts nach Nietzsche und Foucault.* Frankfurt/Main: Campus.

Sayer, Andrew. 1992. *Method in Social Science.* Second Edition. London/New York: Routledge.

Scott, David and Roy Bhaskar. 2015. *Roy Bhaskar—A Theory of Education.* Heidelberg: Springer.

Thompson, Edward P. 1978. *The Poverty of Theory and Other Essays.* New York: Monthly Review Press.

Van Dijk, Teun. 1995. "Aims of Critical Discourse Analysis." *Japanese Discourse* 1: 17–27.

Verschueren, Jef. 2001. "Predicaments of Criticism." *Critique of Anthropology* 21 (1): 59–81.

Widdowson, Henry G. 1996. "Reply to Fairclough: Discourse and Interpretation: Conjectures and Refutations." *Language and Literature* 5 (1): 57–69.

————. 2000. "On the Limitations of Linguistics Applied." *Applied Linguistics* 21 (1): 3–25.

Wolf, Frieder Otto. 2008. "Ein Materialismus für das 21. Jahrhundert." In *Kritik und Materialität,* edited by Alex Demirović, 41–59. Münster: Westfälisches Dampfboot.

Worsham, Lynn and Gary A. Olson. 1999. "Hegemony and the Future of Democracy: Ernesto Laclau's Political Philosophy." *JAC* 19 (1): 1–34.

Chapter 9

Semiosis and Discursivity of the Commodity-Form

The Role of the "Commodity-Message Model" in Ferruccio Rossi-Landi's Materialist Semiotics

Giorgio Borrelli

How can a semiotic method be defined as *materialist*? Applying the Marxian analysis of *commodity-form* to research on language and communication, the Italian scholar Ferruccio Rossi-Landi (1921–1985) tried to answer this question. More specifically, Rossi-Landi maintained that the dialectical analysis of the commodity could be fundamentally understood as a *semiotic analysis of the commodity as a message*.

In this paper I aim to illustrate how certain aspects of Rossi-Landi's *materialist semiotics* could have heuristic value with respect to the methodological implications of a materialist analysis of language and discourse. To demonstrate this assumption, I will focus on the dialectical foundations of Rossi-Landi's *homological method*, namely, a method based on the hypothesis according to which *production of material artifacts* and *production of signs and messages* are characterized by a fundamental similarity, due to a common *structure*. Secondly, I will try to explain why the homological method—understood as an analytical device—is coherent with the theoretical (and categorical) framework of the Marxian materialist approach.

First of all, such a coherency lies in the role attributed by Rossi-Landi to the fundamental category of the Marxian critique of political economy: that is, the *commodity*. In line with the semiotic model of Charles W. Morris (1901–1979), Rossi-Landi affirms that a commodity can be interpreted as a *message* to which are connected several layers of *signification* and *interpretation*. Furthermore, just like a message, a commodity is produced and exchanged following specific *programs* and *codes*. Indeed, we could say that Marx—reconstructing the dialectic of value-form, and the valorization process of capital—has disclosed the highly formalized structure of the different programs and codes subtending the production of commodities. From such a perspective, the exchange of commodities in a capitalist economy can be analyzed as a concrete form of nonverbal communication.

Moreover, a commodity could be understood as a sign vehicle designating the *programs* through which the economic sphere of production interprets and satisfies the numerous needs arising in the economic sphere of consumption. Such a thesis implies a corollary: social needs are organized and planned in the economic sphere of production. This means that commodity-form can also be considered as a vehicle of certain forms of *ideology*, which Rossi-Landi understands as a discursive *organization of society and human practice*. To sum up, the commodity could be understood as a crossroads of verbal and nonverbal forms of semiosis.

STRUCTURE AND PURPOSES OF THE STUDY

In the following I will try to explain why certain categories and theoretical models, typical of the Marxian theory, could be relevant for a materialist approach to discourse and language. More specifically, I would like to illustrate why Marxian Dialectical Materialism could be considered as a *semiotic* method. In this regard, I will hypothesize that Marx, through his analysis of the commodity-form, has drawn a theoretical and methodological schema which is *inherently* semiotic. The Italian scholar Ferruccio Rossi-Landi has tried to frame the Marxian theory in such a perspective, considering certain assumptions of the critique of political economy as a pioneering example of nonverbal semiotics. The reason of this hypothesis lies in the fact that Marx implicitly describes the commodity as a *bearer* of several strata of signification. Therefore, Rossi-Landi's *materialistic semiotics* will constitute my theoretical point of reference.

In the next three sections, I will illustrate how the term "materialist" assumes two different—but strictly interrelated—meanings. Such a polysemy depends on the fact that Rossi-Landi structures his theoretical framework on two analytical levels. The first level is based on the semiotic model of Charles W. Morris; it regards the relation between *signs* and *bodies*. In this case, meaning is constructed through an opposition to what Rossi-Landi defines as "idealist semiotics." The second level refers explicitly to the relationship between sign systems and the material processes of social reproduction.

In the fifth section—in line with Rossi-Landi's *commodity-message model*—I will try to explain that the commodity-form can be analyzed as the bearer of three different—but strictly connected—semiotic levels: (a) the level constituted by the dialectic between production and consumption; (b) the level of the valorization process of capital; (c) the level of ideological discourse.

In what follows, I will try to explain how the several forms of nonverbal and verbal semiosis are implied in each of these fundamental layers.

MATERIALIST SEMIOTICS AND THE MARXIAN METHOD

"Materialist semiotics" is the formula with which Rossi-Landi summed up the goal of his research. From a very general point of view, the term obviously refers to Marxian-Engelsian dialectical and historical materialism, implying a refusal of *idealism, naturalism,* and *mechanistic materialism.*

In his *Ideas for a Manifesto of Materialistic semiotics* (1974), Rossi-Landi affirms that: "a materialistic semiotics must be a semiotics founded on social reality, on the actual ways in which [humans] interact among themselves and with the rest of the living and nonliving world. It cannot examine sign systems apart from the other social processes with which they are functioning all along" (Rossi-Landi 1992, 278). In my opinion, such an assumption connects Rossi-Landi's materialist semiotics with certain fundamental theses of Critical Discourse Analysis (CDA), as developed by Fairclough. More specifically, according to Fairclough, CDA focusses on the "relations between discourse and other social elements (power relations, ideologies, institutions, social identities, and so forth)" (Fairclough 2012, 1).

From such a perspective, the concept of "discourse" refers to all the "semiotic ways of construing aspects of the world (physical, social or mental) which can generally be identified with different positions or perspectives of different groups of social actors" (Fairclouhg 2012, 4). Even if a terminological comparison between the materialist-semiotic approach and CDA is beyond the purposes of this paper, I would like just to underline that a parallelism can be established between Fairclough's notion of "discourse" and Rossi-Landi's concept of "ideology." As I will explain in what follows, Rossi-Landi's concept of "ideology" refers to the hypothesis according to which all social relations and behaviors are coordinated by a *general program* corresponding to the perspective from which the ruling class conceives and, therefore, plans the social order. On the opposite side—according to Rossi-Landi—the working class should oppose its own ideological discourse, facing conservative ideology with a revolutionary approach. In the light of this thesis, I will also maintain that *ideology* coincides with the set of *discourses* that define the needs involved in the system of commodity-production; in this sense, ideology organizes the several ways in which those needs should be satisfied by production—obviously, prioritizing the valorization process of capital. From such a perspective, it may be possible to affirm that the general relation between production and consumption is structured according to certain forms of *discourse* and, therefore, that such a relation is ideologically determined.

According to Rossi-Landi, the best way to describe social reality is to approach it in terms of *social reproduction* (*gesellschaftliche Reproduktion*): "social reproduction is the totality of processes by which any society—from a primitive tribe to contemporary highly developed societies—proceeds in time, preserving itself while at the same time administering some changes in its own internal structure." (Rossi-Landi 1992, 278).

Describing social reproduction as the *totality of social processes*, Rossi-Landi follows certain fundamental assumptions of Marx's 1857 *Einleitung*—that is, the introduction to the *Grundrisse* (1857–1858). As is well known, in this unpublished work, Marx criticizes certain methodological incongruences of classical political economy, and, in doing so, he delineates certain fundamental insights of his method. For this reason, *Einleitung* constituted a reference point for several generations of Marxists scholars, especially for those who were interested in detecting and reconstructing the methodological foundations of dialectical materialism. Such an attention also characterized the research of one of the most important Italian Marxist philosophers of twentieth century, Galvano Della Volpe (1895–1968). According to Della Volpe, *Einleitung* contains the elemental core of the Marxian method, which consists of two analytical passages: (a) arising from the concrete to the abstract; (b) going down again from the abstract to the concrete. Della Volpe defines this method as the "concrete-abstract-concrete circle," or method of the "determined abstraction." (Della Volpe 1969, 196) I will now attempt to explain the meaning of this metaphorical reading of Marxian dialectics.

Very briefly, in *Einleitung* Marx maintains that classical political economy starts its analytical procedure by considering "the real and the concrete," (Marx 1973, 100) that is, by considering certain categories in a very general way, without any reference to their specifications. For example, classical political economy starts its analyses considering that population in general is the *subject of production*, overlooking the fact that population is divided in classes, hence, the fact that production is organized according to such a division. Political economy represents the concrete by means of an abstraction—that is, the category of "population"—but such an analytical operation is *undetermined*, because it represents the concrete as a "chaotic" (*ibid.*) totality, that is, a totality in which the several and problematic relations between its parts are not explained. To sum up, classical political economy abstracts from the concrete, stopping its analysis at the level of abstract determinations; hence, its categories are vague, and its abstractions are *undetermined*. Using the metaphor introduced by Della Volpe, classical political economy proceeds from the concrete to the abstract, but it does not return from the abstract to the concrete. On the contrary, *returning from the abstract to the concrete* constitutes the distinctive feature of the Marxian method.

But what does "returning to the concrete" actually mean? According to Della Volpe, such an idea is contained in another passage of the 1857 introduction, in which Marx affirms that the analysis of the concrete should proceed by structuring a complex of more and more specific categories, that is, it must proceed from the general concepts to the "simplest determinations." (ibid.) As a further analytical moment, these simple and abstract categories should be connected to each other in order to create a new schema of the initial concrete, a new *representation* of a totality in which all the *relations* between its parts are clarified and explained. For example, to understand why labor is the source of wealth, it is necessary to connect the category of labor with all the peculiar determinations of the capitalist mode of production, namely, with certain specific categories such as "commodity," "value," "money," "exploitation," etc. In this way, the whole *valorization process of capital* arises as a *new concrete*, as Marx would say, as "the concentration of many determinations, hence unity of the diverse." (ibid.) According to Della Volpe, the initial undetermined totality is now a *structured totality*, a "manifold unity" (*unità molteplice*) (Della Volpe, *Logica*, 196) or a "*determined abstraction*." (ibid.) In this sense, the analytical procedure returns from the abstract to the concrete.

Defining social reproduction as the totality of processes by which a certain society produces and reproduces itself, Rossi-Landi refers exactly to the concept of "structured totality" as theorized by Della Volpe. More specifically, Rossi-Landi presents the category of "social reproduction" as a schema, an *abstract construction* characterized by three analytical levels. The first two levels are methodological devices typical of the Marxian theory: (a) the triad constituted by *production*, *exchange*, and *consumption*—as Marx schematizes in the *Einleitung*; and (b) the relationship between *structure* and *superstructure*—as Marx schematizes in the famous *Vorworth* of 1859; the third level represents the peculiar characteristic of Rossi-Landi's model: (c) the level of *sign systems*. According to Rossi-Landi, Marxist scholars have usually ignored how fundamental the role played by communicative processes is in the dialectics between the three economic moments of production, exchange, and consumption; furthermore, Marxist analyses—as well as their critics— have always considered the relation between structure and superstructure in purely dualistic terms, overlooking the possibility that such a relation has to be explained through the hypothesis of a *mediating element*, hence, that it has to be explained from a *triadic* point of view. Such a mediating element is constituted by *sign systems* which are generated and involved in the general process of social reproduction. Therefore—according to Rossi-Landi—explaining the role of language and communication, the whole process of social reproduction can be structured and analyzed as a more determined totality, that is, as a concrete constituted by further specific determinations.

SIGN SYSTEMS AND SOCIAL REPRODUCTION

To explain the functioning of the *schema of social reproduction*, it would seem appropriate to start from (c) the level of sign systems. The theoretical structure of this level is grounded on the assumption according to which "it is with the whole of his social organization that man *communicates.*" (Rossi-Landi 1977, 16, my italics) Such a hypothesis implies the methodological assumption that the several types of human communication have to be considered as actually *integrated*; this means that every distinction between human forms of communication has not to be considered as "natural," but rather as a result of certain methodological and theoretical choices. On the contrary, Rossi-Landi proposes another methodological approach: adopting certain conceptual instruments typically employed to study nonverbal communication, it could be possible to explain certain aspects of verbal communication, and vice versa. Particularly, it could be possible to analyze economic processes as processes of semiosis, and, consequently, the semiotic character of economics. Indeed, according to Rossi-Landi, economics can be understood as "the study of the nonverbal sign system which makes it possible for particular types of messages, usually called "commodities," to circulate. More briefly, and with a formula: *economics is the study of commodity-messages.*" (Rossi-Landi 1977, 134) To sum up, Rossi-Landi's main hypothesis is that the economic moment of exchange could be understood as a communicative process, but such a process has to be understood in its turn as a *productive* moment, namely, a moment consisting in the human ability to compose, exchange and interpret—that is, to use—every kind of messages. Such a perspective evidences, the methodological role played by (a) the level of production-exchange-consumption such an analytical device explains how the dialectical relations between production, exchange, and consumption characterize also every social communication. From such a perspective, the general exchange process (Verkher) could be understood fundamentally as a communication process, namely, every kind of communication can be understood as *production of signs and messages, exchange of messages, consumption of messages and signs.*

Rossi-Landi defines the human ability of composing, and interpreting messages as *linguistic work*: with a formula, communication *is* linguistic work. In the next section, I will try to explain why such an assumption represents the theoretical root of what Rossi-Landi defines as "homological method." And I will proceed with certain terminological clarification. Now, I would like just to explain why sign systems can be understood as elements of the material process of social reproduction.

According to Rossi-Landi, any sign system "includes as a minimum a code or canon consisting of the materials that are worked on, the tools of the work, and the rules needed for applying them, all these being the products of previous work." (Rossi-Landi 1990, 198) From such a perspective, it should be stated that the *practical-communicative use of language* presents the same fundamental elements of *labor process* as defined by Marx: that is, *the activity conforming to a goal*, the *material* on which work is applied, and work *instruments*. Assuming that sign systems are *products* of linguistic work, Rossi-Landi underlines the *material* and *practical* character of language and communication. More specifically, the *material* character of sign systems emerges from the fact that

> sign systems are systems of artefacts that could not exist in nature without the intervention of man, and if we don't want to admit that something *human* exists for man without the intervention of man himself, we must hold to the principle that every artefact, however understood, is the result of work which man has done and can do again. Generalizing, between any product or human result as absent, and the same result as present, there is a difference that can be explained (for which reason can be given) only in terms of the work carried out by men to obtain it. (Rossi-Landi 1977, 32)

Therefore, *language is work*: indeed, just like work, language produces artifacts. Nevertheless, Rossi-Landi's argumentation implies an inverse perspective: human language constitutes a fundamental element of economic production. Hence, *work is language*. Indeed, if, agreeing with Marx, we consider human work as an activity conforming to a goal [*zweckmässige Tätigkeit*], we must also admit that work is inherently *semiotic*, because that goal is actually a *sign*, that is—as Rossi-Landi maintains—"a conscious or unconscious, desired or endured, 'mental' anticipation of the product," (Rossi-Landi 1977, 40) namely, a *design* or a *project*. Hence, language "determines the finalistic character of work, its taking place according to a *program*;" (ibid., my italics) and a *program* is nothing else but an organized part of a certain sign system, that is, a set of *instructions* which are more or less implicit in certain forms of human social work.

In the light of all these theses, we may reach an understanding of why sign systems should be considered as the mediating element in (b) the relationships between *structure* and *superstructure*. On the structural level, sign systems establish the goals of working processes, playing an active role in the *relations of production*. From a general point of view, according to Rossi-Landi, the economic moment of production could be understood as an *enormous program* which forces the workmen to function as its own instruments, materials, and products.[1] Therefore, it should be affirmed that the level of sign system *organizes* the economic base by positing the goals of production; nevertheless, such a *mediation* corresponds in its turn to a *particular mediation* of the super-structural level. In this theoretical passage emerges one of the most original thesis of Rossi-Landi's semiotics. Assuming that every practical activity is organized following the rules of certain sign systems, it could be possible to hypothesize that all the sign systems are coordinated by a wider program, a general framework controlling certain fundamental processes of social reproduction: such a gigantic program is *ideology*. In this regard, the thesis propounded by Rossi-Landi is that "as a vision of the world, ideology, once it moves beyond a state of mere contemplation, necessarily becomes a purposeful project, a teleological activity which affects the constitution of society as a whole." (Rossi-Landi 1990, 281) This is the thesis of *ideology as social design*, and its main assumption is that every social interaction is inherently *ideological*, because every human behavior—in some measure—is based on a *codified* and *institutionalized* part of the ideological social design.

Considering ideology as social design, it is possible to state that the ideological factor acts at all three levels (structure, sign systems, and superstructure) of social reproduction, and that every-level influences the other two: (a) for example, observing social reproduction from the level of superstructure, one could see that political and juridical institutions—by means of codified sign systems like work and private property legislation—organize *productive forces* in *relations of production*; thus, detecting the role of sign systems one could explain more clearly how superstructure retroacts on structure; (b) focusing on the intermediate level, sign systems are influenced by mode of production in so far as all signs—as outlined above—are artifacts: thus, the global situation of semiosis could be explained considering that signs are materials, instruments, and products of human work; ideological institutions establish programs regulating communication understood as sign production-exchange-consumption; thus, it could be shown how structure and superstructure influence sign systems; (c) in the end, starting from the structure, it is possible to observe that ideology and communication maintain the mode of production (which also means that the former are influenced by the latter).

HOMOLOGICAL METHOD AND THE MATERIALITY OF LANGUAGE: SEMIOTICS BETWEEN *SIGNS* AND *BODIES*

One of the most distinctive features of Rossi-Landi's materialist semiotics consists in what he defines as the *homological method*.

Rossi-Landi maintains that the homological method can be understood as an application of the Marxian analyses of social reproduction to research on language and communication. (see Rossi-Landi 1968, 9) But what does "homological" actually mean? Rossi-Landi borrows this term from biological sciences, where it refers "to a fundamental similarity due to community of descent, to a correspondence in structure and in origin" (Rossi-Landi 1977, 72, note 25) between different species. From such a perspective, homological methods consist in constructing a theoretical model through which certain similarities and correspondences—between boundaries of analysis which appear as completely disconnected—can be identified. (see Ponzio 2008, 8) The result of this theoretical construction is—once again—a *structured totality* in which all the parts are reciprocally connected. More specifically, the homological method consists in connecting the two sub-totalities of *linguistic production* and *material production* in a wider totality constituted by the *human being*, understood—from a Marxian point of view—as *product* of its own *work*. It means that, according to Rossi-Landi, the Marxian thesis on the *anthropogenic* character of work should be extended, including the thesis on the anthropogenic character of *language*, understood in its *verbal* and *nonverbal* dimension: human beings produce themselves through their social work, and, in this sense, mankind is the result of the general process of social reproduction; but a relevant part of social reproduction is constituted by *linguistic production*. From such a perspective, human *language*, that is, the human ability of producing and interpreting signs and messages, can be understood as *work*.

In this regard, a terminological—and, of course, theoretical—clarification seems opportune. Rossi-Landi uses the noun "language" or, the adjective "linguistic," referring to the verbal sign systems, but he clarifies that such a term could refer implicitly also to nonverbal communication and nonverbal sign systems. Indeed, for Rossi-Landi verbal and nonverbal sign systems are both *primary modeling systems*, that is, they are two manifestations of the human *syntactical capacity*, (see Sebeok 2003, 178) that is the human capacity of generate, communicate, and interpret meaningful signs in general (hence, nonverbal signs also).[2]

In the light of these considerations a question could arise: Are all of these assumptions coherent with a Marxian theoretical framework? The reason for this doubt is easily explained by the fact that—as is well known—a coherent Marxian theory of language does not exist. Obviously, considering the work of Marx in its entirety, it is possible to find several and, of course, particularly interesting references to the concept of "language"; nevertheless, as Fredric Jameson affirms, this is not enough to ground a "materialist theory of language." (Jameson 1981, 45) Furthermore, Jameson criticizes those theories which are based "on a tacit homology between the 'production' of language in writing and speech, and economic production," (ibid.) including "the rich and suggestive work of Ferruccio Rossi-Landi, which turns explicitly on the exploration of language production." (Jameson 1981, 45, note 24) More specifically, the author of *The Political Unconscious* maintains that the homological method can be contested for two strictly connected lacks: (a) homological method is an ideological construct of intellectuals, which "seek to glamorize their tasks—which can for the most part be subsumed under the rubric of the elaboration, reproduction or critique of ideology—by assimilating them to real work on the assembly line and to the experience of resistance of matter in genuine manual labor" (ibid.); (b) homological method grounds its epistemic statute on a mechanical and naturalistic concept of "matter," referring, for example, to the Marxian[3] allusion to "the sonorous vibration of language in air and space." (ibid.)

One might agree with Jameson's view of the incoherent behavior of "intellectuals," their *intellectual* dishonesty, but this is not the case of Rossi-Landi. Just like Jameson, Rossi-Landi has often criticized such ideological behavior; furthermore, in several passages of his papers, Rossi-Landi affirms that his conception of linguistic production does not consist in an *isomorphic representation* of the work on the assembly line, and that his idea of "materiality" does not coincide with the idea of purely "observable" or "perceivable" matter; moreover, Rossi-Landi has criticized this latter assumption rigorously since his studies on the sign theory of Charles W. Morris, and the claim to theorizing a behavioristic semiotics based on observation. However, although the general purpose of Morris's theory should be contested, its theoretical model of *semiosis* should be preserved. A semiotic theory based on observation cannot exist, because the property of being *a sign of something else* is not an observable property. On the contrary, being *a sign of something else* is—as Morris himself maintains—a *relational property*, which can be assigned to a specific object only with reference to a specific schema, that is, to an *abstract model* representing a "*global situation,*" (Rossi-Landi 1977, 25) a totality in which all the functions of the parts are specified, and all the relations among them are posited.

But what does "semiosis" mean? From a very general point of view, "the process in which something functions as sign may be called semiosis." (Morris 1938, 3) To describe such a process, Morris constructs a set of "special" or "technical" terms, such as: *sign vehicle, designatum, interpretant,* and *interpreter*; each of these terms denotes a *relational property* that a certain thing takes on "by participating in the functional process of semiosis." (Morris 1938, 4.) The explication of the logic of semiosis can be condensed in a formula: semiosis is a process in which "something takes account of something else mediately, that is, by means of a third something. Semiosis is accordingly a mediated-taking-account-of. The *mediators* are sign vehicles; the takings-account-of are *interpretants*; the agents of the process are *interpreters*; what is taken account of are *designata*." (ibid.)

As Rossi-Landi shows, Morris's formulation expresses the possibility of a materialist foundation of semiotics; indeed, his theoretical model is inherently characterized by three fundamental—and strictly connected—assumptions:

(a) semiosis has to be considered as a processual and structured totality, or as Morris would say, as a "global situation"; (b) the notion of "sign vehicle" implies the fact that "every sign must contain in itself both sign and non-sign portions" (Rossi-Landi 1992, 285); (c) emphasizing the role of the agents in the semiosis, Morris himself has recognized that every human semiosic and interpretative process can be understood as *social practice*. From such a perspective, sign vehicles can be understood as the *material* part of the sign, namely, the *matter* on which a certain type of linguistic work is expended. Such a linguistic work constitutes the *designative* part of the sign. Therefore, the *designatum* coincides with the particular program which a certain social actor has *inscribed*[4] in the sign vehicle, and the *interpretant* coincides with the manner in which those particular programs should be executed—that is, interpreted—by other interpreters. Obviously, the fact that the sign vehicle constitutes the *material* part of the sign does not imply the *vehicle* should be necessarily a *material* object; indeed, the vehicle can be also another *sign*, supporting further level of *designation*.

Starting from all of these theses, Rossi-Landi is able to explain the difference between idealist and materialist semiotics: the first approach maintains that "all bodies *are* signs." (Rossi-Landi 1977, 271, my italics) On the contrary, materialist semiotics recognizes that all "bodies *can be* signs." (ibid., my italics) This means that being a "sign"—as well as being the *material* part of the sign—is not an inherent quality of a certain object, but it is a property deriving from the position occupied by that object in the practical process of semiosis.

THE *COMMODITY-MESSAGE MODEL*: BETWEEN SEMIOSIS AND DISCOURSE

From the point of view of materialistic semiotics, "a sign is a sign because it is the center of a network of social relation, or because it belongs to such a network." (Rossi-Landi 1977, 274) And, "the logic of this statement is similar to the logic of the statement that a commodity is not a material thing because it is a social relation. From this it doesn't follow that a commodity doesn't have a material body—indeed, without a material body, the bearer of its use-value, no piece of goods would ever be able to enter the social relations which make of it a commodity." (*ibid.*)

Starting from such an assumption, Rossi-Landi maintains that when goods circulate in the form of commodities they *are* messages. Also in this case, the structure of social practice constitutes a methodological lens through which the functioning of language and communication can be analyzed and explained: when a human sign is generated to be exchanged, then such a human sign becomes a message; and this process could be based on communicative programs—derived from previous sign work—which are independent from the awareness of the sender and receiver.

Rossi-Landi underlines that the Marxian analysis of *commodity-form* could be understood fundamentally as a *semiotic analysis of commodity as message*; more specifically, the *internal contradiction* between *use-value* and *exchange value* constitutes a distinction between two levels of signification. Precisely, "a commodity appears on the market as the bearer of several layers of signification; interpretation must distinguish between these different layers and trace them back to the sign-system they belong to." (Rossi-Landi 1977, 127)

From such a perspective, a semiotic analysis of the use-value must coincide with an examination of the totality of semiosic practices (verbal and nonverbal) which are implied in the dialectics between production and consumption; more specifically, on the one hand, such an analysis should investigate how the economic sphere of production interprets and satisfies—but also, determines—the numerous needs arising in the economic sphere of consumption; therefore, starting from the level of production, we could analyses the use-value of a commodity as a semiotic program concerning the way in which an artifact must function to satisfy a specific need. On the other hand, the semiotic analyses should investigate how the moment of consumption accepts and executes the programs established by the production, or reacts against them establishing alternative programs, namely, linguistically redefining the sphere of needs and desires.

Nevertheless, this latter is just one layer of signification, and, furthermore, a layer which generally regards the artifact understood as a product—as a use-value —rather than its commodity dimension. On the contrary, commodity—according to Rossi-Landi—derives its semiotic specificity from certain particular social relationships and programs of communication; (see Rossi-Landi 1977, 127) for example, the fact that a commodity is exposed in a shop window represents an important part of the sign work which is necessary to codify a product into a commodity; but the exchange value—which is the peculiar aspect of commodity—is not implied in these layers of signification. Rather, the semiotic level which posits the peculiar character of commodity is constituted by what it could be defined—from a Marxian point of view—as the *valorization process of capital*; although Rossi-Landi does not analyze the semiotic implications this level, it could be possible—in my opinion—to identify such a Marxian concept with the highly formalized structure of the different programs and codes subtending the production and the circulation of commodities. According to Rossi-Landi, in analyzing this structure, Marx developed a pioneering analysis of nonverbal communication. Hence, the semiotic character of the valorization process could be probably identified with the fact that capital functions as a code, a particular form semiosis which imposes specific designative aspects to certain objects and signs—reducing them to the role of its sign vehicles: for example, according to the logic of capital every product of work is commodity, and a certain value has to be *realized* every time that a certain commodity is sold on the market. The *meaning* of a product does not consist in the fact that it can satisfy a certain need, but in the fact that it must realize surplus value for the capital.

To conclude, I would like to refer to a third level of signification which is connected to the commodity-form. It should be stated that commodity can be understood as a sign vehicle of that particular form of semiosis represented by the *ideology*. More specifically, I am referring to the totality of myths, imagines, and narrations which are more or less transmitted by marketing and advertising, and which are organized according to certain specific forms of ideological discourse. From such a perspective, a commodity could be understood as the sign vehicle through which the general program of ideology organizes the sphere of social needs, and structures the desires of the collective unconscious.

CONCLUSION

In this paper I have tried to illustrate how Rossi-Landi's *materialist semiotics* could represent a heuristic instrument for the materialist analysis of language and discourse.

In this regard, I have proposed to start from a fundamental assumption of Rossi-Landi's theory: in order to postulate the *materialist* dimension of language, it is necessary to assume that language is *work*, and that every human social sign system is an articulate product of such work.

According to Rossi-Landi, it is possible to hypothesize the *"material"* character of language because every human (verbal and nonverbal) communication presents in itself the elements of the working process as described by Marx. Human signs do not exist "in Nature," but, rather, they are the result of human work: work oriented by signs, work performed on signs by means of other signs. On the other hand, if we are able to hypothesize the "linguistic" character of work, this is because all labor processes take place according to certain organized signs systems and forms of communication.

From a general point of view, all these theses imply the necessity to include certain Marxian categories in the study of language and discursivities. Rossi-Landi demonstrated how such inclusion is coherent with the dialectical-materialist approach. Indeed—according to Rossi-Landi—the overlap between dialectical materialism and semiotics—understood as the study of verbal and nonverbal sign systems—emerges clearly from the analysis of commodity-form: Marx himself adopted a *crypto-semiotic method* in his investigations of commodity fetishism and critique of the categories of classical political economy.

Even if a coherent Marxian theory of language is not readily available, as already stated, we know that Marx refers to the concepts of *language* and *sign* in several passages of his writings. The following quotation, in fact, can be linked with what Rossi-Landi affirms: "every commodity is a sign (Zeichen), since, as value, it is only the material envelope (sachliche Hülle) of the human labor spent on it." (see Marx 1976, 185, translation slightly modified by me)[5]

Starting from this quotation, Rossi-Landi proposed to interpret commodities as messages transmitting information "on human labor, on the manner in which society is organized, on exploitation." (Rossi-Landi 1972, 222) I have attempted to reconnect this thesis with the semiotic background of Rossi-Landi's theory, that is, the model of semiosis as structured by Charles W. Morris: from such a perspective the commodity can be understood as a sign vehicle consisting of different layers of signification, that is, a message referring to different codes.

To conclude, I would like to underline that Rossi-Landi's theory represents a *pioneering* attempt at applying the Marxian critique of political economy to studies on language and communication. On the one hand, his theoretical proposal has the merit of illustrating how fundamental the set of instruments produced by semiotics may prove to be for other critical approaches; on the other hand, his approach also demonstrates that the Marxian critique of political economy can contribute to a better understanding of semiotic processes. In the light of all these considerations, I believe that, explaining the *material* character of language, Rossi-Landi's semiotics represents an important support for the several materialist approaches in Discourse Studies.

NOTES

1. In my opinion, this latter assumption has a theoretical base in the Marxian concept of *Zwecksetzung*, that is, the activity of positing goals, characterizing every mode of production—although Rossi-Landi does not explicitly refer to such a category.

2. For an in-depth analysis on the theoretical relations between Sebeok and Rossi-Landi see Ponzio and Petrilli (2004, 207–222).

3. As is well known, in *The German Ideology*, Marx and Engels affirm that "the 'mind' is from the outset afflicted with the curse of being 'burdened' with matter, which here makes its appearance in the form of agitated layers of air, sounds, in short, of language" (Marx and Engles 1998, 49)

4. I believe such a theoretical assumption could be interpreted as a link with the *Actor Network Theory* as structured by Latour and Law. Cf. Latour (2006, 81–124); Law (1999, 1–14).

5. In his translation of *Capital*, Ben Fowkes renders the German word "Zeichen" with the English word "symbol." I disagree with this terminological choice for two reasons: first of all, the word "symbol" has the German word "(das) Symbol" as its equivalent, and Marx does not use this term in the above-mentioned excerpt; secondly, from a semiotic perspective, a symbol is a particular type of sign: explained in a very synthetic manner, a symbol is a sign that refers to other signs (see Morris 1946). Obviously, it cannot be demonstrated that Marx used the two different terms following a similar semiotic distinction. Nevertheless, it seems opportune to specify that Marx uses—for example—"Symbol" and "Zeichen" to illustrate two different acceptations of the sign-character of money in general: for example he defines *paper-money* as the *paper-symbol* (*Papiersymbol*) of the coin, understood in turn as the *sign of value* [Das Vertzeichen]. Fawkes' translation eliminates these subtle—but probably important—terminological nuances, gathering the different meanings under the umbrella-term "symbol." (see Marx 1976, 221–227). Instead, all these differences are maintained in the Italian translation of *Capital* by Fineschi and Sgrò (see Marx 2011, 138–143).

BIBLIOGRAPHY

Della Volpe, Galvano. 1969. *Logica come scienza storica*. Rome: Editori Riuniti.

Fairclough, Norman. 2012. "Critical Discourse Analysis." Accessed August 12, 2016. https://www.academia.edu/3791325/Critical_discourse_analysis_2012_

Jameson, Fredric. 1981. *The Political Unconscious. Narrative as a Socially Symbolic Act*. London: Routledge.

Latour, Bruno. 2006. "Dove sono le masse mancanti? Sociologia di alcuni oggetti di uso comune." In *Il senso degli oggetti tecnici*. Edited by Alvise Mattozzi, 81–124. Rome: Meltemi.

Law, John. 1999. "After ANT: complexity, naming and topology." In *Actor-Network and After*, edited by John Law and John Hassard, 1–14, Oxford/Klee: Blackwell-The Sociological Review.

Marx, Karl. 1973. *Grundrisse. Introduction to the Critique of Political Economy*. Translated by Martin Nicolaus. New York: Vintage Books.

———. 1976. *Capital. A Critique of Political Economy. Volume One*. Translated by Ben Fowkes. London: Penguin Books.

———. 2011. *Il capitale. Critica dell'economia politica. Libro primo. Il processo di accumulazione del capitale (1863–1890)*. Edited by Roberto Fineschi, translated by Delio Cantimori, Roberto Fineschi, Giovanni Sgrò. Naples: La città del Sole.

Marx, Karl and Friedrich Engels. 1998. *The German Ideology*. Amherst/New York: Prometheus Books.

Morris, Charles W. 1938. "Foundations of the Theory of Signs. " In *International Encyclopedia of Unified Science, Vol. I, 2*. Edited by Otto Neurath, Rudolf Carnap, Charles W. Morris. Chicago: The University of Chicago Press.

———. 1946. *Sings, Language and Behaviour*. New York: Prentice-Hall.

Ponzio, Augusto. 2008. *Linguaggio, lavoro e mercato globale. Rileggendo Rossi-Landi*. Milan/ Udine: Mimesis.

Ponzio, Augusto and Susan Petrilli. 2004. "The concept of language. Ferruccio Rossi-Landi and Thomas A. Sebeok." In *Athanor. Lavoro immateriale*. Edited by Susan Petrilli, 207–222. Rome: Meltemi.

Rossi-Landi, Ferruccio. 1968. *Il linguaggio come lavoro e come mercato*. Milan: Bompiani.

———. 1972. *Semiotica e ideologia*. Milan: Bompiani.

———. 1977. *Linguistics and Economics*. The Hague/Paris: Mouton.

———. 1990. *Marxism and Ideology*. Oxford: Clarendon Press.

———. 1992. *Between signs and non-signs*. Edited by Susan Petrilli. Amsterdam/Philadelphia: John Benjamins.

Sebeok, Thomas A. 2003. *Segni. Una introduzione alla semiotica*. Edited by Susan Petrilli. Rome: Carocci.

Chapter 10

Desire, Queer Politics, and the Materiality of Experience

Early Asexual Discourses in Online Communities

Julia Maria Zimmermann

Since the linguistic turn, classic materialist approaches have undergone notable change, most often toward increasing insignificance (Coole and Frost 2010, 3), while matter kept challenging constructivist queer theory. Theorists such as Judith Butler (1993), Elizabeth Grosz (1994), or Anne Fausto-Sterling (2000) were among the theorists involved in the debate. Generally, and both in everyday language as well as philosophical discourse, materiality is used in its substantial meaning, that is, to denote anything which is made up of atoms. Accordingly, in many discourse theoretical approaches, including queer theories, materiality plays a role as a medium of discourse, or as the "other" of language, namely the body (Coole and Frost 2010, 8). In some social constructionist approaches, materiality is seen as "raw-matter" which becomes only intelligible through discursivation. While constructionist gender and queer scholars, for example, Butler, soon admitted that materiality indeed played a role—that "bodies matter" (Butler 1993)—their take on materiality remains somewhat unclear. Arguably, matter becomes agent materiality through discursive shaping only. This conception is by no means new, in fact, it goes back to Aristotelian thought (Coole 2010, 95). Additionally, it may imply that the only reality of experience, in the end, is that which can be accessed through discourses. Although it has been criticized in more "materialist" approaches from feminist phenomenological and feminist biological perspectives (Fausto-Sterling 2000), the dilemma of access to, and intelligibility of experiences, has not been solved satisfactorily. This chapter does not intend to offer a final solution to this dilemma, but to present and discuss a case study example, in which the (in)accessibility to material experiences is both enabled through discursivation and challenging the discourse. Early asexual discourses provide a fruitful perspective on this intersection. Here, subjects seek to "make sense" of a specific constitution—the lack of sexual attraction—that is experienced in a "neomaterial" fashion: the

145

absence of attraction is experienced as an active, unruly force for which not only no words but, moreover, no conception at all exist.

New materialisms suggest an alternative conception of materialization as "a complex, pluralistic, relatively open process" (Coole and Frost 2010, 7). While being engaged in various academic fields and deploying very different conceptions of materiality, they share an inspiration by twentieth-century discoveries in natural sciences which define "materialities" as processes on a subatomic level and in a non-substantial, indeterminate fashion (Coole and Frost 2010, 10–15):

> The point [...] for new materialisms is that theoretical physics' understanding of matter is now a long way from the material world we inhabit in our everyday lives and that it is no longer tenable to rely on the obsolete certainties of classical physics earlier materialists did. [...] [F]orces, charges, waves virtual particles, and empty space suggest an ontology that is very different from the substantialist Cartesian or mechanistic Newtonian accounts of matter. [...] In fact, it is evident from new materialist writing that forces, energies, and intensities (rather than substances) and complex, even random, processes (rather than simple, predictable states) have become the new currency. (Coole and Frost 2010, 11–12)

With this conception of materiality as intrinsically dynamic and active, it comes as no surprise that many queer theorists embraced desire as such a materiality. This, however, all but facilitates a valid distinction between materiality and discourse. "Materiality," in this sense, is more than the "substantial" which can be experienced sensually and intersubjectively.[1] Rather, some forms of materiality can be located solely in subjective experiences, especially when linked to bodily experiences. Intersubjective communication can render these materialities intelligible, but only by means of discursive formations: language, definitions, and images. When discourses are missing, materiality remains unintelligible, albeit not necessarily unconscious.

In this chapter, I will define "materiality" very generally as that which becomes the object of the discursive production of meaning and which in return activates and shapes discursive processes. In short, these two entities intersect. "Intersection," here, is understood in the classic sense: Materiality and discourse are two distinct conceptions that can be separated analytically. However, in empirical observation they are hardly distinguishable and are no longer reducible to materiality or discourse alone, but mutually affect and shape each other.

NEW MATERIALISMS IN EMPIRICAL QUEER THEORY

Generally, the rise of new materialisms took queer theories by storm. Seemingly out of a sudden, the materiality of the body was "rediscovered" (as if it had been lost in the first place). Authors from a natural scientific background, like Fausto-Sterling, challenged linguistic and/or social constructionist notions of sex and gender. Their argumentation that both, bodily matter and discursive construction, exist and intersect, may be regarded as one kind of materialist discourse studies. In the first chapter of "Sexing the Body" (2000), the biologist Fausto-Sterling comes, in revision of previous feminist approaches to the materiality of sex and gender to a preliminary conclusion that mainly draws on Elizabeth Grosz's approach (Fausto-Sterling 2000, 13–25). According to Grosz, materiality exists prior to the production of its meaning through discourses. However, it is not possible for "raw matter" to exist independently from the discursive production of meaning. She employs the image of a Möbius strip, a topological puzzle in which the outside and the inside of a ribbon appear as twisted. Grosz imagines the subject's psyche as being constituted through the twisted interdependence of material/physical bodily manifestations on the "inside" and discourses and cultural meaning on the "outside." Finally, the location on the inside or the outside, that is, the differentiation between matter and discourse, becomes impossible (Grosz 1994). This connection between materiality and discourse is somewhat different from Butler's suggestion. It notably introduces a spatial and temporal aspect which is suspended in Butler's theory once the connection between materiality and discourse is established. Grosz also affirms that there is "no body as such: there are only *bodies*—male or female, black, brown, white, large or small—and the gradations in between." (Grosz 1994, 19) Grosz, in these and the following few words, rejects each notion of "the (meta) body" for the sake of the contextualized existence of actual bodies in all their different shapes, ages, positions, etc. Despite not completely devoid of certain discursive notions, particularly notions of gender, race, age, etc., which render bodies classifiable and thus comparable, Grosz rejects idealist conceptions of bodies in favor of concrete material phenomena. A very similar discussion about the validity of ideal definitions versus material experience that is arguably at odds with it can be witnessed in many contributions during the early asexual discursivation process, which will be shown later.

Materiality, in this sense, can be understood as inherently diverse, resisting most attempts of universalization and normalization, at least to a certain degree. This characteristic of materiality establishes its "queerness," an observation I borrow from Karen Barad (2012a). "Queerness," here, is understood in its original, literal sense, as something which lies obliquely to norms, idealizations, and discourses assumed to be universal. In the contemporary sense, "queer" designates desire which resists heteronormative adjustments, a desiring established as "natural," "universal," and "ideal." The manifestations of these "queer" desires reveal the lack of "material" heterosexuality in some persons, and denounce discourses on sexuality as ignorant toward material experiences. Queer theory therefore constitutes its constructionist approach on materiality by resisting specific discourses.

However, it retains some problematic assumptions. When gender and queer theorists try to address the problem of materiality and corporeal experience, they seem to face the difficulty of discerning the localization of material/ bodily experience. There is a silent agreement that externally visible and locatable sex/gender characteristics—namely genitals—are not the materiality they have in mind, and instead consider these characteristics as signs which become discursive markers for sex/gender, sexuality as well as material body experience itself only through discursive meaning and corporeal mapping (Grosz 1994, 34). Thus, the reference to these signs as "true" materiality, while opposing their truth as signifiers of sex/gender is, from a theoretical perspective, unsatisfactory. I think this difficulty arises mainly from an understanding of materiality as stable, measurable, and locatable. However, such a definition of materiality facilitates the political use of bodies and corporeal experiences, including sexual desires. I define these argumentations, which are discursive enunciations, as "physicalisations," as a specific way of the discursive production of meaning through objectifying unintelligible material experiences. In the end, a valid distinction between materiality, or corporeality, and discourse in not possible, since the two intersect and constitute each other interdependently. This, I concede, is a sincere problem for methodological considerations. The way, however, it is sometimes solved, is no less problematic, particularly for asexuality research:

> Eros, desire, life forces run through everything, not only specific body parts or specific kind [*sic*!] of engagements among body parts. Matter itself is not a substrate or a medium for the flow of desire. Materiality itself is always already a desiring dynamism, a reiterative reconfiguring, energized and energizing, enlivened and enlivening. (Barad 2012c, 59)

I think there is a crucial problem in this conception: Barad defines matter as erotic, or libidinal, as maybe voluptuous and driven. This renders matter intelligible, although not locatable. However, this description of matter supposes a universality (that of the erotic) which is quite as problematic as the criticized notion that every human is male or female exclusively. While I adopt the notion of a fluid, dynamic materiality, I reject its definition as "erotic," or within any other positivist form. Unfortunately, erotic (or libidinal) universalism is not only very common in queer theory, but also it can be defined as its very base, particularly when queer theory is informed by psychoanalytical, Freudian and Lacanian, notions. Thus, Grosz, to quote but one example among many others from Adrienne Rich (1980)[2] through Judith Butler (1990)/ (1993) to Sara Ahmed (2006, 67–68), states:

> The body is libidinally invested. The subject always maintains a relation of love (or hate) toward its own body because it must always maintain a certain level of psychical and libidinal investment. No person lives his or her body merely as a functional instrument or a means to an end. Its value is never simply or solely functional, for it has a (libidinal) value in itself. (Grosz 1994, 32)

Without forestalling too much, I can already point out that narrations of many asexuals on their body indeed lack any trace of "libidinal investment" and are not seldom seen as "instruments or means to an end."

While queer theories may be oblique to heteronormative discourse, and do so on the base of resisting materialities in queer persons, they are not at all independent of discourses. In fact, I even want to argue that discourses enable, rather than restrict, queer materialities. Notably, I am not talking about the fact that queer identities are only constructible on a discursive foundation—as it is coined by Foucault in his famous quote that the sodomist was an aberration, but the homosexual is a species (Foucault 1990, 43). I take this for granted. Rather, I claim that the experience of desire—or lack thereof—may also be the result of discourses. Partly, this has been examined and questioned by Adrienne Rich on compulsory heterosexuality (Rich 1980). Partly, and this is the point I want to make here, it is the proliferation of discourses on sexuality that enables subjects to gain awareness of their subjective desire, particularly when it resists normative discourses. Far from arguing in favor of an "inborn" (read: pre-discursive), essentialist sexual orientation, but being equally skeptic toward radical constructionist approaches, I claim that material queer desires and experiences are to some degree enabled through discourses, though not created by them. Thus, if we maintain my previous definition of materiality, that is, that it is diverse and therefore, to a certain degree, resists attempts of normalization, this, again, is a definition based upon a specific—postmodern—set of discourses which enable the acknowledgement and construal of diversity rather than attempting to universalize and/or classify material phenomena.

THE MATERIALITY OF ABSENCE: ASEXUALITY

While it may be very well comprehensible to understand desire as a material experience, and thus as part of materiality in general, this may seem odd when talking about asexuality—defined, for the moment, as the very absence of desire.[3]

A person who does not (exclusively) experience heterosexual desire may define themselves as homo- or bisexual and accord their bodily experiences. Similarly, a person who does not identify with the assigned sex/gender may define themselves (or be defined) as the (!) other sex/gender. In these cases, the unintelligible can become intelligible, and ultimately physicalized, for example, with regard to "wrong" sex characteristics in the case of trans persons, thanks to already existing discursive offers. The material experience of these individuals, however, may be different, for example, neither conforming to the assigned sex/gender nor any other. The same may apply to sexual desire. When coping with materiality, we need to take into account the paradox, but in fact very common, materiality of absence. Here again, we can refer to neo-materialist approaches, namely Karen Barad. In an essay on "Nothingness" (Barad 2012b), she ponders on the ontology of the void, or rather, that which is beyond measurability. Since measurements, to her, "are material-discursive practices of mattering" (Barad 2012b, 7), the failure to measure occurrences, either scientifically (that which I have dubbed "physicality") or linguistically (which would be the methodology of discourse analysis), all too often leads to the denial of ontology per se. This, Barad argues, is a false conclusion. Instead, she reflects upon the virtuality of the void, and concludes: "Virtual particles are experimenting with the im/possibilities of non/being, but that doesn't mean they aren't real, on the contrary" (Barad 2012b, 13), and: "Nothingness is not absence, but the infinite plentitude of openness." (Barad 2012b, 16) This openness allows for a potentially infinite procreation of materialist discourses.

I would like to name one example. If we take for instance the discursive introduction of asexuality as a sexual orientation towards no sex/gender, we deal exactly with this kind of discursivation and materialization of the void (i.e. the nothingness of sexual attraction). Narrative interviews with asexual persons could, and maybe would in many cases, show that this absence of sexual attraction, while neither localizable nor "substantial," is experienced nonetheless in a material, albeit vague and indeterminate fashion. Only the relatively recent labeling as "asexual" renders this experience intelligible. However, while academic research, particularly in sexology and psychology[4], less so in social sciences and humanities[5], is growing without a doubt, the bodily experiences of asexuals have scarcely been considered.

By now, we are able to communicate a certain experience lived by some people. At the same time, though, and although natural science on asexuality is far from being established, no physical foundation of asexuality could be established: no lack in hormones, no difference in arousal compared to non-asexual persons (Brotto/ Yule 2011, 707), no connection to mental or physical illnesses, no genetic peculiarity, etc.[6]

Asexuality, arguably more than every other sexual orientation, can be defined as a manifestation of the void, as material experience and its subsequent discursivation.

There is another important aspect: the asexual discourse is a bottom-up discourse created mainly by asexual persons themselves. Thus, it is not an expert's discourse trickling down, and not even a discourse which has been (re-)appropriated by asexuals, as it is the case in LGBT "queerness." As it is subjective, the asexual discourse allows statements and enunciations as productive of meaning which, in other discourses, would be invalidated as "void": The argumentation "but for me, personally, it is like xyz" is valid, and has already been productive in asexual discourse, as we will see later. For example, asexuals who experience little and/or circumstantial sexual attraction created discourses on gray-asexuality and the asexual spectrum. Asexuals who do or do not experience non-sexual forms of interpersonal attraction, such as romantic attraction, created the analytical differentiation between sexual, romantic, platonic, aesthetic, and sensual attraction. Queer/Feminist asexuals navigated through discourses on sex-positivity and struggled to situate themselves as, for example, personally repulsed by sexual behavior, but sex-positive on a societal level.

This proliferation of discourses nevertheless shows one central principle of discourse: During the process of discursivation, more precisely, the process of naming material experiences these experiences become fixated. The virtual particle, the "plentitude of openness," is both, actual and enclosed. To sum up, asexual material experience relied and continues to rely on discourses on sexuality, corporeality as well as gender and identity in order to become manifest and viable. On the other hand, the asexual discourse coined, so far, predominantly by asexuals themselves, relies on materiality and lived experiences as a guide and corrective of discursivation.

In the following section, I will illustrate this material-discursive practice of mattering and discursivation in the early asexual online community.

CASE STUDY: THE HUMAN AMOEBA.
EARLY ASEXUAL DISCOURSES

Apart from the very theoretical and hypothetical use of the term "asexuality,"[7] there was literally no concept for the non-existence of sexual desire/sexual interest in persons, and even less an umbrella term until the late 1990s. The reportedly common experience of many "asexuals" was a feeling of brokenness and loneliness, a conviction to be "the only one who feels like that." The arguably first public self-description of asexuality was an online article, published on May 20, 1997, by Zoe O'Reilly, entitled "My life as an amoeba" (O'Reilly 1997). It was the first publication in which an asexual person used the term "asexual" as a self-definition, and as a term to describe their experience of not experiencing sexual desire. The wording of an experience that hitherto had neither a name nor a legitimate existence also initiated a debate on the "correct" definition of asexuality, a definition in which not only (self-declared) asexuals, but also psychologists and other theorists have since taken part in.

O'Reilly's article is purely based on personal experiences; it is a biographical piece. Obviously, she did not intend to give the term "asexuality" a broader definition beyond her own, which is based on the *asexual* procreation of amoebas. Asexuality, in O'Reilly's article, is defined as the "lack of sexuality," which refers to an innate disposition, although it employs the term "sexuality" in a very unspecific way. Still, being reflective of discourses on coming out, asexuality is defined as a sexual orientation and thus connected to an existing discourse of sexuality. Alternatively, she describes an asexual life as a lifestyle "abstaining from sex," and hence a more or less conscious action. This latter definition was debated and ultimately relinquished in the inter-community discourse. Another definition of O'Reilly's, however, has become the crucial criterion for identifying as asexual, and indeed, as a queer person generally—the self-perception as asexual:

> Some might say that we aren't really asexual, we just want to think we are. Remember this quote, "I think, therefore I am." Add a couple words, "I think I'm asexual, therefore I am." (O'Reilly 1997)

In the comments to that article, many persons confessed having the same feelings, sharing the same disinterest in sexuality. This may, in retrospect, be considered the first asexual community-building ever, which was consolidated by persons sharing their email addresses and homepages, seeking help and advice or inviting discussion on various issues. It is worthwhile to analyze some of these confessions, since they offer paths of discursivation and knowledge-building on asexuality based upon previously inapt material, subjective experiences.

The dating of these comments is a bit tricky, since no time stamps are given. According to the internet archive Wayback Machine, the 27 remarks were posted between June 1997, shortly after the publication of the article, and May 2005. Note that I will give all quotations below in original spelling and grammar.[8]

Many commentators share highly personal and even intimate biographical narratives in which the subjective experience of something that is dubbed as a "lack of attraction/sex drive/ orientation," as "disinterest" or even "disgust" occurs as a materiality which had not been nameable previously. Sometimes, discovering the absence of sexual desire is only the result of a deliberate self-discovery and thus intelligible as a failed intersection of discourse (universal sexuality) and materiality (lack thereof). Thus, the confessions often express a perceived misfit between personal/material experience and the (lacking) discourse which enables them to "make sense" of their experiences within their social environment:

> Physically, I'm male, but there's nothing inside to tell me what I am, no drive. (Gary)
>   When I reached puberty I kept waiting for those 'feelings' to come. They never. (Anonymous)
>   I feel funny writing this. I am a 27 year old man and my family and friends are wondering why I don't date. There's no way to explain to them that I have no interest in sex. (Jeremy)
>   After discovering a little bit about my sexuality, and then finding a name for it. I've decided it's probably asexuality! (Michelle)

For the most part, the unnameable experience of absence leads to a disconnection from a society which is imagined as constituted by a collective experience of sexuality. Of course, this collective experience is a highly discursive imputation. To the "asexual" outsider, the discourse on "normal" sexual behavior must be identic with the material experience they expect in their (supposedly) sexual fellows, but to which they themselves have no access due to their lack of comparable experiences. Thus, "asexuals" can only match their experience to a discourse which completely erases even the possibility that the absence of sexual feelings can be real. Instead of questioning a discourse which "asexuals" need to take for granted for worse or better, they tend to question the actuality of their own experience and/or their place within a society which is discursively constituted around various sexual attractions.

> I see some bodies as more aesthetically beautiful than others, but I don't want to have sex with any of them. I don't understand one-night-stands or drunken sex. I feel so excluded from society. (Rachel)
>   i've never been in a romantic relationship (yup, 21 and never been kissed), and right now that upsets me a lot, because i feel so abnormal. (irene)
>   You can't imagine what a relief it is [to know about asexuality]. I have to admit I am still "in the closet" about it though. [...] I don't know when (if ever) I will tell everyone my true feelings. Maybe when there is more out there about us. As society is right now, I don't think people see asexuality as a "legit" preference. They assume something is wrong with you or something happened to cause you to feel that way. (Amy)
>   I did not even know there is such thing as asexuality until I was 25. Could you believe it really confused me, until I found out that was really me? Now I'm finally getting it managed by myself, but it still is non-understandable and even unbearable to some of my people to approve the fact that I have no interest in sex. (Jyrgen)

This disconnection from a discursive society, however, appears surmountable, now that a label—and with it, the first step into a discourse of one's own—exists:

Somehow, having a label makes me feel better. (Anonymous [II])

After the publication of O'Reilly's article, the term "asexuality" became known more widely, although it was not yet considered the fixed name for this orientation, in which many diverse experiences and ways of experiencing "asexuality" gathered. Discussions on terminology brought about such self-descriptions as "asexual," "antisexual," "non-sexual," "celibate," etc.

In 2000, the first asexual online community was established: The Yahoo! Group "Haven for the Human Amoeba," which exists until today, despite a tangible declining of contributions after 2006. In 2001, contributors were mainly occupied with discourse labor and the formulation of definitions of asexuality.

Early attempts to define asexuality revolve around the (unspoken) question whether asexuality was a deliberate choice, a lifestyle, and thus a synonym to celibacy, or an inborn condition and thus equivalent to the then-common discourse in sexology. In short, the debate centered on the position that asexuality could take within a complex discursive landscape. "Asexuals" decided to take the second path and define asexuality as a biological disposition. As David Jay, AVEN founder, put it in a forum debate in August 2001:

The reason that the contraversy over the word celibate came up is because I [...] expressed a problem with it. Namely that celibacy implies a choice, whereas asexuality implies a state. If I tell someone that I'm celibate they'll ask why, if I tell someone I'm asexual they'll ask how, and I for me the second question is more appropriate (if alot less answerable.). (bloodyredcommie [David Jay], August 22, 2001)[9]

In closing the ranks with sexology and queer discourse, "asexuals" somewhat accepted the discourse which roots sexual orientation within the body and therefore highlights the "material" aspect. As Przyblo points out, summarizing the constructionist argument made by Foucault about the medicalization, biologization and, ultimately, essentialism of sexuality in modern scientific research: "This search for the truth of sex, on and in the body, is evident throughout the scientific work on asexuality" (Przybylo 2012, 233). It thus tries to "prove" the existence of "real" asexuality in predictable physical and medical factors:

This view that sexuality, and asexuality in particular, might be discovered somewhere within the body is not however endemic to scientific studies of asexuality but operates as part of broader scientific and popular discourses which identify sex and sexuality as a biological imperative. Within the biological imperative, sexuality is manifest in the body and sex is an expression of one's innermost self [...]. (Przybylo 2012, 235)

Although I unconditionally agree with Przybylo's criticism, I would like to stress another point. Sexuality, and asexuality, is not simply "discovered somewhere within the body." It is searched for and ultimately discovered within certain body areas that have been marked as "sexual" previously in discourses on sexuality, particularly genitals and hormones. Brotto and Yule's (2011) failed attempt to "discover" asexuality in the vaginal responses of their female participants, is not a random sign for a "biological imperative." Rather, it shows how much "the body" is topographed through sexual discourses. When sexuality is located within the body (note that in this case, it is not a "material," individual body but a discursive, or ideal, body), this is never an "innocent," pre-discursive body, but a fundamentally sexualized body. In this cycle, the discourse on sexuality and the (discursivated) body mutually validate each other.

This is, however, certainly not the corporeal materialism that asexuals necessarily have in mind when claiming the "inbornness" of their orientation. Rather, they are informed by an increasing awareness and debate on the definition of sexuality and identity that is generally based on self-determination, thus favoring a subjective experience of corporeal materiality to an objectifiable definition. To asexuals, this stance may be particularly convincing: Sexual feelings simply cannot be located anywhere when no sexual feelings exist. At this point, neo-materialist approaches that decidedly break with measurable notions of matter, succor asexual (and postmodern) notions of subjective materiality:

I don't think sexual orientation altogether is strictly biological construct, by the way. It isn't measurable or detectable much the same way the malfunction of some organs is, so I won't expect it to be given so much medical attention, unless it is connected with some issues that ARE medical (hormone issues, psychiatric-mental health issues..). (Wild Seven, on AVEN, October 16, 2005)[10]

However, whether located or locatable in the body or not, as early as August 2001, a new discussion about the most suitable definition of asexuality arose when a Haven for the Human Amoeba user shared their libidinal experiences and found that they could not fit them into an asexual discourse, either:

My main purpose for this post was a to deal with a problem I'm having. Most people in this club have expressed the definition of asexual as having no sex drive. I for one have a sex drive, but I don't act on my sexual drives like a normal person I guess. What I mean, is I'm not really attracted to guys or girls, I don't hit on guys or girls, I don't look for romantic relationships, but yet I masterbate, quite often. [...] That's my view on asexualism. Its not about having a sex drive or not, that would be called impotentcy. Its about the desire to NOT have sex. If it is possible to have a desire to NOT do something. (absofsteel19, August 24, 2001)[11]

In a way, absofsteel19 not only demands a revision of the valid definition of asexuality based on their subjective experiences—which is the point I am obviously making here—but refers to a possible bodily perception which, at least in their eyes, seems incompatible with the current discourse of desire: the desire to not desire. Within a discursive formation in which drives are per definition directed towards an entity (humans, animals, objects, or the self), with the possibility, of course, to not reach the desired goal and thus experience distress, the desire of absence somewhat constitutes the absurd situation in which an individual desires to be deceived in order to obtain satisfaction. Had asexual discourses previously operated with the usual equation of sexual drive/sexual desire/sexual attraction, with asexuality meaning experiencing none of them, absofsteel now posed a riddle which could not that easily be solved. One solution, offered by David Jay, was the introduction of a non-directed sex drive, that is, the possibility to experience sexual feelings without them being directed to a specific person or a specific gender more generally, and thus being different from sexual drives attracted by the same/another/either gender. This definition was again based upon material intimate experiences he himself discovered, albeit not until absofsteel had challenged the up-to-then accepted asexual discourse:

But the basic gyst of it is that you can have a sex drive without it actually going anywhere. If I examine myself I can see that I have the mechanics of sexuality in me, I can become sexually aroused and sex, while somewhat odd and disgusting-seeming, seems like something that would feel good on some physical level. The thing is that that drive to have sex doesn't get associated with anyone. So I never meet someone and feel like I want to have a sexual relationship WITH THAT PERSON, so my sex drive doesn't really manifest itself in my interactions with people. Since my sex drive doesn't really, well, drive me to do anything (other than masterbate occassionally), I don't pay it much heed, and for all purposes am asexual. (bloodyredcommie, August 25, 2001)[12]

Very soon, discussions on the definition of asexuality gained multiple dimensional levels that distinguished sexual experiences usually considered as the same:

Bascially I compare asexuality (and other sexualities) to a stereo system
Sexuality = Stereo
Sex drive = Volume (note: this stereo has no volume control)

Orientation = The radio station that's playing (hetero, homo, bi, and whatever else you can think of, there is also no control for this).

Now here's where asexuality comes in. Each stereo is set at a certain volume, but if your volume is all the way down, you can't hear it. If you can't hear it, how do you know what's playing? You don't. And so through that, asexuality is born.

Technically everyone has a sex drive, but in a basic sense it's possible to not have one. The stereo is on, but you can't hear what's playing, so there's no point in listening. For some the volume is just high enough for them to have a little interest, such as masturbation, but nowhere near high enough for them to want to have actual sex with someone. There is still no interest in intercourse, so they still fall under the term "asexual." (montgomery_erickson, August 30, 2001)[13]

I still think that there's more than that, that you can lose the attraction aspect and still have the sex drive. To extend your metaphor, you can have the volume at a low-but-audible level, but have the radio tuned to static. Then you won't bother concentrating on it because its not a particularely [sic] interesting thing to listen to. (bloodyredcommie, August 30, 2001)[14]

Both definitions obviously lack the language to describe properly what they experience as "asexual" or as an asexual "truth." This is presumably due to the fact that prevalent discourses on sexuality do not fit asexual experiences, or that asexual experiences do exist, but are not intelligible in any discourse on sexuality. Thus, the commentators rely on interdiscursive metaphors to make themselves comprehensible, dubbed as "Stereo-Theory."

In the months to follow, the struggle for an all-encompassing definition of asexuality went on. Both, personal experiences and communicability were at stake. Hinderliter summarizes this struggle in the following observation:

The consensus opinion (at least the one expressed the most) was that asexuality is undefinable—each person had their own reason for calling themself asexual, and there was too much diversity in their (still very small) asexual community for any one definition to cover everyone. However, people also agreed that it would be useful to have a definition that they could give to people—having a definition would be helpful for asexual visibility. (Hinderliter 2009)

By the end of September 2001, the usual definition for asexuality as "someone who does not experience sexual attraction" (in David Jay's words) seemed the more or less agreed-upon minimal definition. However, as Hinderliter (2009) states, this was merely a "PR definition" for external communication purposes, while within the community, identifying as asexual is as easy (or difficult) as "when the term rings for you, go for it":

No single definition encompasses all asexual people, so the common theme is that asexuals are people who call themselves asexual because they disidentify [sic!] with sexuality—i.e. they prefer not to have sex, and this affects how they go about forming relationships. [...] In this context, I think the definition 'a person who does not experience sexual attraction' was intended to fill the need of a definition to be used for the purpose of asexual visibility rather than as the one that the community was based on. (Hinderliter, 2009)

This relative discursive openness, or, alternatively, the discursive approach of a "brick box" which leaves the exact definition of the asexual experience—comprising sex drive, romantic and/or platonic preferences, sexual activity etc.—to the respective individual is, in my opinion, not only very "postmodern" in a discursive sense. Moreover, it leaves much room for the acknowledgement and validity of material subjective experiences. While this may lead to a proliferation of discourses—asexuals have ceased to use "asexuality" as singular and moved to "asexualities" or "asexual spectrum" a long time ago—it also engages with materialism to an extent that constitutes a novelty—and a challenge—for traditional discourses on (queer) sexuality.

OUTLOOK: METHODOLOGICAL CHALLENGES

In this paper, I have offered some thoughts on how intersections between discourse and materiality become visible in queer contexts. The case of asexuality provides, in my opinion, some very challenging insights on this intersection, particularly since asexuality, as a sexual orientation and identity category, is recent and therefore can be researched "from scratch" through online communities. Additionally, subjective narrative and (scientific) discourses on asexuality often are equiprimordial. "Informed" asexual subjects simultaneously challenge and transform queer discourses on sexuality, while queer discourses on sexuality sooner or later will have to acknowledge the materiality of absence.

What is the materiality of absence's challenge for Discourse Studies? Obviously, the detection of plainly unintelligible materiality is not easy, if not impossible. There might be an imperative for alternative, "queerer" methods of data collection and analysis. Still, in my opinion, Discourse Studies, as dealing with the production and communication of meaning, is a well-equipped approach to detect materialities of absence, queerness, and the unintelligible, exactly because it deconstructs linguistic structures. Utterances such as feeling "weird," "broken," "different," or not being able to name the experience, can be read as traces of unintelligibility. The use of metaphors and images can, as we have seen, act as a bridge between subjective materialities and deficient discourses. In any case, researchers need to accept thoroughly the subject's expertise. The "void" needs to be accepted as "the void" (and not, e.g. "the repressed"). Furthermore, the materiality of experience needs to be acknowledged as a reality, even though words are lacking. Subjective expertise may seem as though it clashes with constructionist notions. Blurred meanings need to be taken seriously, for rather than posing an unsolvable riddle, they point at the productive breaking points of discourse.

NOTES

1. On the "intersensual" materiality of experience, see Connolly (2010).

2. Rich denounces heterosexual desire in women as an institution compelled on them by patriarchy. In comparison to that, she defines the „Lesbian continuum" as ranging from "asexual" to sexual relationships between women. However, she does not acknowledge asexuality in women, if not as a result from sexual oppression (Rich 1980, 654).

3. On the problems of definition of asexuality, see Gazzola/ Morrison (2012, 23).

4. Among others, Bogaert (2004, 2006, 2015); Brotto (2010); (Brotto/ Yule 2011); (Chasin 2011).

5. The most notable being Cerankowski/Milks (2010); Cerankowski/ Milks (2014); Przybylo/ Cooper (2014).

6. For an overview on these items, see Bogaert (2006) or Brotto/ Yule (2016).

7. I am using this term with inverted commas when designating those persons who experience no sexual attraction, desire, and/or drive and would thus later be defined and/or self-define as "asexual." Note, however, at that time, the self-definition as an "asexual" was almost unknown.

8. The comments can be retrieved via http://web.archive.org/web/20020 612021943/; http://dispatches.azstarnet.com/zoe/amoeba2.htm; accessed on March 23, 2017.

9. https://groups.yahoo.com/neo/groups/havenforthehumanamoeba/conversations/messages/100; accessed on March 23, 2017.

10. http://www.asexuality.org/en/topic/11643-medical-journals/; accessed on March 23, 2017.

11. https://groups.yahoo.com/neo/groups/havenforthehumanamoeba/conversations/messages/125; accessed on March 23, 2017.

12. https://groups.yahoo.com/neo/groups/havenforthehumanamoeba/conversations/messages/132; accessed on March 23, 2017.

13. https://groups.yahoo.com/neo/groups/havenforthehumanamoeba/conversations/messages/140; accessed on March 23, 2017.

14. https://groups.yahoo.com/neo/groups/havenforthehumanamoeba/conversations/messages/141; accessed on March 23, 2017.

BIBLIOGRAPHY

Ahmed, Sara. 2006. *Queer Phenomenology. Orientations, Objects, Others.* Durham/ London: Duke University Press.

Barad, Karen. 2012a. "Nature's Queer Performantivity." *Kvinder, Køn & Forskning* 25–53.

———. 2012b. "What Is the Measure of Nothingness? Infinity; Virtuality; Justice | Was ist das Maß des Nichts? Unendlichkeit, Virtualität, Gerechtigkeit." *100 Notes—100 Thoughts / 100 Notizen—100 Gedanken No. 099.* Kassel: Documenta (13).

———. 2012c. "Matter feels, converses, suffers, desires, yearns and remembers." In *New Materialism: Interviews & Cartographies*, by Rick Dolphijn and Iris van der Tuin. Open Humanities Press.

Anthony Bogaert. 2004. "Asexuality: Prevalence and associated factors in a national probability sample." *Journal of Sex Research* 41: 279–287.

———.2006. "Toward a conceptual understanding of asexuality." *Review of General Psychology* 10 (3): 241–250.

———.2015. "Asexuality: what it is and why it matters." *Journal of Sex Research* 52 362–379.

Brotto, Lois A. 2010. "Asexuality: A Mixed-Methods Approach." *Archives of Sexual Behavior 39* 599–618.

Brotto, Lori A, and Morag A. Yule. 2011. "Physiological an Subjective Sexual Arousal in Self-Identified Asexual Women." *Archives of Sexual Behaviour* 40: 699–712.

———.2016. "Asexuality: Sexual Orientation, Paraphilia, Sexual Dysfunction, or None of the Above?" *Archives of Sexual Behavior 45.*

Butler, Judith. 1990. *Gender Trouble: Feminism and the Subversion of Identity.* London/New York: Routledge.

———.1993. *Bodies that Matter. On the Discursive Limits of "Sex."* London/New York: Routledge.

Cerankowski, Karli, and Megan Milks. 2010. "New Orientations: Asexuality and Its Implications for Theory and Practice." *Feminist Studies* 36: 650.

———. 2014. *Asexualities: Feminist and Queer Perspectives.* New York: Routledge.

Chasin, CJ DeLuzio. 2011. "Theoretical Issues in the Study of Asexuality." *Archives of Sexual Behaviour* 40: 713–723.

Connolly, William. 2010. "Materialities of Experience." In *New Materialisms: Ontology, Agency, and Politics*, by Diana Coole and Samantha Frost, 178–200. Durham/London: Duke University Press.

Coole, Diana. 2010. "The Inertia of Matter and the Generativity of the Flesh." In *New Materialisms: Ontology, Agency, and Politics*, by Diana Coole and Samantha Frost, 92–115. Durham/London: Duke University Press.

Coole, Diana, and Samantha Frost. 2010. "Introducing the New Materialisms." In *New Materialisms: Ontology, Agency, and Politics*, by Diana Coole and Samantha Frost, 1–43. Durham/ London: Duke University Press.

Fausto-Sterling, Anne. 2000. *Sexing the Body: Gender Politics and the Construction of Sexuality.* New York: Basic Books.

Foucault, Michel. 1990. *A History of Sexuality. Volume 1: An Introduction.* New York: Random House.

Gazzola, Stephanie B., and Melanie A. Morrison. 2012. "Asexuality: an emergent sexual orientation" In *Sexual Minority Research in the New Millenium*, by Todd G. Morrisson, 21–44. New York: Nova Science Publishers.

Grosz, Elizabeth. 1994. *Volatile Bodies. Toward a Corporeal Feminism.* Bloomington/ Indianapolis: Indiana University Press.

Hinderliter, Andrew C. 2009. "Asexuality: The History of a Definition." Accessed October 25, 2016. http://www.asexualexplorations.net/home/history_of_definition.html

O'Reilly, Zoe. 1997. "My life as a human amoeba" On: *StarNet Dispatches*. Published: 30 May. Accessed October 14, 2016. http://web.archive.org/web/20020601161040/ http://dispatches.azstarnet.com/zoe/amoeba.htm

Przybylo, Ela. 2012. "Producing facts: Empirical asexuality and the scientific study of sex." *Feminism Psychology* 23 (2): 224–242.

Przybylo, Ela, and Danielle Cooper. 2014. "Asexual Resonances: Tracing a Queerly Asexual Archive." *GLQ: A Journal of Lesbian and Gay Studies 20* 306–309.

Rich, Adrienne. 1980. "Compulsory Heterosexuality and Lesbian Existence." *Signs* 631–660.

Index

About the Authors and Editors

Ligia Mara Boin Menossi de Araújo holds a doctorate in Linguistics from the Federal University of São Carlos (UFSCar) and is currently conducting postdoctoral research at the University of São Paulo (USP) in French Discourse Analysis and philology, under the supervision of Prof. Dr. Manoel Mourivaldo Santiado-Almeida.

Giorgio Borrelli finished his PhD in "Theory of Language and Sciences of the Sign," in 2015, at the University of Bari "Aldo Moro" (Italy). The title of his dissertation is "Per una semiotica materialistica. Ferruccio Rossi-Landi e dintorni" [For a materialistic semiotics. Ferruccio Rossi-Landi and surroundings]. His research interests are focused on the general science of signs as a theoretical and methodological instrument for social research. More specifically, he is interested in the relation between semiotics and the dialectical-materialistic approach to the Social Sciences. He is a teaching assistant and exam committee member in Semiotics and Philosophy of Language at the University of Bari "Aldo Moro."

Johannes Beetz is a doctoral researcher at the Centre for Applied Linguistics at the University of Warwick, the United Kingdom. He studied sociology, philosophy, and American studies at the Johannes Gutenberg-University in Mainz, Germany. He is a member of the ERC DISCONEX project, DiscourseNet, and a founding member of the DIPE research group on Discourse, Ideology, and Political Economy. His research investigates the discursive practices of researchers in the social science. His research interests include Critical Theory and Marxism, Discourse Studies, and post-Structuralist Theory.

Jean-Jacques Courtine is 2018 Leverhulme Trust Visiting Professor at Queen Mary, University of London, Honorary Professor of European Studies at the University of Auckland, Professor Emeritus at the Universities of Sorbonne Nouvelle (Paris III) and California (Santa Barbara). He has worked and published extensively on discourse analysis, the history of the body, of gender, and of emotions. Most recent books: *History of Virility*, co-ed. with Alain Corbin and Georges Vigarello (New York, Columbia University Press, 2016); Histoire des émotions (History of Emotions), gen. co-ed. with Alain Corbin and Georges Vigarello, 3 vol. (Paris: Le Seuil, 2016–2017).

Benjamin Glasson, PhD, teaches politics at the University of Melbourne. He has published in the fields of political theory, cultural studies, and psychoanalysis, including in the *Journal of Political Ideologies, Psychoanalysis, Culture and Society*, and *Continuum: Journal of Media and Cultural Studies.* His chief research interest is the relationship between knowledge production and belonging in late modern societies. He is particularly interested in how affect, identity, and desire mediate between expert and political discourses, as well as in the changing relations of knowledge and authority as societies and communication networks grow more complex and fragmented.

Benno Herzog is Associate Professor at the Department of Sociology and Social Anthropology, University of Valencia, Spain. He has worked and conducted research in Germany (Universities of Frankfurt and Mainz), the United Kingdom (University of Manchester, Open University, and University of Warwick), and Brazil (Federal University of Paraíba). His research focuses on social critique and critical theory of society, discourse theory and discourse analysis, and migration and discrimination.

Manuel Iretzberger, MA, studied Governance and Public Policy, and Philosophy at the Universities of Passau and Turku. His research interests include Critical Theory, Political Philosophy, and International Relations. He is currently writing his PhD thesis on "Statehood and Sovereignty From a Critical-Realist Perspective" at the chair of International Relations in Passau, where he also teaches and provides research training for exchange students. He is a scholar at the Rosa Luxemburg Foundation (Berlin) and currently lives in Munich.

Leiser Baronas, Roberto a doctorate in Linguistics, is Associate Professor at the Department of Letters, Federal University of São Carlos (UFSCar), Professor in the PhD Graduate Program in Linguistics—PPGL/UFSCar, CNPq grantee for research productivity, and coordinator of the Laboratory for Epistemological Studies and Multimodal Discursivities—LEEDIM/CNPq/UFSCar.

Helio Oliveira is a doctoral researcher in Linguistics in the Institute of Language Studies at the University of Campinas, Brazil (UNICAMP), member of the Formulas and Stereotypes: Theory and Analysis (FEsTA) research group and held a scholarship of the São Paulo Research Foundation (FAPESP Proc. 2015/19670–1) during a research stay at the Ecole des Hautes Etudes in Sciences Sociales (EHESS), Paris. His research interests include racist discourse and the Black Consciousness Movement, taking Discourse Analysis as the major theoretical basis.

Laura Pantzerhielm is a research fellow at WZB Berlin Social Science Center and a doctoral student in Political Science at Freie Universität Berlin. Her research interests lie at the intersection between International Relations (IR) and political theory and include post-structuralist discourse analysis, post-Marxist theories of the Political, IR theory, and IR norms research. Laura Pantzerhielm holds a Master's degree in International Affairs and Human Rights from Institut d'Études Politiques de Paris (Sciences Po) and an MA in Political Science from Freie Universität Berlin.

Marco Antonio Almeida Ruiz is a doctoral researcher in Linguistics at the Federal University of São Carlos (UFSCar) and PhD student in sociology at École des Hautes Études en Sciences Sociales—EHESS/Paris (cotutelle de thèse). His research centers on historical and epistemological conditions of French Discourse Analysis in Brazil and France under the supervision of Prof. Dr. Roberto Leiser Baronas and Prof. Dr. Johannes Angermuller. FAPESP grantee, process 2014/22526–7 and process 2015/20984–0.

Veit Schwab is a doctoral researcher in the Centre for Applied Linguistics and the Department for Politics and International Studies at the University of Warwick (United Kingdom). He is a member of the Network for Critical Border and Migration Regime Research (kritnet) and DiscourseNet, and an associate member of the ERC DISCONEX project at Warwick. His research interests include Critical Migration Studies, Discourse Theory and Analysis, as well as post-structuralist and critical theories in Politics and International Studies. From October 2012 to October 2013, he worked as a Research Fellow and part-time teacher in the Geschwister Scholl Institute for Political Science (GSI) at Ludwig-Maximilians-Universitat München (University of Munich).

Julia Maria Zimmermann, studied Sociology, Philosophy, and Social and Economic History at the University of Jena. In 2017, she obtained a PhD in social sciences at the University of Luxembourg. Her thesis is about the discursive co-construction of gender and Europeanization in debates in the European Parliament between 1999 and 2014. She has worked as a research assistant at the chairs of sociological theory and knowledge sociology in Jena and as a researcher at the University of Luxembourg. Her main interests of research are gender and queer theory, with an emphasis on asexuality, discourse studies, social theory, social inequality, and knowledge sociology.

Lightning Source UK Ltd.
Milton Keynes UK
UKHW041456110719
345969UK00006B/262/P

9 781498 558150